ALGEBRAIC
THEORY
of
LATTICES

PETER CRAWLEY

*Brigham Young
University*

ROBERT P. DILWORTH

*California Institute
of Technology*

PRENTICE-HALL, INC.
Englewood Cliffs, N.J.

Library of Congress Cataloging in Publication Data

CRAWLEY, PETER,
  Algebraic theory of lattices.

  Bibliography: p. 193
  1. Lattice theory. I. Dilworth, Robert Palmer.
joint author. II. Title.
QA171.5.C7   512'.7   72–7595
ISBN 0–13–022269–0

To the Memory
of
Morgan Ward

10   9   8   7   6   5   4   3   2   1

Printed in the United States of America

PRENTICE-HALL INTERNATIONAL, INC., *London*
PRENTICE-HALL OF AUSTRALIA, PTY, LTD., *Sydney*
PRENTICE-HALL OF CANADA, LTD., *Toronto*
PRENTICE-HALL OF INDIA PRIVATE LIMITED, *New Delhi*
PRENTICE-HALL OF JAPAN, INC. *Tokyo*

CONTENTS

iii

PREFACE

Our purpose in this book is two-fold: first, to illustrate the depth and beauty of lattice theory by systematically developing a body of results at the *heart* of the subject including a representative sample of its most profound results; and second, as lattice theoretic techniques are useful in many branches of mathematics, to broadly illustrate the more important tools and techniques of lattice theory. A glance at the contents will reveal that this book is not encyclopedic. For example, it includes none of the theory of orthomodular lattices, pseudo-complemented lattices, multiplicative lattices, partially ordered systems such as lattice-ordered groups or rings, or lattices of continuous functions. Such topics as Boolean algebras, combinatorial geometries, and continuous geometries are treated very incompletely. Generally, our focus is on lattice structure theory, and we have tended to include those results that give insight into how lattices are put together and how they behave under certain assumptions. Also, the reader will note the absence of "applications;" we have involved other branches of mathematics only insofar as they give lattice theoretical insights.

Our approach is to quickly pass over the elementary aspects of the subject and to concentrate on the more difficult results. Indeed, many of the more routine proofs are left as exercises for the reader. At several points, the frontier of lattice theory is touched, and here the relevant open problems and conjectures are discussed. Most of the results in the book have appeared earlier in print, though in a number of instances our proofs are new; and in the majority of cases we have noted the authorship of a particular theorem. The absence of a provenance, however, should not be construed as a claim to originality.

As far as partially ordered sets and lattices are concerned, the book is self-contained. We do assume a familiarity with the basics of set theory and "modern algebra" (e.g., the rudimentary aspects of groups, rings, fields and vector spaces).

This book has grown out of notes prepared for courses in lattice theory

v

at the California Institute of Technology, taught by us individually and to-gether during the preceding five years. And it incorporates the suggestions and criticisms of a number of students and colleagues. Particularly, we acknowledge with appreciation the contributions of Richard A. Dean and Bjarni Jónsson.

Peter Crawley
R. P. Dilworth

NOTATIONAL NOTE

Throughout this book we adopt the following set theoretical notational con-ventions: set-union, set-intersection, set-inclusion and proper inclusion are denoted by the familiar rounded symbols $\cup$, $\cap$, $\subseteq$ and $\subset$, respectively; for two sets A and B, the set of those elements in A but not in B is denoted by $A - B$, and when B consists of a single element b, we write $A - B = A - b$. The empty set is denoted by $\varnothing$; $|A|$ denotes the cardinality of a set A.

1

PARTIALLY
ORDERED SETS

A *partially ordered set* is a system consisting of a nonempty set P and a binary relation $\leq$ in P such that the following conditions are satisfied for all x, y, $z \in P$:

   (1) $x \leq x$.
   (2) If $x \leq y$ and $y \leq x$, then $x = y^{(1)}$.
   (3) If $x \leq y$ and $y \leq z$, then $x \leq z$.

The relation $\leq$ is a *partial order* in the set P, and P is said to be *partially ordered* by the relation $\leq$. Although the set P is only the domain of the partial order $\leq$, we will usually follow the custom of identifying P with the partially ordered set. Also, the partial orders of most partially ordered sets will be denoted by the same symbol, $\leq$.

If x and y are elements of the partially ordered set P, we also write $y \geq x$ in case $x \leq y$. We write $x < y$ if $x \leq y$ and $x \neq y$, and we say that x is *less* than y. Again, when $x < y$, we write $y > x$ and say that y is *greater* than x. The formulas $x \not\leq y$ and $y \not\geq x$ both mean that $x \leq y$ does not hold.

Partially ordered sets abound in mathematics. A rather uninspiring example is any set together with the relation of logical identity. A familiar example is a set of real numbers together with the so-called *natural ordering*: $x \leq y$ if $y - x$ is nonnegative. Another example is the set of positive integers together with the relation $\leq$ defined by: $x \leq y$ if x divides y. Note that in the last two examples, the set of positive integers becomes the domain of two different partial orders. A particularly important example of a partially ordered set is the set of all subsets of a given set X together with the relation of set-inclusion.

Certain partially ordered sets may be diagrammatically represented. To describe this, we need the concept of covering. If x and y are elements of a partially ordered set P, $x < y$, and there is no element $z \in P$ such that

---

(1) The symbol $=$ will always denote logical identity. Its negation will be denoted by $\neq$

1

$x < z < y$, then we say that x is *covered* by y (or y *covers* x), and we write $x \prec y$ (or $y \succ x$).

Consider a finite partially ordered set P. On the page, draw a small circle for each element in P in such a way that the circle associated with an element x lies above the circle associated with an element y whenever $x > y$. Then, whenever $x \succ y$, connect the circles associated with x and y by a line segment. We call the resulting figure a *diagram* and say that the partially ordered set P is *represented* by this diagram. Since in P, $x > y$ if and only if there is a finite sequence of elements $z_0, z_1, \ldots, z_n \in P$ such that $x = z_0 \succ z_1 \succ \cdots \succ z_n = y$, a diagram which represents P determines the partial order of P. Moreover, if we define two partially ordered sets P_1 and P_2 to be *isomorphic* if there is one-to-one map f of P_1 onto P_2 such that, for all $x, y \in P_1$,

$$x \leq y \text{ if and only if } f(x) \leq f(y),$$

then it is easily verified that two finite partially ordered sets are isomorphic if and only if they can be represented by the same diagram.

For example, the reader might check that Fig. 1-1 represents the set of

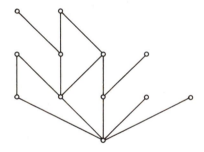

Fig. 1-1

integers $\{1, 2, \ldots, 12\}$ with $x \leq y$ if x divides y and that Fig. 1-2 represents the set of all subsets of $\{1, 2, 3\}$ partially ordered by set-inclusion.

In connection with the definition of isomorphism given above, it is convenient to define a map f of a partially ordered set P_1 to a partially ordered set P_2 to be *order-preserving* if $f(x) \leq f(y)$ whenever $x \leq y$.

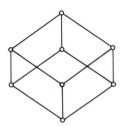

Fig. 1-2

If S is a subset of a partially ordered set P, then there is at most one element $a \in S$ such that $a \geq x$ for all $x \in S$. Such an element a, if it exists, is called the *greatest* element of S. Similarly, if S contains an element b such that $b \leq x$ for all $x \in S$, then b is called the *least* element of S. A distinction should be made between greatest elements and maximal elements. An element $a \in S$ is called a *maximal* element of S if there is no element $x \in S$ with $x > a$. Certainly the greatest element of S (if one exists) is a maximal element of S; on the other hand, it may happen that S contains many maximal elements but no greatest element. The same considerations apply to minimal elements: An element $a \in S$ is a *minimal* element of S if there is no $x \in S$ such that $a > x$.

A partially ordered set P with the property that each of its nonempty subsets contains a maximal element is said to satisfy the *ascending chain condition*. If each nonempty subset of P contains a minimal element, then P satisfies the *descending chain condition*. These names come from the following alternative formulations: P satisfies the ascending chain condition if and only if it contains no infinite sequence of elements $a_1, a_2, a_3, \ldots$ such that $a_1 < a_2 < a_3 < \cdots$; it satisfies the descending chain condition if and only if it contains no infinite sequence of elements $a_1, a_2, a_3, \ldots$ such that $a_1 > a_2 > a_3 > \cdots$.

Two elements x and y in a partially ordered set P are called *comparable* if either $x \leq y$ or $y \leq x$. Two elements that are not comparable are *noncomparable*. If S is a subset of P with the property that any two elements in S are comparable, then S is called a *chain* (or *totally ordered set*). When a chain S further satisfies the descending chain condition, we refer to S as an *ascending well-ordered chain*. Similarly, S is a *descending well-ordered chain* if it satisfies the ascending chain condition. We leave it to the reader to verify that *all the chains of a partially ordered set P are finite if and only if P satisfies both the ascending chain condition and the descending chain condition.*

If a partially ordered set P is the set-union of k chains, k a positive integer, then any set of $k + 1$ elements of P contains at least two elements which belong to the same chain and hence are comparable. The converse of this observation is our first theorem:

1.1: *If a partially ordered set P has the property that each of its subsets with $k + 1$ elements contains at least one pair of comparable elements, then P is the set-union of k chains.*[2]

PROOF: The proof of Theorem 1.1 is in two parts; the first part is a proof of the theorem in the case of finite partially ordered sets, while the second part completes the proof in the general case. The first part, as given here, is due to Tverberg.[3]

[2] R. P. Dilworth [32].
[3] H. Tverberg [85].

Suppose then that P is a finite partially ordered set, and suppose that k is the maximal number pairwise noncomparable elements in P. The proof proceeds by induction on the number of elements in P. Let C be a maximal chain in P. If the set $P - C$ contains no subset of k pairwise noncomparable elements, then by the induction hypothesis, $P - C$ is the set-union of $k - 1$ chains, so that P is the set-union of k chains.

Assume that $P - C$ contains a subset $S = \{s_1, \ldots, s_k\}$ of k pairwise noncomparable elements. Set

$$P_* = \{x \in P \mid x \leq s \text{ for some } s \in S\},$$
$$P^* = \{x \in P \mid x \geq s \text{ for some } s \in S\}.$$

Since every element of P is comparable with some element in S, it follows that $P = P_* \cup P^*$. Moreover, the maximality of the chain C ensures that the greatest element of C does not belong to P_* and least element of C does not belong to P^*. Thus by the induction hypothesis we must have

$$P_* = D_1 \cup \cdots \cup D_k \quad \text{and} \quad P^* = E_1 \cup \cdots \cup E_k,$$

where each D_i and each E_i is a chain. Also, we can assume that the D_i's and E_i's have been numbered in such a way that $s_i \in D_i$ and $s_i \in E_i$ for each $i = 1, \ldots, k$. But then $C_i = D_i \cup E_i$ is a chain of P for each i, and consequently

$$P = P_* \cup P^* = C_1 \cup \cdots \cup C_k$$

is the set-union of k chains.

To complete the proof in the infinite case, some set-theoretic tool equivalent to the Axiom of Choice is needed. The most convenient form for our purposes here is Zorn's lemma, which we digress momentarily to describe.

An element a in a partially ordered set P is said to be an *upper bound* of a subset $S \subseteq P$ if $a \geq x$ for every $x \in S$. Similarly, a is a *lower bound* of S if $a \leq x$ for every $x \in S$.

The following statement, usually known as Zorn's lemma, is equivalent to the Axiom of Choice and will be assumed to hold throughout:

If every chain of a nonempty partially ordered set P has an upper bound, then P has a maximal element.

(The reader may find it instructive to derive Zorn's lemma from the Axiom of Choice.)

Continuing with the proof of 1.1, let P be a (possibly infinite) partially ordered set, and suppose that the maximal number of pairwise noncomparable elements in P is an integer k. This part of the proof is made by induction on the integer k.

Let us define a subset C of P to be *strong* if for every finite subset $S \subseteq P$ there is at least one representation of S as a set-union of k chains such that $C \cap S$ is contained in one of these chains. Since the theorem is true for finite partially ordered sets, each strong set is a chain. Let $\mathcal{P}$ denote the collection of all strong subsets of P, and consider $\mathcal{P}$ as partially ordered by set-inclusion. Observe that the subset $\{x\}$ is strong for every element $x \in P$. (This statement also uses 1.1 in the finite case!) In particular, $\mathcal{P}$ is nonempty. Next, suppose that $\mathcal{C}$ is a chain of $\mathcal{P}$. Set $\bar{C} = \bigcup_{C \in \mathcal{C}} C$. If S is a finite subset of P, then

$$S \cap \bar{C} = S \cap \bigcup_{C \in \mathcal{C}} C = \bigcup_{C \in \mathcal{C}} S \cap C,$$

and as $S \cap \bar{C}$ is finite and the sets $S \cap C$ $(C \in \mathcal{C})$ form a chain of subsets of P, it follows that $S \cap \bar{C} = S \cap C_0$ for some $C_0 \in \mathcal{C}$. Consequently, the fact that C_0 is strong implies that $\bar{C}$ is strong. Furthermore, $\bar{C}$ is certainly an upper bound of the chain $\mathcal{C}$. Thus the assumptions of Zorn's lemma are satisfied by $\mathcal{P}$, and hence $\mathcal{P}$ contains a maximal element M.

Consider $P - M$. Suppose this set contains k pairwise noncomparable elements $a_1, \ldots, a_k$. Then the maximality of M implies that the set $M \cup \{a_i\}$ is not strong for each $i = 1, \ldots, k$, and hence for each i there is a finite subset S_i of P with the property that in any representation of S_i as a set-union of k chains, no one of these chains contains $S_i \cap (M \cup \{a_i\})$. Note that a_i is necessarily in S_i for each i, since M is strong. Set

$$S = S_1 \cup \cdots \cup S_k.$$

Inasmuch as M is strong, there are k chains $K_1, \ldots, K_k$ such that $S = K_1 \cup \cdots \cup K_k$, $a_i \in K_i$ for each i, and $S \cap M \subseteq K_n$ for some n. Put $K'_i = S_n \cap K_i$ for each $i = 1, \ldots, k$. Then $S_n = K'_1 \cup \cdots \cup K'_k$, and

$$S_n \cap M \subseteq S_n \cap S \cap M \subseteq S_n \cap K_n = K'_n.$$

But $a_n \in S_n \cap K_n = K'_n$, and therefore $S_n \cap (M \cup \{a_n\}) \subseteq K'_n$. This last formula, however, contradicts the choice of S_n, and we conclude that $P - M$ contains at most $k - 1$ pairwise noncomparable elements. By the induction assumption, $P - M$ is the set-union of $k - 1$ chains. And as M is a chain, P is the set-union of k chains, completing the proof of the theorem.

Theorem 1.1 does not hold if k is allowed to be infinite. To see this, let Ω denote the first ordinal number of cardinality that of the continuum, and let f be a one-to-one map of Ω to the real numbers. Let P be that partially ordered set whose elements are the ordered pairs $\langle \xi, f(\xi) \rangle$ $(\xi < \Omega)$ and whose partial order $\leq$ is defined by

$$\langle \xi, f(\xi) \rangle \leq \langle \eta, f(\eta) \rangle \text{ if } \xi \leq \eta \text{ and } f(\xi) \leq f(\eta).$$

Let S be any subset of P such that any two ordered pairs in S are noncomparable, and put

$$W = \{\xi \mid \langle \xi, f(\xi) \rangle \in S\}.$$

W is then a set of ordinal numbers and hence is an ascending well-ordered chain. Observe that if $\xi, \eta \in W$ and $\xi < \eta$, then the noncomparability of

$\langle \xi, f(\xi) \rangle$ and $\langle \eta, f(\eta) \rangle$ implies that $f(\xi) > f(\eta)$. Therefore

$$\{f(\xi) | \langle \xi, f(\xi) \rangle \in S\}$$

is a set of real numbers which, under the natural order, is a decending well-ordered chain. Such a set of real numbers is necessarily countable, and consequently S is countable. In a similar way it follows that any chain of P is also countable. Thus P is an uncountable partially ordered set in which every chain as well as every set of pairwise noncomparable elements is countable.

An example such as the foregoing is not possible, however, if we require all chains and sets of pairwise noncomparable elements to be finite, for *if every chain and every set of pairwise noncomparable elements in a partially ordered set P is finite, then P is finite.* (The proof is an exercise.)

Our next theorem shows that every partial order can be refined to a total order.

1.2: *If P is a partially ordered set, then there exists a partial order R in the set P such that the set P together with R is a chain, and, for all $x, y \in P$, $x \leq y$ implies $x \, R \, y$.*[4]

PROOF: Let $\mathcal{P}$ be the set of all relations R in the set P such that

(1) R is a partial order in P.
(2) For all $x, y \in P$, $x \leq y$ implies $x \, R \, y$.

Considering binary relations as sets of ordered pairs, partially order $\mathcal{P}$ by set-inclusion. Note that $\mathcal{P}$ is nonempty since the relation $\leq$ is in $\mathcal{P}$. Furthermore, it is easily checked that the set-union of any chain of relations in $\mathcal{P}$ is again in $\mathcal{P}$, and consequently $\mathcal{P}$ contains a maximal element R_0 by Zorn's lemma.

Suppose that the set P together with R_0 is not a chain; i.e., there exist two elements $u, v \in P$ such that neither $u \, R_0 \, v$ nor $v \, R_0 \, u$. Define the relation R_1 in the set P by the following rules:

(a) If $x \, R_0 \, y$, then $x \, R_1 \, y$.
(b) If $x \, R_0 \, u$ and $v \, R_0 \, y$, then $x \, R_1 \, y$.

Clearly R_0 is a subset of R_1, and R_1 satisfies condition (2). Also, $x \, R_1 \, x$ for every $x \in P$. Suppose that $x, y, z \in P$ and that $x \, R_1 \, y$ and $y \, R_1 \, z$. Then one of the four following situations must occur:

(1) $x \, R_0 \, y$ and $y \, R_0 \, z$.
(2) $x \, R_0 \, y$, $y \, R_0 \, u$, and $v \, R_0 \, z$.

[4] E. Szpilrajn [80].

(3) $x\,R_0\,u$, $v\,R_0\,y$, and $y\,R_0\,z$.
(4) $x\,R_0\,u$, $v\,R_0\,y$, $y\,R_0\,u$, and $v\,R_0\,z$.

Situation (4) is impossible since it yields that $v\,R_0\,u$. Situation (1) yields that $x\,R_0\,z$, and therefore $x\,R_1\,z$. If (2) occurs, then $x\,R_0\,u$ and $v\,R_0\,z$, whence $x\,R_1\,z$. Similarly, $x\,R_1\,z$ if (3) occurs. Therefore $x\,R_1\,y$ and $y\,R_1\,z$ imply that $x\,R_1\,z$. Suppose $x = z$. In this case (2) and (3) are also impossible, for each yields $v\,R_0\,u$. This leaves (1), whence $x = y$. Consequently $x\,R_1\,y$ and $y\,R_1\,x$ imply $x = y$. Thus the set P is partially ordered by R_1, and we conclude that $R_1 \in \mathcal{P}$. But as $u\,R_1\,v$, R_1 is greater than R_0, contrary to the maximality of R_0. We infer that the set P together with R_0 is a chain, and the proof is complete.

Partially ordered sets have the following useful property: when one of them is turned upside down, it is again a partially ordered set. More precisely, for a given partially ordered set P, let $\hat{P}$ be that system consisting of the elements of P together with the binary relation $\leq^{\char94}$ defined by the rule

$$x \leq^{\char94} y \quad \text{if} \quad y \leq x.$$

The system $\hat{P}$ is then a partially ordered set, which we will refer to as the *dual* of P. The name, of course, is suggestive of the fact that the dual of $\hat{P}$ is just P.

For a given statement made in the partially ordered set P, we can form the *dual statement* by replacing each of the relations $\leq$ and $\geq$ by the other whenever they occur in the original statement. For example, the dual of the statement "P satisfies the ascending chain condition" is the statement "P satisfies the descending chain condition." We say that a statement is a *self-dual statement* if, whenever the statement is true in a partially ordered set P, it is also true in $\hat{P}$. Both of the statements "P is a chain" and "all chains in P are finite" are self-dual, while the statement "P satisfies the ascending chain condition" is not. Notice that whenever a self-dual statement holds in a partially ordered set P, then the dual of this statement also holds in P.

The value of these considerations is this: If, as a consequence of certain self-dual statements, another statement is shown to hold in a partially ordered set P, then this statement must also hold in $\hat{P}$, and consequently the dual of the derived statement must hold in P. For instance, since Zorn's lemma holds, so does the dual statement: If every chain in a nonempty partially ordered set P has a lower bound, then P has a minimal element.

Occasionally we will encounter a statement to be proved that consists of two parts, the second part being the dual statement of the first. When such a statement is to be derived from a set of self-dual properties, our work is cut in half; we need only derive the first part and then remark that the second follows "by duality."

2

LATTICES

With the definitions of upper and lower bounds in mind, we can define least upper and greatest lower bounds, the underlying concepts of lattice theory. Let P be a partially ordered set, and S a subset of P. We say that an element $a \in P$ is a *join* (or *least upper bound*) of S if a is an upper bound of S, and $a \leq x$ for every upper bound x of S. Similarly, b is a *meet* (or *greatest lower bound*) of S if b is a lower bound of S, and $b \geq y$ for every lower bound y of S. Joins or meets do not always exist; when one does, it is unique.

If the join of the subset S exists in the partially ordered set P, then we denote this join by either of the formulas

$$\bigvee S \qquad \text{or} \qquad \bigvee_{s \in S} s.$$

When S is a two-element set, say $S = \{x, y\}$, we write

$$\bigvee \{x, y\} = x \vee y.$$

The meet of S, when it exists, is denoted by

$$\bigwedge S \qquad \text{or} \qquad \bigwedge_{s \in S} s,$$

and

$$\bigwedge \{x, y\} = x \wedge y.$$

A partially ordered set in which every pair of elements has a join and a meet is called a *lattice*. A partially ordered set in which *every* subset has a join and a meet is called a *complete lattice*.

Lattices too occur in abundance. For example, any chain is a lattice. The set of positive integers, where $x \leq y$ means that x divides y, is a lattice; here the join of x and y is their least common multiple, and their meet is the greatest common divisor. For any set X, the set of all subsets of X partially ordered by set-inclusion is a complete lattice; the join of any collection of subsets is the set-union, and the meet is the set-intersection. For future use, this lattice will be referred to as "the lattice of all subsets of X." If G is an operator group, then the set of all admissible subgroups of G partially ordered by set-inclusion is a complete lattice, as is the set of all admissible normal subgroups of G under set-inclusion; in both cases, the meet of a subset of the lattice is the set-intersection, and the join is the admissible subgroup generated by the set-union. These two lattices will be referred to as "the lattice of all admissible subgroups of G" and "the lattice of all admissible normal subgroups of G," respectively.

It should be noted that the defining property of a lattice is a self-dual property, as is the defining property of a complete lattice. Consequently the dual of any lattice is again a lattice, and the dual of a complete lattice is complete. Moreover, joins in the lattice L coincide with meets in $\hat{L}$, and meets in L coincide with joins in $\hat{L}$.

It is implicit in the definition of complete lattice that the empty set $\varnothing$ has a join and a meet. In this regard $\bigvee \varnothing$ exists in a partially ordered set P if and only if $\bigwedge P$ exists, in which case $\bigvee \varnothing = \bigwedge P$. Dually, $\bigwedge \varnothing$ exists in P if and only if $\bigvee P$ exists, and when one exists the two are equal.

Notice further that the definition of complete lattice can be significantly shortened: *If every subset of a partially ordered set P has a join, then P is a complete lattice.* To prove this, let S be any subset of P, and set

$$S_* = \{x \in P \,|\, x \leq s \text{ for all } s \in S\}.$$

Then $a = \bigvee S_*$ exists in P, and it is an easy exercise to verify that a is the meet of S in P. Consequently every subset of P also has a meet, so that P is a complete lattice. The dual statement also holds: If every subset of a partially ordered set P has a meet, then P is a complete lattice. These considerations, however, do not apply to the definition of lattice; it is very easy to write down examples of partially ordered sets that are not lattices but in which every pair of elements has a meet.

For a lattice, completeness depends only on the existence of joins of chains:

2.1: *If every ascending well-ordered chain in a lattice L has a join, then L is a complete lattice.*

PROOF: Let S be any subset of L. As above, let S_* denote the set of all lower bounds of S. Let $\mathcal{P}$ be the collection of all ascending well-ordered chains in S_*, and define a partial order $\leq$ in $\mathcal{P}$ by the rule

$$C \leq D \text{ if } C = D \text{ or } C = \{x \in D \,|\, x < d\} \qquad \text{for some } d \in D.$$

$\mathcal{P}$ is nonempty since it contains the empty set, and an application of Zorn's lemma yields a maximal element $M \in \mathcal{P}$. By assumption, M has a join, $a = \bigvee M$. Certainly a is a lower bound of S. If a is not the greatest lower bound, there is an element $b \in S_*$ such that $b \not\leq a$, and we infer that $a \vee b \in S_*$ and $a \vee b > a$, so that $M \cup \{a \vee b\}$ is an ascending well-ordered chain in

S_*, contrary to the maximality of M. Thus $a = \bigwedge S$, and it follows that L is a complete lattice.

If a lattice L is complete, and for each subset $S \subseteq L$ we define $S^c = \{x \in L \mid x \leq \bigvee S\}$, then the map $S \longrightarrow S^c$ satisfies the conditions

(1) $S \subseteq S^c$.
(2) $S \subseteq T$ implies $S^c \subseteq T^c$.
(3) $(S^c)^c = S^c$.

Conversely, let X be an arbitrary set. A map $S \longrightarrow S^c$ of the set of all subsets of X to itself is a *closure operator* if (1)–(3) hold. Define a subset $S \subseteq X$ to be *closed if* $S = S^c$. Then the set of all closed subsets of X, partially ordered by set-inclusion, is a complete lattice (the set-intersection of any family of closed sets is again closed).

Closure operators provide a powerful technique for constructing complete lattices. They allow us, for example, to enlarge any partially ordered set to a complete lattice. For if P is a partially ordered set, and for each subset $S \subseteq P$ we define $S^c = \{x \in P \mid x \leq s$ for some $s \in S\}$, then the mapping $S \longrightarrow S^c$ is a closure operator, and the map $x \longrightarrow \{x\}^c$ of P to the lattice of all closed subsets of P is one-to-one and order-preserving, and its inverse is order-preserving. These closed subsets of P are called *o-ideals*; we shall put them to use in Chap. 10. Even more important examples of complete lattices obtained from closure operators are the lattices of ideals and normal completions described in Chap. 9.

If L is a lattice, then it is readily verified that the following five conditions hold for all $x, y, z \in L$:

(1) $x \vee x = x \wedge x = x$.
(2) $x \vee y = y \vee x$ and $x \wedge y = y \wedge x$.
(3) $x \vee (y \vee z) = (x \vee y) \vee z$ and $x \wedge (y \wedge z) = (x \wedge y) \wedge z$.
(4) $x \vee (x \wedge y) = x \wedge (x \vee y) = x$.
(5) The conditions $x \wedge y = x$, $x \vee y = y$, and $x \leq y$ are equivalent.

On the other hand, if in a set L two binary operations $\vee$ and $\wedge$ are defined such that (1)–(4) hold for all $x, y, z \in L$, and if we now define a relation $\leq$ in L by

$$x \leq y \text{ if } x \wedge y = x,$$

then L together with this relation $\leq$ is a lattice in which the join and meet of two elements $x, y \in L$ are, respectively, $x \vee y$ and $x \wedge y$. (The proofs of the foregoing assertions are left as an exercise.)

Viewing lattices as systems with two binary operations leads us to the concepts of sublattice, homomorphism, and isomorphism. We say that a nonempty subset M of a lattice L is a *sublattice* of L if $x \vee y, x \wedge y \in M$

whenever x, $y \in M$. It should be emphasized that the indicated joins and meets in the preceding sentence are those in L. A subset of a lattice L might itself be a lattice relative to the partial order of L and yet not be a sublattice of L; for example, if L is the lattice of all subsets of $\{1, 2, 3\}$, then the subset $\{\varnothing, \{1\}, \{2\}, \{1, 2, 3\}\}$, partially ordered by set-inclusion, is a lattice, but it is not a sublattice of L. Also, sublattices need not be closed under infinite joins and meets. If a lattice L is complete and a subset M of L has the property that $\bigvee S$, $\bigwedge S \in M$ for every nonempty subset $S \subseteq M$, then we say that M is a *complete sublattice* of L.

If a is an element of a lattice L, then each of the subsets

$$\{x \in L \mid x \geq a\} \quad \text{and} \quad \{x \in L \mid x \leq a\}$$

is a sublattice of L; they will be denoted by $1/a$ and $a/0$, respectively. Also, if $a \geq b$ in L, then the subset

$$\{x \in L \mid a \geq x \geq b\}$$

is a sublattice, which we denote by a/b. Sublattices of this type are referred to as *quotient sublattices*.

The collection of all the sublattices of a lattice L together with the empty set forms a complete lattice under set-inclusion, inasmuch as a nonempty set-intersection of any set of sublattices of L is again a sublattice. In particular, if X is any subset of L, there is a least sublattice of L that contains X—the set-intersection of those sublattices containing X. We will refer to this least sublattice as the *sublattice of L generated* by X. If the only sublattice containing X is L itself, we say that L is *generated* by X.

When we speak of a homomorphism, we will always mean a mapping that preserves finite meets and joins. Specifically, we define a mapping f of a lattice L to a lattice M to be a *homomorphism* if, for all x, $y \in L$,

$$f(x \vee y) = f(x) \vee f(y) \quad \text{and} \quad f(x \wedge y) = f(x) \wedge f(y).$$

A one-to-one homomorphism is called an *isomorphism*. Two lattices L and M are isomorphic (in symbols, $L \cong M$) if there exists an isomorphism of L onto M. An isomorphism of a lattice onto itself is an *automorphism*.

This definition of isomorphism views lattices as systems with two binary operations, while in the previous chapter the concept of isomorphic partially ordered sets was defined in terms of order-preserving maps. The reader should verify that when restricted to lattices, the two definitions coincide: *A one-to-one map f of a lattice L onto a lattice M is an isomorphism if and only if f and its inverse are order-preserving.*

For example, there are exactly five isomorphically distinct lattices having five elements; each five-element lattice is represented by one of the diagrams in Fig. 2-1.

We will want to consider identities in lattices, and therefore we need the concept of a lattice polynomial. Given a nonempty set X, we define a

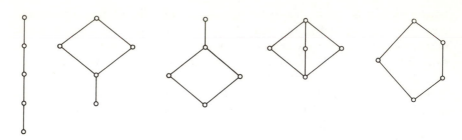

Fig. 2-1

lattice polynomial over X of *rank* r by induction as follows: Each element of X by itself is a lattice polynomial over X of rank 1; if p and q are lattice polynomials over X of ranks r and s, respectively, then the symbols

$$(p \vee q) \qquad \text{and} \qquad (p \wedge q)$$

are both lattice polynomials over X of rank $r + s$.[1] Notice that if p is a lattice polynomial over X, then there is some finite subset $Y \subseteq X$ such that p is a lattice polynomial over Y.

Let $W(X)$ denote the collection of all lattice polynomials over X. Since $(p \vee q) \in W(X)$ and $(p \wedge q) \in W(X)$ whenever $p, q \in W(X)$, the set $W(X)$ is naturally endowed with two binary operations $\vee$ and $\wedge$, and the system consisting of $W(X)$ together with these two operations will be referred to as the *word algebra* over X.

The word algebra is useful because of the following freeness property: *If f is any map of the set X to a lattice L, then f extends to a homomorphism φ of $W(X)$ to L.* Here a map φ of $W(X)$ to a lattice L is a *homomorphism* if, for all $p, q \in W(X)$,

$$\varphi((p \vee q)) = \varphi(p) \vee \varphi(q) \qquad \text{and} \qquad \varphi((p \wedge q)) = \varphi(p) \wedge \varphi(q).$$

The extension φ, of course, is constructed inductively: If $p \in X$, then $\varphi(p) = f(p)$, and if $\varphi(p)$ and $\varphi(q)$ have been defined, then $\varphi((p \vee q)) = \varphi(p) \vee \varphi(q)$ and $\varphi((p \wedge q)) = \varphi(p) \wedge \varphi(q)$.

Now let p and q be two lattice polynomials over X. We say that a lattice L satisfies the *lattice identity*[2]

$$p = q$$

if $\varphi(p) = \varphi(q)$ for every homomorphism φ of $W(X)$ to L.

This concept of a lattice satisfying an identity can also be formulated without reference to the word algebra. Let $X = \{x_1, \ldots, x_n\}$ be a nonempty

---

[1] In practice when we write lattice polynomials, superfluous parentheses will be dropped; e.g., $(x \vee (y \wedge z))$ will be more simply written $x \vee (y \wedge z)$.

[2] The reader will note that our notation for lattice identities violates our rule of using the symbol $=$ only for logical identity.

finite set. Let L be any lattice, and let L^n denote the set of all ordered n-tuples of elements of L. For each n-tuple $\langle a_1, \ldots, a_n \rangle \in L^n$ and each lattice polynomial p over X we define the lattice element

$$p(a_1, \ldots, a_n) \in L$$

by induction on the rank of p: If $p = x_k$, then $p(a_1, \ldots, a_n) = a_k$; if $p = (p_1 \vee p_2)$, then

$$p(a_1, \ldots, a_n) = p_1(a_1, \ldots, a_n) \vee p_2(a_1, \ldots, a_n),$$

with a dual definition in the case that $p = (p_1 \wedge p_2)$. It should now be apparent that, for any two lattice polynomials p and q over X, the lattice L satisfies the lattice identity $p = q$ if and only if

$$p(a_1, \ldots, a_n) = q(a_1, \ldots, a_n)$$

for each $\langle a_1, \ldots, a_n \rangle \in L^n$.

Conditions (1)–(4) above are examples of lattice identities that are satisfied by every lattice. In the next chapter we will consider some lattice identities that are not generally satisfied. Under any circumstances it is clear that if a lattice L satisfies a given lattice identity, then every sublattice and every homomorphic image of L satisfies this identity.

Most of the results obtained in subsequent chapters will involve some type of finiteness condition. The most stringent such condition that we will impose is the requirement that the lattice itself be finite. More general is the requirement that the lattice satisfy both the ascending and descending chain conditions, and more general still that it satisfy just one of the chain conditions.

The descending chain condition is generalized still further by the atomicity conditions. An element that covers the least element of a lattice L will be referred to as an *atom* of L. If a lattice L (perhaps with no least element) has the property that the sublattice a/b contains an atom whenever $a > b$ in L, we say that L is *strongly atomic*. The lattice L is said to be *weakly atomic* if, for every pair of elements $a, b \in L$ with $a > b$, there exist elements u, $v \in L$ such that $a \geq u \succ v \geq b$. And L is *atomic* if it has a least element and the sublattice $a/0$ contains an atom for each $a > 0$. Each strongly atomic lattice is weakly atomic, and each strongly atomic lattice having a least element is atomic. But despite the name, weak atomicity is not implied by atomicity. (Example?) So far we can immediately point to several classes of strongly atomic lattices, e.g., the lattice of all subsets of a set, the lattice of all subgroups of a torsion abelian group, and the lattice of all subspaces of a vector space.

The ascending chain condition also has an important generalization. An element c in a complete lattice L is called *compact* if whenever $c \leq \bigvee S$ there exists a finite subset $T \subseteq S$ with $c \leq \bigvee T$. We define a lattice L to be *compactly generated* if L is complete and each of its elements is a join of compact elements. It is perhaps surprising that this class of lattices, defined in a fairly complicated way, arises so naturally. The lattice of all subsets of a set is compactly generated, the compact elements being the finite subsets. Both the lattice of all admissible subgroups of an operator group and the lattice of all admissible normal subgroups are compactly generated; in the first case the compact elements are the finitely generated admissible subgroups, and in the second case they are the admissible normal closures of finite subsets of the group. This last example illustrates a very general situation: If in a set A a number of finitary operations are defined, then the set of all sub-algebras of A and the set of all congruence relations in A (considered as sets of ordered pairs) form compactly generated lattices under set-inclusion.

We have already suggested that the ascending chain condition implies compact generation: *Every element of a complete lattice L is compact if and only if L satisfies the ascending chain condition.* Suppose the lattice L satisfies the ascending chain condition, a is any element of L, and $a \leq \bigvee S$. Look at the set of all elements of the form $\bigvee F$, where F is a finite subset of S. This set contains a maximal element, say $\bigvee T$, because L satisfies the ascending chain condition, and the maximality of $\bigvee T$ requires that $\bigvee T = \bigvee S \geq a$. Thus a is compact. The reader can supply the proof of the converse.

In a compactly generated lattice L the join of two compact elements is again compact, but the meet of two compact elements need not be compact. (Example?) The property of compact generation is also inherited by complete sublattices: *If L is a compactly generated lattice and K is a complete sublattice of L, then K is compactly generated.* (The proof is an exercise.) Moreover, compact generation and the atomicity conditions are interrelated. In the first place:

2.2: *Every compactly generated lattice is weakly atomic.*

PROOF: Suppose that $a > b$ in a compactly generated lattice L. Then there is a compact element $c \in L$ such that $a \geq c$ but $b \not\geq c$; i.e., $a \geq b \vee c > b$. Set $P = \{x \in L \,|\, b \vee c > x \geq b\}$. P is nonempty since $b \in P$. Considering P as partially ordered by the restriction to P of the partial order of L, let C be any chain of P, and $d = \bigvee C$. Certainly $b \vee c \geq d \geq b$. If $b \vee c = d$, then $c \leq d = \bigvee C$, and the compactness of c implies that there is a finite subset $T \subseteq C$ such that $c \leq \bigvee T$. But T is a finite chain, so that if x is the largest member of T we have $x = \bigvee T \geq c$ and hence that $x \geq b \vee c$, contrary to the fact that $x \in P$. Consequently $b \vee c > d$, and $d \in P$. The hypotheses of Zorn's lemma are therefore satisfied, and we conclude that P contains a maximal element v. Now $a \geq b \vee c > v \geq b$, and the maximality of v ensures that there is no element $z \in L$ with $b \vee c > z > v$. Thus $a \geq b \vee c \succ v \geq b$, completing the proof.

Compact generation, too, has a useful generalization. Let us define a lattice L to be *upper continuous* if L is complete and, for every element $a \in L$ and every chain C in L, $a \wedge \bigvee C = \bigvee_{x \in C} a \wedge x$. The lattice L is *lower continuous* if its dual lattice is upper continuous, and it is *continuous* if it is both upper and lower continuous.

2.3: *Every compactly generated lattice is upper continuous.*

PROOF: Observe first that when $y \geq z$ in a compactly generated lattice L and $c \leq y$ implies $c \leq z$ for every compact element $c \in L$, then $y = z$. (Proof?) We will use this observation to prove 2.3. Note that inasmuch as $a \geq \bigvee_{x \in C} a \wedge x$ and $\bigvee C \geq \bigvee_{x \in C} a \wedge x$, we certainly have that

$$a \wedge \bigvee C \geq \bigvee_{x \in C} a \wedge x.$$

On the other hand, if c is a compact element with $c \leq a \wedge \bigvee C$, then $c \leq a$ and $c \leq \bigvee C$, and because of the compactness of c, there is a finite subset $T \subseteq C$ such that $c \leq \bigvee T$. Again, if x_0 is the largest element of T, then $x_0 = \bigvee T \geq c$, whence $c \leq a \wedge x_0 \leq \bigvee_{x \in C} a \wedge x$. And with the remark at the beginning of the proof in mind, the conclusion of 2.3 follows.

At several points we will actually need an alternative form of upper continuity.

2.4: *If a is an element of an upper continuous lattice L, S is a subset of L, and $\mathcal{S}$ is the set of all finite subsets of S, then*

$$a \wedge \bigvee S = \bigvee_{F \in \mathcal{S}} a \wedge \bigvee F.$$

PROOF: This is trivial when S is finite, so we proceed by induction on the cardinality of S. Assuming that 2.4 holds for every subset of L of cardinality less than $|S|$, arrange the elements in S in a (possibly transfinite) sequence x_0, $x_1, \ldots, x_\xi, \ldots (\xi < \lambda)$, where λ is the least ordinal number with $|\lambda| = |S|$. Set $S_\xi = \{x_\eta \mid \eta < \xi\}$. Then $|S_\xi| < |S|$ for each $\xi < \lambda$, and the elements $\bigvee S_\xi \ (\xi < \lambda)$ form a chain in L. Consequently if $\mathcal{S}_\xi$ denotes the set of all finite subsets of S_ξ,

$$a \wedge \bigvee S = a \wedge \bigvee_{\xi < \lambda} \bigvee S_\xi = \bigvee_{\xi < \lambda} a \wedge \bigvee S_\xi$$
$$= \bigvee_{\xi < \lambda} \bigvee_{F \in \mathcal{S}_\xi} a \wedge \bigvee F = \bigvee_{F \in \mathcal{S}} a \wedge \bigvee F,$$

completing the proof.

This alternative form shows that in the presence of upper continuity every atom is compact: *If a is an element of an upper continuous lattice L such that the sublattice $a/0$ satisfies the ascending chain condition, then a is compact.* For if $a \leq \bigvee S$ and $\mathcal{S}$ is the set of all finite subsets of S, then $a =$

$a \wedge \bigvee S = \bigvee_{F \in \mathfrak{F}} a \wedge \bigvee F$, and inasmuch as a is compact in $a/0$, it follows that $a = a \wedge \bigvee F \leq \bigvee F$ for some finite subset $F \subseteq S$.

In view of the preceding results, one might be tempted to guess that each weakly atomic upper continuous lattice is compactly generated. This is not the case, however, as shown by the following example due to Jeffrey Leon. Let C be the chain of nonnegative integers with a largest element ∞ adjoined. Let L be the set of all functions f on the nonnegative integers to C with the property that $f(i) = \infty$ for all but finitely many i, together with the "zero" function 0 defined by $0(i) = 0$ for all i. Define a partial order $\leq$ in L by

$$f \leq g \text{ if } f(i) \leq g(i) \qquad \text{for all } i.$$

L is then a complete lattice in which arbitrary joins as well as finite meets are computed componentwise. And it is easy to check that L is upper continuous and that $1/f$ is atomic whenever $f \neq 0$. On the other hand, if $f \neq 0$, then there is some integer k such that $f(k) = \infty$, and if we define the functions $f_n (n = 0, 1, \ldots)$ by $f_n(i) = f(i)$ when $i \neq k$ and $f_n(k) = n$, then f is the join of the f_n's, but the join of any finite subset of f_n's is less than f. Thus 0 is the only compact element of L.

We conclude this section with two theorems, the first characterizing completeness in terms of a fixed point property and the second showing that most infinite lattices contain an abundance of large sublattices.

2.5: *A lattice L is complete if and only if every order-preserving map f of L to itself has a fixed point, i.e., $f(a) = a$ for some $a \in L$.*[3]

PROOF: Suppose L is complete and f is an order-preserving map of L to itself. Set $A = \{x \in L \mid f(x) \geq x\}$ and $a = \bigvee A$. If $x \in A$, then $x \leq a$, and as f is order-preserving, $x \leq f(x) \leq f(a)$. $f(a)$ is therefore an upper bound of A, whence $a \leq f(a)$. This last relation implies that $f(a) \leq f(f(a))$, showing that $f(a) \in A$. Hence $f(a) \leq a$, and the equality $f(a) = a$ follows.

To prove the converse, assume that L is a lattice that is not complete. Theorem 2.1 yields that L contains a descending well-ordered chain C that does not have a meet. And if we let C_* denote the set of all lower bounds of C, it follows as in the proof of 2.1 that C_* contains a maximal ascending well-ordered chain D. Observe that if there were an element $x \in L$ such that $c \geq x \geq d$ for all $c \in C$ and $d \in D$, then x would be a lower bound of C, and since C does not have a meet, an element $y \in C_*$ would have to exist with $y \nleq x$, and as $x \vee y \in C_*$ and $x \vee y > x$, the set $D \cup \{x \vee y\}$ would be an ascending well-ordered chain in C_*, contradicting the maximality of D. Therefore there is no element $x \in L$ such that $c \geq x \geq d$ for all $c \in C$ and $d \in D$.

[3] A. Tarski [84], A. C. Davis [23].

We are now ready to define an order-preserving map that does not have a fixed point in L. For each $x \in L$, set

$$C(x) = \{c \in C \mid x \not\leq c\}, \qquad D(x) = \{d \in D \mid x \not\geq d\}.$$

As we observed above, for a given $x \in L$ either $C(x)$ or $D(x)$ is nonempty; if $C(x)$ is nonempty, define $f(x)$ to be the greatest element in $C(x)$; if $C(x)$ is empty, define $f(x)$ to be the least element in $D(x)$. Now for any $x \in L$ either $x \not\leq f(x)$ or $x \not\geq f(x)$, so f does not have a fixed point. It remains only to show that f is order-preserving.

Let x and y be elements in L with $x \leq y$. If $C(x)$ is empty but $C(y)$ is not, then $f(x) \in D$, while $f(y) \in C$, so that $f(x) \leq f(y)$. If both $C(x)$ and $C(y)$ are empty, then again $f(x) \leq f(y)$ because $D(y) \subseteq D(x)$. Finally, if $C(x)$ is nonempty, then $C(y)$ is also nonempty, and inasmuch as $C(y) \supseteq C(x)$, it follows that $f(x) \leq f(y)$. Thus f is order-preserving, and the proof is complete.

In connection with 2.5 the reader might show that if a partially ordered set P has a largest element and satisfies the descending chain condition, then every order-preserving map of P to itself has a fixed point. In particular there exist partially ordered sets that are not lattices but in which every order-preserving map has a fixed point. This suggests the following problem, which appears to be open: Describe those (finite) partially ordered sets in which each order-preserving map has a fixed point.

2.6: *If a lattice L has regular cardinality α, then one of the following conditions holds:*

(1) *There is an element $a \in L$ such that $a/0 \neq L$ and $|a/0| = \alpha$.*
(2) *There is an element $b \in L$ such that $1/b \neq L$ and $|1/b| = \alpha$.*
(3) *L has a least element 0 and a greatest element 1, and it contains a subset A of cardinality α such that, for every two distinct elements $x, y \in A$, $x \wedge y = 0$ and $x \vee y = 1$.*[4]

Observe that if condition (3) holds, then any subset of A together with 0 and 1 forms a sublattice of the lattice L. Consequently 2.6 has the following corollary: *If a lattice L has a regular cardinality α, then L has an infinite chain of sublattices each of cardinality α.*

PROOF OF 2.6: Assume that both (1) and (2) fail in the lattice L. Let $x \in L$ be any element that is neither the least element nor greatest element (if either

---

[4] T. Whaley [87]. Recall that a cardinal α is *regular* if it is infinite and it is not the sum of fewer than α cardinals each less than α. An infinite cardinal that is not regular is called *singular*.

exists). For any element $y \in L$, set

$$S(x, y) = \{z \in L \,|\, z \vee x = y\},$$
$$T(x, y) = \{z \in L \,|\, z \wedge x = y\}.$$

Certainly $z \in S(x, z \vee x)$, and therefore

$$L = \bigcup_{y \geq x} S(x, y).$$

Moreover, if $y_1 \neq y_2$, then $S(x, y_1)$ and $S(x, y_2)$ are disjoint, so that

$$\alpha = |L| = \sum_{y \geq x} |S(x, y)|.$$

Now by assumption $|1/x| < \alpha$ and α is regular, and therefore there is some element $y_0 > x$ for which $|S(x, y_0)| = \alpha$. Clearly, $S(x, y_0) \subseteq y_0/0$, and this implies that $|y_0/0| = \alpha$. But the only way this last equality can hold is for L to have a greatest element 1 and $y_0 = 1$. Moreover, if $1 > y \geq x$, then $|y/0| < \alpha$, and it follows that $|S(x, y)| < \alpha$. Thus

$$|L - S(x, 1)| = \Big| \bigcup_{1 > y \geq x} S(x, y) \Big| = \sum_{1 > y \geq x} |S(x, y)| < \alpha.$$

By duality, L has a least element 0, and $|L - T(x, 0)| < \alpha$. At this point, set

$$C(x) = S(x, 1) \cap T(x, 0) = \{z \in L \,|\, z \vee x = 1 \text{ and } z \wedge x = 0\}.$$

The inequalities above yield that

$$|L - C(x)| \leq |L - S(x, 1)| + |L - T(x, 0)| < \alpha.$$

And we emphasize that this last inequality holds for any element $x \neq 0, 1$.

To complete the proof, it suffices to construct an element x_ξ for each ordinal number $\xi < \alpha$ such that $x_\xi \neq 0, 1$ and $x_\xi \in C(x_\eta)$ whenever $\xi \neq \eta$. Proceeding by induction, suppose that we have the elements $x_\xi (\xi < \mu)$ with the required properties for some ordinal $\mu < \alpha$. Then as α is regular, $\mu < \alpha$, and each $|L - C(x_\xi)| < \alpha$, we must have

$$\Big| L - \bigcap_{\xi < \mu} C(x_\xi) \Big| = \Big| \bigcup_{\xi < \mu} (L - C(x_\xi)) \Big| \leq \sum_{\xi < \mu} |L - C(x_\xi)| < \alpha.$$

In particular, the set $\bigcap_{\xi < \mu} C(x_\xi)$ is not empty, and we take x_μ to be any one of its elements. This completes the proof.

The reader should devise an example to show that 2.6 fails without the assumption that the cardinality of the lattice is regular. Whether the corollary to 2.6 remains true without this assumption of regularity, however, is an open question.

3

DISTRIBUTIVE, MODULAR
AND
SEMIMODULAR LATTICES

The study of distributive lattices begins with the following theorem, the proof of which is left as an exercise for the reader.

3.1: *If a lattice satisfies any one of the following identities, then it satisfies all three:*

(1) $(x \vee y) \wedge (x \vee z) \wedge (y \vee z) = (x \wedge y) \vee (x \wedge z) \vee (y \wedge z)$.
(2) $x \wedge (y \vee z) = (x \wedge y) \vee (x \wedge z)$.
(3) $x \vee (y \wedge z) = (x \vee y) \wedge (x \vee z)$.

A lattice that satisfies these identities is called a *distributive* lattice.

Not every lattice is distributive. The reader may verify, for example, that of the five lattices with five elements, three are distributive, while two are not. The two which are not distributive are shown in Fig. 3-1. On the other hand, any chain is a distributive lattice, and the lattice of all subsets of a set is always distributive.

We say that a lattice L is *modular* if, for all $a, b, c \in L$,

$$a \geq b \text{ implies } a \wedge (b \vee c) = b \vee (a \wedge c).$$

Alternatively, a lattice is a modular if and only if it satisfies the following identity:

$$(x \vee y) \wedge ((x \wedge y) \vee z) = (x \wedge y) \vee ((x \vee y) \wedge z).$$

Observe that modularity and distributivity are self-dual lattice properties.

Every distributive lattice is modular, but not every modular lattice is distributive. In particular, the lattice on the left in Fig. 3-1 is modular but not distributive, while the lattice on the right in Fig. 3-1 is not even modular. Interestingly enough, these two five-element lattices determine whether or not a particular lattice is distributive or modular. Our next two results formulate this precisely.

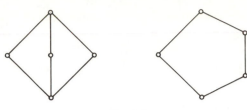

Fig. 3–1

3.2: *A lattice L is modular if and only if L has no nonmodular five-element sublattice.*

PROOF: Let a, b, c be elements of a lattice L, and suppose that $a \geq b$. Then it is easily checked that

$$b \vee c \geq a \wedge (b \vee c) \geq b \vee (a \wedge c) \geq a \wedge c.$$

Moreover, either $b \vee c = a \wedge (b \vee c)$ or $b \vee (a \wedge c) = a \wedge c$ implies that $a \wedge (b \vee c) = b \vee (a \wedge c)$. Now suppose that L is nonmodular, and a, b, c, $\in L$ are such that $a \geq b$ and $a \wedge (b \vee c) \neq b \vee (a \wedge c)$. Then, in view of the preceding remarks,

$$b \vee c > a \wedge (b \vee c) > b \vee (a \wedge c) > a \wedge c.$$

Also

$$c \wedge (a \wedge (b \vee c)) = a \wedge (c \wedge (b \vee c)) = a \wedge c,$$

and because of the inequalities above, we must have $c \wedge (b \vee (a \wedge c)) = a \wedge c$. Similarly,

$$c \vee (b \vee (a \wedge c)) = c \vee (a \wedge (b \vee c)) = b \vee c.$$

Consequently, the elements $b \vee c$, $a \wedge (b \vee c)$, $b \vee (a \wedge c)$, $a \wedge c$, and c form a five-element sublattice of L which is isomorphic to the nonmodular five-element lattice represented in Fig. 3-1. Since every sublattice of a modular lattice is modular, the proof of 3.2 is complete.

3.3: *A lattice L is distributive if and only if L has no nondistributive five-element sublattice.*

PROOF: Again, the necessity is clear, and inasmuch as we possess 3.2 it suffices to show that a modular nondistributive lattice contains a nondistributive five-element sublattice. Suppose a_1, a_2, a_3 are elements of a modular lattice L. Set

$$u = (a_1 \vee a_2) \wedge (a_1 \vee a_3) \wedge (a_2 \vee a_3),$$
$$v = (a_1 \wedge a_2) \vee (a_1 \wedge a_3) \vee (a_2 \wedge a_3),$$
$$e_1 = (a_2 \wedge a_3) \vee (a_1 \wedge (a_2 \vee a_3)),$$
$$e_2 = (a_1 \wedge a_3) \vee (a_2 \wedge (a_1 \vee a_3)),$$
$$e_3 = (a_1 \wedge a_2) \vee (a_3 \wedge (a_1 \vee a_2)),$$

and observe that application of the modular law yields a dual expression for the e_i's:

$$e_1 = (a_2 \vee a_3) \wedge (a_1 \vee (a_2 \wedge a_3)),$$

$$e_2 = (a_1 \vee a_3) \wedge (a_2 \vee (a_1 \wedge a_3)),$$

$$e_3 = (a_1 \vee a_2) \wedge (a_3 \vee (a_1 \wedge a_2)).$$

Let us compute $e_1 \vee e_2$. From the fact that

$$a_1 \wedge a_3 \leq a_1 \wedge (a_2 \vee a_3), \qquad a_2 \wedge a_3 \leq a_2 \wedge (a_1 \vee a_3),$$

and with two applications of modularity, we obtain that

$$\begin{aligned} e_1 \vee e_2 &= (a_2 \wedge (a_1 \vee a_3)) \vee (a_1 \wedge (a_2 \vee a_3)) \\ &= (a_2 \vee a_3) \wedge [a_1 \vee (a_2 \wedge (a_1 \vee a_3))] \\ &= (a_2 \vee a_3) \wedge [(a_1 \vee a_3) \wedge (a_1 \vee a_2)] = u. \end{aligned}$$

By symmetry we have that $u = e_1 \vee e_2 = e_1 \vee e_3 = e_2 \vee e_3$, and duality yields that $v = e_1 \wedge e_2 = e_1 \wedge e_3 = e_2 \wedge e_3$. Notice also that if any two of the elements u, e_1, e_2, e_3, v are equal, then $u = v$. This is clear for any two of e_1, e_2, e_3. If $u = e_1$, then $v = e_1 \wedge e_2 = e_2$, and hence $u = e_2 \vee e_3 = e_3$, whence $u = e_1 \wedge e_3 = v$. The remaining cases follow similarly.

Now if L is nondistributive, there are three elements $a_1, a_2, a_3 \in L$ such that, if u, v, e_1, e_2, and e_3 are defined for these a_i's as above, then $u \neq v$. Therefore, in view of the calculations in the preceding paragraph, the elements u, e_1, e_2, e_3, v form a five-element sublattice of L which is isomorphic to the modular nondistributive lattice in Fig. 3-1, and the proof of 3.3 is complete.

The statements of 3.2 and 3.3 can be recast in the following, often useful, form: *A lattice L is modular if and only if, for all $a, b, c \in L$,*

$$a \geq b, \qquad a \vee c = b \vee c, \qquad \text{and} \qquad a \wedge c = b \wedge c \quad \text{imply} \quad a = b;$$

L is distributive if and only if for all $a, b, c \in L$,

$$a \vee c = b \vee c \qquad \text{and} \qquad a \wedge c = b \wedge c \quad \text{imply} \quad a = b.$$

Perhaps the most ready source of examples of modular lattices comes from other algebraic systems, groups, rings, vector spaces, etc. The reader can show that *for any operator group G the lattice of admissible normal subgroups of G is a modular lattice.* And one of the fundamental properties of operator groups, the second isomorphism theorem, has a lattice-theoretic counterpart.

3.4: *If a and b are elements of a modular lattice L, then the quotient sublattices $a \vee b/a$ and $b/a \wedge b$ are isomorphic.*

PROOF: Define the mapping f of $a \vee b/a$ to $b/a \wedge b$ by

$$f(x) = x \wedge b \qquad\qquad x \in a \vee b/a$$

and define the mapping g of $b/a \wedge b$ to $a \vee b/a$ by

$$g(y) = a \vee y \qquad\qquad y \in b/a \wedge b.$$

If $x \in a \vee b/a$, i.e., $a \vee b \geq x \geq a$, then it follows by modularity that

$$g(f(x)) = a \vee (x \wedge b) = x \wedge (a \vee b) = x.$$

Similarly, $f(g(y)) = y$ for all $y \in b/a \wedge b$. Consequently f and g are inverses of each other, and so both are one-to-one and onto. Since both are also order-preserving, the conclusion of 3.4 follows.

In compactly generated lattices this second isomorphism theorem is equivalent to modularity.

3.5:   *If a compactly generated lattice L has the property that $a \vee b/a \cong b/a \wedge b$ for all a, $b \in L$, then L is modular.*[1]

PROOF: Suppose L is a compactly generated lattice satisfying the hypothesis of the theorem but L is not modular. Then L contains a five-element sublattice $\{a, b, t, u, v\}$ such that $a > b$ and $t \vee a = t \vee b = u$, $t \wedge a = t \wedge b = v$. If a does not cover b, then by 2.2 there exist elements $p, q \in L$ such that $a \geq p \succ q \geq b$. Clearly, $t \vee p = t \vee q = u$ and $t \wedge p = t \wedge q = v$, and consequently the subset $\{p, q, t, u, v\}$ is a nonmodular five-element sublattice in which $p \succ q$. Hence we may assume that the sublattice $\{a, b, t, u, v\}$ was originally picked in such a way that $a \succ b$.

Let T be the set of all ordered triples $\langle x, y, z \rangle$ $(x, y, z \in L)$ such that $u \geq x \geq a$, $y \geq b$, $z \geq v$ and such that the following relations hold:

(1) $t \vee y = u.$
(2) $t \wedge x = z.$
(3) $x \succ y \geq z.$
(4) $a \wedge y = b.$

T is nonempty since the triple $\langle a, b, v \rangle$ is in T. Partially order T by defining $\langle x, y, z \rangle \leq \langle x', y', z' \rangle$ if $x \leq x'$, $y \leq y'$, and $z \leq z'$. Suppose $\langle x_i, y_i, z_i \rangle$ $(i \in I)$ is a chain of elements in T. Set

$$\bar{x} = \bigvee_{i \in I} x_i, \qquad \bar{y} = \bigvee_{i \in I} y_i, \qquad \bar{z} = \bigvee_{i \in I} z_i.$$

Then

$$t \vee \bar{y} = t \vee \bigvee_{i \in I} y_i = \bigvee_{i \in I} t \vee y_i = u,$$

and as the elements $x_i (i \in I)$ and the elements $y_i (i \in I)$ form chains in L, we have

$$t \wedge \bar{x} = t \wedge \bigvee_{i \in I} x_i = \bigvee_{i \in I} t \wedge x_i = \bigvee_{i \in I} z_i = \bar{z}$$

and

$$a \wedge \bar{y} = a \wedge \bigvee_{i \in I} y_i = \bigvee_{i \in I} a \wedge y_i = b.$$

[1] P. Crawley [17]. Cf. M. Ward [86].

Moreover, for each $i \in I$, $a \vee y_i = x_i$ since $x_i \geq a$, $x_i \succ y_i$, and $y_i \not\geq a$. Therefore

$$a \vee \bar{y} = a \vee \bigvee_{i \in I} y_i = \bigvee_{i \in I} a \vee y_i = \bigvee_{i \in I} x_i = \bar{x}.$$

Hence $\bar{x}/\bar{y} = a \vee \bar{y}/\bar{y} \cong a/a \wedge \bar{y} = a/b$, and since $a \succ b$, we must have $\bar{x} \succ \bar{y}$. It follows that $\langle \bar{x}, \bar{y}, \bar{z} \rangle \in T$, and consequently every chain of T has an upper bound. By Zorn's lemma, T contains a maximal element $\langle a_0, b_0, v_0 \rangle$.

The remainder of the proof uses the following lemma; its proof is left to the reader.

A. Let L be a lattice in which $a \vee b/a \cong b/a \wedge b$ for all $a, b \in L$, and let p, q, and r be elements of L with $p \succ q$. Then either $r \wedge p = r \wedge q$ or $r \wedge p \succ r \wedge q$. Similarly, either $r \vee p = r \vee q$ or $r \vee p \succ r \vee q$.

Continuing with the proof of the theorem, notice that $u/b_0 = t \vee b_0/b_0 \cong t/t \wedge b_0 = t/v_0$. Thus, as $u > a_0 \succ b_0$, there must exist an element $v_1 \in L$ such that

$$t > v_1 \succ v_0.$$

Set

$$a_1 = a_0 \vee v_1 \qquad \text{and} \qquad b_1 = b_0 \vee v_1.$$

We will show that the triple $\langle a_1, b_1, v_1 \rangle$ belongs to T.

It is clear that $t \vee b_1 = u$. Now $a_0 \not\geq v_1$ since $t \wedge a_0 = v_0$, and this implies that $a_1 = a_0 \vee v_1 \neq a_0 \vee v_0 = a_0$. Therefore by A and the fact that $v_1 \succ v_0$ we infer that $a_1 \succ a_0$. Computing further,

$$t \wedge a_1 \geq v_1 \succ v_0 = t \wedge a_0,$$

so that $t \wedge a_1 \succ t \wedge a_0 = v_0$ by A. Thus $t \wedge a_1 = v_1$. Just as $a_1 \succ a_0$, it follows that $b_1 \succ b_0$. Consequently $a_1 \neq b_1$, for otherwise $b_1 > a_0 > b_0$, contrary to $b_1 \succ b_0$. Therefore by A and the fact that $a_0 \succ b_0$ we obtain that $a_1 \succ b_1$. Finally, consider $a \wedge b_1$. Inasmuch as $a_0 \geq a > b$ and $b_1 > b$, it follows that $a \wedge b_1 \leq a_0 \wedge b_1 = b_0$. This implies that $b \leq a \wedge b_1 \leq a \wedge b_0 = b$, whence $a \wedge b_1 = b$. We conclude that $\langle a_1, b_1, v_1 \rangle$ satisfies conditions (1)–(4); i.e., $\langle a_1, b_1, v_1 \rangle \in T$. But $\langle a_1, b_1, v_1 \rangle$ is certainly greater than $\langle a_0, b_0, v_0 \rangle$, contrary to the maximal choice of $\langle a_0, b_0, v_0 \rangle$. Thus L must be modular, and the proof of the theorem is complete.

If the assumption of compact generation is dropped, then 3.5 fails, as the following example demonstrates. Let E and F be disjoint chains isomorphic to the real numbers, let $L = E \cup F \cup \{-\infty\} \cup \{\infty\}$, and define in L, $-\infty < x \leq y < \infty$ if and only if both x, y belong to either E or F and $x \leq y$ in that chain to which they belong. L is then a nonmodular lattice, even though $a \vee b/a \cong b/a \wedge b$ for all $a, b \in L$.

By weakening the second isomorphism theorem, we are led to the concept of semimodularity. Specifically, we call a lattice L *semimodular* if, for all $a, b \in L$, $a \succ a \wedge b$ implies $a \vee b \succ b$. The lattice L is *lower semi-*

modular if its dual is semimodular, i.e., if, for all $a, b \in L$, $a \vee b \succ b$ implies $a \succ a \wedge b$. Every modular lattice is both semimodular and lower semimodular. On the other hand, an examination of the proof of 3.5 reveals that every application of the assumption $a \vee b/a \cong b/a \wedge b$, with one exception, actually requires only the weaker assumption that $a \vee b \succ a$ if and only if $b \succ a \wedge b$. The exception occurs in proving the existence of the covering element v_1. However, if the lattice is further assumed to be strongly atomic, then the existence of v_1 follows from this condition. Thus we have:

3.6: *If a compactly generated, strongly atomic lattice L is both semimodular and lower semimodular, then L is modular.*

Group theory again provides examples of semimodular lattices. If the subnormal subgroups of a group G satisfy the ascending chain condition, then the set of all the subnormal subgroups of G is a lower semimodular sublattice of the lattice of all subgroups of G. In particular, the lattice of all subgroups of a finite nilpotent group is lower semimodular, and as demonstrated by the dihedral group of order 8, this lattice is generally nonmodular.

Another source of examples comes from the theory of field extensions. If F is a subfield of a field K, and if we define a subfield S of K to be *relatively algebraically closed* if S contains every element of K which is algebraic over S, then the collection of all relatively algebraically closed subfields of K which contain F, partially ordered by set-inclusion, is a semimodular compactly generated strongly atomic lattice. These lattices, too, are generally nonmodular; e.g., if K is generated over F by three independent transcendental elements x, y, z, then the modular law fails for the relatively algebraically closed subfields

$$A = F(x, y), \qquad B = F(x) \qquad \text{and} \qquad C = F(z, x + yz).$$

We can construct a finite semimodular lattice quite simply by taking the lattice of all subsets of a finite set with, say, n elements, choosing an integer $t \leq n$ and identifying all those subsets with t or more elements. For instance, if this is done with $n = 4$ and $t = 3$, the nonmodular semimodular lattice in Fig. 3-2 is obtained.

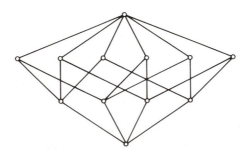

Fig. 3–2

Classically semimodular lattices arose out of certain closure operators. In the preceding chapter we remarked that if X is any set and a map $S \longrightarrow S^c$ of the set of all subsets of X to itself is a closure operator, i.e.,

(1)　$S \subseteq S^c$,
(2)　$S \subseteq T$ implies $S^c \subseteq T^c$,
(3)　$(S^c)^c = S^c$,

then the closed subsets of X form a complete lattice under set-inclusion. If, in addition, this closure operator satisfies the *exchange axiom*,

(4)　$x, y \in X, x \in (S \cup \{y\})^c$ and $x \notin S^c$ imply that $y \in (S \cup \{x\})^c$,

then the complete lattice of closed subsets of X is semimodular, and each of its elements is a join of atoms. (Proof?)

As an illustration, let us apply the preceding paragraph to graphs. Given any graph G without trivial cycles and without double edges, let X be the set of all the edges of G. Define a subset S of X to be closed if S has the property that it contains all the edges comprising a cycle whenever it contains all but one of the edges of this cycle, and for any subset $S \subseteq X$ define S^c to be the least closed subset containing S. Conditions (1)–(4) are now easily verified, and consequently the closed subsets of X form a complete semimodular lattice called the *edge lattice* of G. For example, if G is the graph shown in Fig. 3-3, then the edge lattice of G is isomorphic to Fig. 3-4.

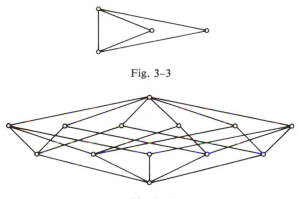

Fig. 3–3

Fig. 3–4

In a compactly generated strongly atomic lattice, semimodularity is also equivalent to an apparently weaker condition:

3.7:　*If a compactly generated, strongly atomic lattice L has the property that, for all $a, b \in L, a, b \succ a \wedge b$ imply $a \vee b \succ a, b$, then L is semimodular.*

PROOF: Suppose that $a, b \in L$ are such that $a \succ a \wedge b$. Set

$$T = \{x \in L \mid a \wedge b \le x \le b \text{ and } a \vee x \succ x\}.$$

Then $a \wedge b \in T$, so that T is nonempty. Suppose $x_i (i \in I)$ is a chain of elements in T, and let $\bar{x} = \bigvee_{i \in I} x_i$. If $y \in L$ is such that $a \vee \bar{x} > y \geq \bar{x}$, then as $y \not\geq a$ and $a \vee x_i > x_i$, we have

$$y = y \wedge (a \vee \bar{x}) = y \wedge \bigvee_{i \in I} a \vee x_i = \bigvee_{i \in I} y \wedge (a \vee x_i) = \bigvee_{i \in I} x_i = \bar{x}.$$

Therefore $a \vee \bar{x} > \bar{x}$. And inasmuch as $a \wedge b \leq \bar{x} \leq b$, $\bar{x} \in T$. By Zorn's lemma, T contains a maximal element u. If $b > u$, then by the strong atomicity of L there is an element p such that $b \geq p > u$. Now $p \not\geq a$, and therefore

$$p, a \vee u > u = p \wedge (a \vee u).$$

Consequently $(a \vee u) \vee p = a \vee p > p$. But this means that $p \in T$, contrary to the maximal choice of u. Hence $b = u \in T$, and we conclude that $a \vee b > b$.

3.8: *If a semimodular lattice L has a finite maximal chain containing, say, n elements, then every chain of L contains at most n elements.*

PROOF: Let the least and greatest elements of L be 0 and 1, respectively, and let the n-element maximal chain of L be

$$0 = x_0 \prec x_1 \prec \cdots \prec x_{n-1} = 1.$$

The proof of 3.8 is by induction on the integer n.

Let C be any finite chain of L, and let c be the least element of $C - 0$. If $c \geq x_1$, then $C - 0$ is a chain of $1/x_1$, and the induction assumption yields that $C - 0$ has at most $n - 1$ elements, giving the desired conclusion. Consequently we may assume that $c \not\geq x_1$. Suppose $c \geq a > b > 0$. Then $a \wedge x_1 = b \wedge x_1 = 0 \prec x_1$, and hence $a \vee x_1 > a$ and $b \vee x_1 > b$. Thus $b \vee x_1 = a \vee x_1 > a > b$ is impossible, and therefore we must have that $a \vee x_1 > b \vee x_1$. This observation, together with the fact that all chains of $1/x_1$ are finite, yields that all chains of $c/0$ are finite, so that, in particular, $c/0$ contains an atom p.

Inasmuch as $p \neq x_1$, we have $p, x_1 > p \wedge x_1 = 0$, so that $z = p \vee x_1 > p, x_1$. All the chains of $1/x_1$ contain at most $n - 1$ elements, and therefore if Z is a maximal chain of $1/z$, then Z contains at most $n - 2$ elements. On the other hand, $Z \cup \{p\}$ is a maximal chain with at most $n - 1$ elements in $1/p$, and the induction yields that $C - 0$ has at most $n - 1$ elements.

Note that 3.8 has the following corollary: *If a semimodular lattice L has a finite maximal chain, then any two maximal chains of L contain the same number of elements.*

3.9: *If a semimodular, strongly atomic lattice L satisfies the ascending chain condition and has a least element, then every chain of L is finite.*

PROOF: Assume that 3.9 is not true. Let a be a maximal element in the set

$$\{x \in L \,|\, 1/x \text{ contains an infinite chain}\}.$$

Then a is not the greatest element of L, and hence there is an element $b \in L$ such that $b \succ a$. Every chain of $1/b$ is finite, and if B is a maximal chain of $1/b$, then $B \cup \{a\}$ is a finite maximal chain of $1/a$. But then 3.8 yields that every chain of $1/a$ is finite, a contradiction.

Theorem 3.8 allows us to introduce the idea of dimension in semimodular lattices with finite chains. We say that a semimodular lattice has *dimension* n if it has a maximal chain containing exactly $n + 1$ elements. A semimodular lattice is *finite dimensional* if it has dimension n for some nonnegative integer n; otherwise the lattice is *infinite dimensional*. Also, an element a in a semimodular lattice for which the sublattice $a/0$ has dimension n will be referred to as an *n-dimensional element* or a *finite dimensional element*. Observe that *if an element a in a semimodular lattice is a join of finitely many finite dimensional elements, then a is a finite dimensional element.* (Proof?)

Now suppose that L is a finite dimensional semimodular lattice. For each element $x \in L$, let $\delta(x)$ denote the dimension of $x/0$. This defines a function δ on L to the nonnegative integers, which we call the *dimension function* of L.

3.10: *The dimension function δ of a finite dimensional semimodular lattice L has the following properties:*

(1) $\delta(x) = 0$ *if and only if x is the least element of L.*
(2) $x \prec y$ *if and only if $x \le y$ and $\delta(y) = \delta(x) + 1$.*
(3)   *For all x, $y \in L$, $\delta(x \vee y) + \delta(x \wedge y) \le \delta(x) + \delta(y)$.*

Moreover, the lattice L is modular if and only if

(4)   *For all x, $y \in L$, $\delta(x \vee y) + \delta(x \wedge y) = \delta(x) + \delta(y)$.*

The proof of 3.10 is left as an exercise for the reader. We also leave the proof of the following as an exercise: If a distributive lattice L has finite dimension n, then L contains at most 2^n elements.

Thus far we have mentioned four isomorphically distinct distributive lattices of dimension 3: the four-element chain, the lattice of all subsets of a three-element set, and the two five-element distributive lattices of dimension 3. There is only one more, shown in Fig. 3-5.

A modular lattice of dimension 2 is determined, up to isomorphism, by the number of its atoms. If L is a modular lattice of dimension 3, u is the join of all the atoms of L, and u is *less* than the greatest element of L, then the sublattice $u/0$ is of dimension 2, and there is an atom a of L such that every element which is greater than an atom belongs to the two-dimensional sublattice $1/a$. (The reader should devise a proof of this last assertion.) Consequently a modular lattice of dimension 3 in which the greatest element is not a join of atoms is determined, up to isomorphism, by the number of

Fig. 3–5

its atoms and the number of its two-dimensional elements. For example, such a lattice with four atoms and five two-dimensional elements is represented by Fig. 3-6.

Modular lattices of dimension 3 in which the greatest element is a join of atoms are no longer determined by the number of atoms and number of two-dimensional elements. Figures 3-7 and 3-8 represent nonisomorphic

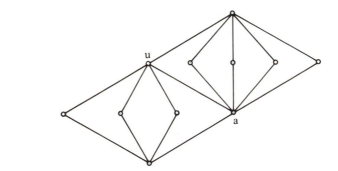

Fig. 3–6

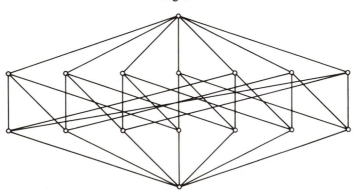

Fig. 3–7

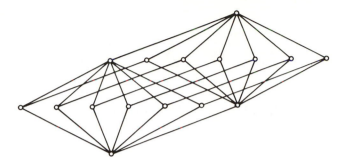

Fig. 3–8

modular lattices of dimension 3, both having seven atoms and seven two-dimensional elements.

The description of all those semimodular lattices of dimension 3 in which the greatest element is not a join of atoms is only slightly more complicated than the modular case. We leave this project to the reader, with a single nonmodular example, Fig. 3-9.

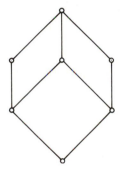

Fig. 3–9

4

COMPLEMENTED LATTICES

When a lattice L has a least element 0 and a greatest element 1, we can speak of complements in L. Specifically, by a *complement* of an element a in the lattice L we mean an element $a' \in L$ such that

$$a \wedge a' = 0 \qquad \text{and} \qquad a \vee a' = 1.$$

We say that a lattice is *complemented* if it has a least element and a greatest element and each of its elements has a complement. A lattice L (not necessarily with least and greatest elements) is called *relatively complemented* if the quotient sublattice a/b is complemented for each pair of elements $a > b$ in L.

We have already seen some complemented lattices. Both the lattice of all subsets of a set and the lattice of all subspaces of a vector space are complemented; in fact, they are also relatively complemented. On the other hand, none of the elements of a chain has a complement, except the least and greatest elements when they both exist.

Other examples of complemented lattices appear in Chap. 3. Our first theorem shows, for instance, that the edge lattice of a graph is relatively complemented.

4.1: *Let L be an upper continuous semimodular lattice. If the greatest element of L is a join of atoms, then L is both atomic and complemented. Consequently if every element of L is the join of atoms, then L is relatively complemented.*

PROOF: Let 0 and 1 denote, respectively, the least and greatest elements of L. Choose any nonzero element $x \in L$. If A is the set of all the atoms of L, then by 2.4 we have

$$x = x \wedge 1 = x \wedge \bigvee A = \bigvee_{F \in \alpha} x \wedge \bigvee F,$$

where α is the set of all finite subsets of A. But at least one of the elements $x \wedge \bigvee F$ is not 0, and each of the elements $x \wedge \bigvee F$ is finite dimensional because of the semimodularity of L, and so there must exist an atom p with $x \geq p$.

Now use upper continuity and Zorn's lemma to obtain an element u that is maximal with respect to the property

$$x \wedge u = 0.$$

If $x \vee u \neq 1$, there is an atom p such that $p \not\leq x \vee u$, and the semimodularity of L requires that $u \vee p \succ u$. Suppose $x \wedge (u \vee p) \neq 0$. As we have just seen, there is an atom q such that $q \leq x \wedge (u \vee p)$. Certainly $u \not\geq q$ since $x \geq q$, and semimodularity again shows that $u \vee q \succ u$. But $u \vee p \geq q$, and therefore $u \vee p \geq u \vee q \succ u$. This last formula combined with the fact that $u \vee p \succ u$ yields that $u \vee p = u \vee q$, and this shows that $x \vee u \geq q \vee u \geq p$ a contradiction. Thus we must have $x \wedge (u \vee p) = 0$. This, however, contradicts the maximality of u, and we conclude that $x \vee u = 1$. Hence L is both atomic and complemented when 1 is a join of atoms.

If every element is a join of atoms, and $a > b$ in L, then

$$a = \bigvee \{ p \vee b \mid a \geq p \succ 0 \text{ and } b \not\geq p \},$$

and as each of the elements $p \vee b$ is an atom of a/b, the preceding paragraphs show that L is relatively complemented.

It is not true that every element of an upper continuous semimodular lattice is a join of atoms when the greatest element is a join of atoms. Figure 4-1 is a semimodular lattice in which the greatest element is a join of atoms but not every element is a join of atoms—nor is the lattice relatively complemented.

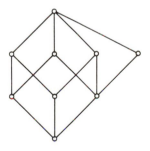

Fig. 4–1

Our next theorem shows, however, that these differences disappear in the face of modularity. First a useful lemma:

4.2: *Every complemented modular lattice is relatively complemented.*

PROOF: If $a \geq x \geq b$ in a complemented modular lattice L and y is a complement of x in L, then the element $a \wedge (b \vee y) = b \vee (a \wedge y)$ is a complement of x in a/b, as desired.

4.3:   *The following conditions in a complete modular lattice L are equivalent:*

(1)   *L is complemented and compactly generated.*
(2)   *L is complemented, strongly atomic, and upper continuous.*
(3)   *L is complemented, atomic, and upper continuous.*
(4)   *L is upper continuous and every element of L is a join of atoms.*
(5)   *L is upper continuous and its greatest element is a join of atoms.*

PROOF: It is clear that (2) implies (3) and (4) implies (5). We need to show, therefore, that (1) implies (2), (3) implies (4), and (5) implies (1). Throughout the proof 0 and 1 will denote the least and greatest elements of L, respectively.

Assume that (1) holds. L is then upper continuous by 2.3. If $a > b$ in L, then by 2.2 there exist elements u, v with $a \geq u \succ v \geq b$; and if p is a complement of v in the sublattice u/b, it follows from lower semimodularity that $p \succ b$, and hence that L is strongly atomic.

Assume that (3) holds. Let x be any element of L, and set

$$v = \bigvee\{p \mid x \geq p \succ 0\}.$$

If $x > v$, then there is a complement w of v in $x/0$, and as w is necessarily non-zero, there is an atom p with $p \leq w$. But then $v \not\geq p$, contrary to the definition of v. Thus $x = v$, and (4) holds. Notice that we have actually proved a little more: *Every element of a complete, relatively complemented, atomic lattice is a join of atoms.*

Finally, assume that (5) holds. Theorem 4.1 and Lemma 4.2 combine to show that L is then complemented and that each of its elements is a join of atoms. In Chap. 2 we noted that each atom in an upper continuous lattice is compact, whence L is compactly generated. This completes the proof.

If every element of a complemented lattice L has exactly one complement, then we say that L is *uniquely complemented*. We say that a complemented lattice L has *unique comparable complements* if no element of L has two distinct comparable complements. In view of 3.2 and 3.3, every complemented distributive lattice is uniquely complemented, while every complemented modular lattice has unique comparable complements. Unfortunately, the converses do not hold; in Chap. 16 we will show that every lattice, in particular a nonmodular lattice, is a sublattice of some uniquely complemented lattice. Still, there seems to be a close relationship between unique complements and distributivity and between unique comparable complements and modularity, as the following two theorems indicate.

4.4:   *Every complemented atomic lattice having unique comparable complements is modular.*[1]

[1] J. E. McLaughlin [68].

PROOF: Throughout the proof, L denotes a lattice which satisfies the hypotheses of 4.4 and whose least and greatest elements are 0 and 1, respectively. The proof is made in several steps, as follows.

A. If $x, p \in L$, $p \succ 0$, and $p \vee x > x$, then $1 \succ x \vee t$ for any complement t of $p \vee x$.

First, observe that

$$p \vee (x \vee t) = (p \vee x) \vee t = 1 > x \vee t,$$

since t cannot be a complement of both $p \vee x$ and x. In particular, $p \nleq x \vee t$, and therefore $p \wedge (x \vee t) = 0$; i.e., $x \vee t$ is a complement of p. If $1 > y \geq x \vee t$, then it follows that y must also be a complement of p, and as comparable complements are unique, we conclude that $y = x \vee t$.

B. For every $x \neq 1$ in L there is an element q such that $1 \succ q \geq x$.

Statement B is immediate from A and shows that the dual of L is also atomic. Since complementation and the uniqueness of comparable complements are self-dual properties, the dual of any statement we now derive in L must also hold in L. In particular, the dual statement of A must hold:

C. If $x, q \in L$, $q \prec 1$, and $q \wedge x < x$, then $0 \prec x \wedge t$ for any complement t of $q \wedge x$.

D. If $x, p \in L$ and $p \succ x \wedge p = 0$, then $x \vee p \succ x$.

Set $a = p \vee x$, and let b be a complement of a. Then $1 \succ x \vee b$ by A. Let $t = a \wedge (x \vee b)$. The condition $t = a$ implies that $x \vee b \geq a$ and hence that $x \vee b = 1$, a contradiction. Thus $t < a$. We next observe that if $a > y \geq x$, then $t \geq y$. In particular, this will show that $a \succ t$. To prove our observation, note that $p \vee y = a$ and $p \succ p \wedge y = 0$, and consequently $1 \succ y \vee b$ by A. But $y \vee b \geq x \vee b$ and $1 \succ x \vee b$, so that we must have $x \vee b = y \vee b \geq y$, which yields that $t \geq y$. Now choose a complement w of t. If $x \vee (a \wedge w) \neq a$, then by the observation above, $t \geq x \vee (a \wedge w) \geq a \wedge w$, which implies that $0 = t \wedge w \geq a \wedge w$. And as $1 = t \vee w \leq a \vee w$, we have that a and t are complements of w, an impossibility. Thus $x \vee w \geq x \vee (a \wedge w) = a$. From this it follows that x is also a complement of w, for

$$x \vee w \geq a \vee w \geq t \vee w = 1,$$

and $x \wedge w \leq t \wedge w = 0$. We conclude that $x = t$, whence $x \vee p = a \succ x$.

E. If $x > y$ in L, then there exists $p \in L$ such that $x \geq p \succ 0$ and $y \ngeq p$. Similarly, there exists $q \in L$ such that $y \leq q \prec 1$ and $x \nleq q$.

Suppose $y \geq p$ whenever $x \geq p \succ 0$. Choose a complement v of y. Then v is not a complement of x since $x > y$, and therefore $x \wedge v > 0$. Hence there is an atom p such that $x \wedge v \geq p$. But then $y \geq p$, which gives $v \wedge y \geq p$, a contradiction. The second part of the statement follows by duality.

F. If $x, y \in L$, then $x \succ x \wedge y$ if and only if $x \vee \cdot y \succ y$.

If $x \succ x \wedge y$, then by E there exists $p \succ 0$ such that $x = p \vee (x \wedge y)$. Consequently by D,

$$x \vee y = p \vee (x \wedge y) \vee y = p \vee y \succ y.$$

Duality yields the opposite implication.

G. For each $x \in L$, the sublattices $x/0$ and $1/x$ are complemented.

Suppose that $x \geq y$. Choose any complement v of y, and put $z = x \wedge v$. Then clearly $y \wedge z = 0$. In view of E, to show that $y \vee z = x$, we need only show that $y \vee z \geq p$ whenever $x \geq p \succ 0$. To this end, assume that $x \geq p \succ 0$. If either $y \geq p$ or $v \geq p$, then $y \vee z \geq p$ as desired, so we may assume that $y \wedge p = v \wedge p = 0$. In this case $y \vee p \succ y$, and it follows from E and C that

$$s = v \wedge (y \vee p) \succ 0.$$

Note also that $z \geq s$. Moreover, $(p \vee s) \vee y = p \vee y \succ y$, which implies that

$$p \vee s \succ (p \vee s) \wedge y = r.$$

Now $r \wedge s = 0 \prec s$ so that $r \vee s \succ r$, and inasmuch as $p \vee s \geq r \vee s \succ r$, we conclude that $y \vee z \geq r \vee s = p \vee s \geq p$. Again, the second part of G follows by duality.

We are now ready to complete the proof of 4.4. Suppose $x, y, z \in L$ are such that $x \geq y$, $x \vee z = y \vee z$, and $x \wedge z = y \wedge z$. Using G, pick a complement u of $x \wedge z$ in the sublattice $z/0$, and pick a complement v of $x \vee z$ in the sublattice $1/u$. Then

$$x \vee v \geq y \vee v = y \vee (y \wedge z) \vee u \vee v = y \vee z \vee v = 1,$$

and

$$y \wedge v \leq x \wedge v = x \wedge (x \vee z) \wedge v = x \wedge u = x \wedge z \wedge u = 0.$$

Consequently x and y are two comparable complements of v, and therefore $x = y$. Thus L is modular, and the proof of 4.4 is complete.

4.5: *Every uniquely complemented atomic lattice is distributive.*[2]

[2] T. Ogasawara and U. Sasaki [74], J. McLaughlin [68]. Cf. G. Birkhoff and M. Ward [13].

PROOF: With 4.4 established, it suffices to prove that *a uniquely complemented modular lattice is distributive*. Assume, therefore, that L is a uniquely complemented modular lattice and that $x, y, z \in L$ are such that $x \lor z = y \lor z$ and $x \land z = y \land z$. Using 4.2, choose a complement u of $x \land z$ in the sublattice $z/0$, and choose a complement v of $x \lor z$ in the sublattice $1/u$. Then, just as in the proof of 4.4, it follows that v is a complement of both x and y in L. Thus $x = y$, and it follows that L is distributive.

Customarily, complemented distributive lattices are called *Boolean algebras* (after G. Boole). Since complementation and distributivity are self-dual properties, the dual lattice of Boolean algebra is also a Boolean algebra. In fact, the reader should verify that *the mapping which takes every element of a Boolean algebra L into its (unique) complement is an isomorphism of L onto its dual lattice*.

A complete Boolean algebra L is *infinitely distributive*; i.e., if $x \in L$ and S is a subset of L, then $x \land \bigvee S = \bigvee_{s \in S} x \land s$. To see this, set $u = \bigvee S$ and $v = \bigvee_{s \in S} x \land s$, and note that $x \land u \geq v$. If x' is the complement of x, then for each $s \in S$,

$$s = s \land (x \lor x') = (s \land x) \lor (s \land x') \leq v \lor x',$$

and therefore $u \leq v \lor x'$. Consequently

$$x \land u \leq x \land (v \lor x') = (x \land v) \lor (x \land x') = x \land v \leq v,$$

and the equality $x \land u = v$ follows.

In the presence of distributivity, infinite distributivity is equivalent to upper continuity. Using 2.4, it can easily be shown that *every distributive upper continuous lattice is infinitely distributive*.

A more restrictive infinite distributive law is that of complete distributivity. We say that a complete lattice L is *completely distributive* if, for every doubly indexed family of elements $x_{i,j} (i \in I, j \in J)$ in L, we have

$$\bigwedge_{i \in I} \bigvee_{j \in J} x_{i,j} = \bigvee_{f \in J^I} \bigwedge_{i \in I} x_{i,f(i)},$$

where J^I denotes the set of all functions on I to J. The last theorem of the chapter shows that the only complete Boolean algebras that satisfy this strong distributive law are those with which we are already familiar.

4.6: *The following conditions in a Boolean algebra L are equivalent:*

(1) *L is complete and completely distributive.*
(2) *L is complete and atomic.*
(3) *L is isomorphic to the Boolean algebra of all subsets of a set.* [3]

---

[3] A. Tarski [82].

PROOF: Since for any set X, the lattice of all subsets of X is completely distributive, (3) implies (1). It remains, therefore, to show that (1) implies (2) and (2) implies (3). Suppose that the Boolean algebra L is complete and completely distributive. Let $0 = \bigwedge L$ and $1 = \bigvee L$, and for each element $a \in L$, set

$$x_{a,0} = a, \qquad x_{a,1} = a', \quad .$$

where a' denotes the complement of a. Then with $J = \{0, 1\}$, complete distributivity yields that

$$1 = \bigwedge_{a \in L} (a \vee a') = \bigwedge_{a \in L} \bigvee_{j \in J} x_{a,j} = \bigvee_{f \in J^L} x_f,$$

where $x_f = \bigwedge_{a \in L} x_{a, f(a)}$. Let $f \in J^L$ be such that $x_f \neq 0$. If $x_f \geq b > 0$ for some element $b \in L$, then

$$x_f \leq x_{b, f(b)}.$$

Now $f(b) = 0$, for otherwise $b \leq x_f \leq x_{b, f(b)} = b'$, contrary to $b \neq 0$. Therefore $x_{b, f(b)} = b$, and this implies that $x_f = b$. It follows that each x_f greater than 0 is an atom of L, and consequently 1 is a join of atoms. By 4.1 this is enough to ensure that L is atomic.

Assume that L is complete and atomic. Let A denote the set of all atoms of L, and for each $x \in L$, set

$$\phi(x) = \{a \in A \,|\, x \geq a\}.$$

ϕ is then a mapping of L to the set of all subsets of A. Observe that if p is an atom of L and $B \subseteq A$, then $p \leq \bigvee B$ implies $p \in B$, for otherwise

$$p = p \wedge \bigvee B = \bigvee_{a \in B} p \wedge a = 0,$$

a contradiction. This fact implies that ϕ is onto. Moreover, inasmuch as L is relatively complemented, $x = \bigvee \phi(x)$ for each $x \in L$, and it follows that ϕ is one-to-one and that $\phi(x) \subseteq \phi(y)$ if and only if $x \leq y$. Thus ϕ is an isomorphism of L onto the Boolean algebra of all subsets of A.

Complete atomic Boolean algebras do not comprise all Boolean algebras. For example, if X is an infinite set, then the lattice L consisting of all finite subsets of X and their complements, under set-inclusion, is a Boolean algebra which is not complete. If E is the set of real numbers, then the collection of all regular open subsets of E, partially ordered by set-inclusion, is a complete Boolean algebra without any atoms. (Here an open subset of E is regular if it coincides with the interior of its closure.)

If R is the set of all rational numbers, and we define a half-open interval to be a subset of R which is either empty or of one of the forms

$$\{x \,|\, x < b\}, \qquad \{x \,|\, a \leq x < b\}, \qquad \text{or} \qquad \{x \,|\, a \leq x\},$$

then the collection of all finite set-unions of half-open intervals, under set-inclusion, is a countable Boolean algebra with no atoms. It is a curious fact that, up to isomorphism, this is the only such Boolean algebra. We leave it to the reader to prove that *any two countable Boolean algebras with no atoms are isomorphic*.

Just as there is a close relationship among distributivity, atomicity, and unique complementation, the continuity of complete Boolean algebras suggests the possibility of a similar relationship among distributivity, continuity, and unique complementation. In this regard the following question remains open: If L is a complete uniquely complemented lattice and if L is continuous, is L a Boolean algebra?

5

FINITE
DECOMPOSITION THEORY

A natural problem that arises in the study of an algebraic system is that of representing its elements as images of some canonical set of elements under a specific operation of the system. Usually this canonical set is taken to be those elements that cannot be further so represented. An elementary example of this is the representation of rational integers as products of primes.

Another fundamental problem is that of representing the system as a whole as a direct or subdirect product of simpler systems. In the study of lattices these two problems are not unrelated. For, as we will see in a later chapter, the representations of a lattice L as a direct or subdirect product correspond to certain meet representations of the least element in the lattice of congruence relations of L, and the uniqueness of the subdirect product representations is a reflection of the uniqueness of the meet representations.

In the next three chapters we will be concerned with the existence and uniqueness of certain meet representations in a lattice. This initial chapter focuses on the finite case.

We say that an element q in a lattice L is *irreducible* if, for all $x, y \in L$,

$$q = x \wedge y \text{ implies } q = x \text{ or } q = y.$$

If a is an element of the lattice L, then a representation

$$a = q_1 \wedge \cdots \wedge q_n$$

of a as a meet of finitely many irreducible elements $q_1, \ldots, q_n$ is called a *finite decomposition* of a. This finite decomposition is *irredundant* if, for each $i = 1, \ldots, n$,

$$a \neq q_1 \wedge \cdots \wedge q_{i-1} \wedge q_{i+1} \wedge \cdots \wedge q_n.$$

If an element in a lattice has a finite decomposition, then it has an irredundant finite decomposition; by deleting superfluous irreducible elements, the original finite decomposition can be refined to an irredundant one. Finite decompositions, however, do not always exist. Observe, for example, that the lattice of all finite subsets of an infinite set X has no irreducible elements. Consequently, just to assert the existence of finite decompositions, some additional assumption is needed; classically the assumption imposed is the ascending chain condition. The reader can easily verify that *if a lattice L satisfies the ascending chain condition, then every element of L has an irredundant finite decomposition.*

Distributivity insures uniqueness.

5.1: *An element in a distributive lattice has at most one irredundant finite decomposition.*[1]

PROOF: Suppose an element a in a distributive lattice L has two irredundant finite decompositions

$$a = q_1 \wedge \cdots \wedge q_n = r_1 \wedge \cdots \wedge r_m.$$

Then for a given i,

$$q_i = q_i \vee a = q_i \vee (r_1 \wedge \cdots \wedge r_m) = (q_i \vee r_1) \wedge \cdots \wedge (q_i \vee r_m),$$

and since q_i is irreducible, there is some j such that $q_i = q_i \vee r_j \geq r_j$. Similarly, there is an integer k such that $r_j \geq q_k$. Therefore $q_i \geq r_j \geq q_k$, and the irredundance of the decompositions implies that $q_i = r_j = q_k$. In the same way it follows that each r_j must equal some q_i, and hence the two finite decompositions are identical.

The modular nondistributive five-element lattice shows that the foregoing uniqueness theorem does not extend to include modular lattices. A weak "uniqueness" does hold, however, in the modular case.

5.2: *If a is an element of a modular lattice L and a has two finite decompositions*

$$a = q_1 \wedge \cdots \wedge q_n = r_1 \wedge \cdots \wedge r_m,$$

then for each q_i there is an r_j such that

$$a = q_1 \wedge \cdots \wedge q_{i-1} \wedge r_j \wedge q_{i+1} \wedge \cdots \wedge q_n.$$

Moreover, this resulting finite decomposition is irredundant if the finite decomposition $a = q_1 \wedge \cdots \wedge q_n$ is irredundant.

PROOF: Set

$$\bar{q}_i = q_1 \wedge \cdots \wedge q_{i-1} \wedge q_{i+1} \wedge \cdots \wedge q_n,$$

and for each $j = 1, \ldots, m$, set $s_j = r_j \wedge \bar{q}_i$. Then $a \leq s_j \leq \bar{q}_i$ for each j. Furthermore, the modularity of L implies that

$$q_i \vee \bar{q}_i / q_i \cong \bar{q}_i / q_i \wedge \bar{q}_i = \bar{q}_i / a,$$

[1] G. Birkhoff [10].

and as q_i is irreducible in L and hence in the sublattice $q_i \vee \bar{q}_i/q_i$, it follows that a is irreducible in the sublattice $\bar{q}_i/a$. But $a = s_1 \wedge \cdots \wedge s_m$ is a representation of a as a meet of elements in $\bar{q}_i/a$, and therefore $a = s_j$ for some j. The irredundance of this resulting finite decomposition is an easy consequence of the irredundance of the finite decomposition $a = q_1 \wedge \cdots \wedge q_n$, and the proof of this part is left to the reader.

Repeated application of 5.2 yields the theorem of Kurosh and Ore: *If a is an element of a modular lattice, then the number of irreducible elements in any irredundant finite decomposition of a is unique.*[2]

Several questions are raised by 5.2. For instance, under the hypotheses of 5.2, is it true that each r_j can replace some q_i? The answer to this is supplied by the following theorem, which summarizes all that is known about this replacement process.

5.3: *If a is an element of a modular lattice L and if*

$$a = q_1 \wedge \cdots \wedge q_n = r_1 \wedge \cdots \wedge r_n$$

are two irredundant finite decompositions of a, then

(1)   *For each q_i there is an r_j such that*

$$a = q_1 \wedge \cdots \wedge q_{i-1} \wedge r_j \wedge q_{i+1} \wedge \cdots \wedge q_n$$
$$= r_1 \wedge \cdots \wedge r_{j-1} \wedge q_i \wedge r_{j+1} \wedge \cdots \wedge r_n.$$

(2)   *There is a permutation π of the integers $1, \ldots, n$ such that, for each $i = 1, \ldots, n$,*

$$a = q_1 \wedge \cdots \wedge q_{i-1} \wedge r_{\pi(i)} \wedge q_{i+1} \wedge \cdots \wedge q_n.\text{[3]}$$

PROOF: For each integer $i = 1, \ldots, n$, set

$$\bar{q}_i = q_1 \wedge \cdots \wedge q_{i-1} \wedge q_{i+1} \wedge \cdots \wedge q_n,$$
$$\bar{r}_i = r_1 \wedge \cdots \wedge r_{i-1} \wedge r_{i+1} \wedge \cdots \wedge r_n.$$

And for the purposes of this proof, define an element $s \in L$ to be a *superdivisor* if $s \geq a$ and, for all $x \in L$, $s \wedge x = a$ implies $x = a$. With this bit of notation and terminology, the proof now proceeds in a number of steps. The proof of the first is left to the reader.

A. If s and t are superdivisors, then $s \wedge t$ is a superdivisor.

B. If q is an irreducible element, $q \geq a$, and $x > q$, then x is a superdivisor.

For if $x \wedge y = a$, then using modularity,

$$q = q \vee a = q \vee (x \wedge y) = x \wedge (q \vee y),$$

[2] A. Kurosh [64], O. Ore [75].
[3] R. Dilworth [31].

and as q is irreducible and $q \neq x$, we must have $q = q \vee y$. Hence

$$y = q \wedge y = q \wedge x \wedge y = q \wedge a = a,$$

and it follows that x is a superdivisor.

C. If s is a superdivisor, then $q_i \vee (s \wedge \bar{q}_i)$ is also a superdivisor for each $i = 1, \ldots, n$.

By B, if $q_i \vee (s \wedge \bar{q}_i)$ is not a superdivisor, then $q_i \geq s \wedge \bar{q}_i$. But then $s \wedge \bar{q}_i = s \wedge q_i \wedge \bar{q}_i = a$, which implies that $\bar{q}_i = a$, contrary to the irredundance of the finite decomposition $a = q_1 \wedge \cdots \wedge q_n$.

D. If $s_1, \ldots, s_i$ are superdivisors and $x \geq s_1 \wedge \bar{q}_1, s_2 \wedge \bar{q}_2, \ldots, s_i \wedge \bar{q}_i$, then there is a superdivisor s such that $x \geq s \wedge q_{i+1} \wedge \cdots \wedge q_n$.

Certainly $x \geq s \wedge q_1 \wedge \cdots \wedge q_n$ for any superdivisor s. Let k be the largest integer such that $x \geq s \wedge q_k \wedge \cdots \wedge q_n$ for some superdivisor s. We would like to show that $k > i$. Suppose this is not the case. Then $x \geq s_k \wedge \bar{q}_k$, and with $s' = s \wedge s_k$ we have

$$x \geq (s' \wedge q_k \wedge \cdots \wedge q_n) \vee (s' \wedge \bar{q}_k)$$
$$= s' \wedge q_{k+1} \wedge \cdots \wedge q_n \wedge (q_k \vee (s' \wedge \bar{q}_k)).$$

But $q_k \vee (s' \wedge \bar{q}_k)$ is a superdivisor by C, and therefore $s'' = s' \wedge (q_k \vee (s' \wedge \bar{q}_k))$ is a superdivisor by A. Consequently $x \geq s'' \wedge q_{k+1} \wedge \cdots \wedge q_n$, contrary to the maximality of k.

E. If q is an irreducible element and $q \geq a$, then $a = q \wedge \bar{q}_i$ if and only if $q \not\geq s \wedge \bar{q}_i$ for every superdivisor s.

Suppose $a = q \wedge \bar{q}_i$ and $q \geq s \wedge \bar{q}_i$ for some superdivisor s. Then

$$s \wedge \bar{q}_i = s \wedge q \wedge \bar{q}_i = s \wedge a = a,$$

which implies that $\bar{q}_i = a$, an impossibility. Conversely, suppose that $q \not\geq s \wedge q_i$ for all superdivisors s. Now

$$q \geq q \wedge \bar{q}_i = (q \wedge \bar{q}_i) \vee (q_i \wedge \bar{q}_i) = (q_i \vee (q \wedge \bar{q}_i)) \wedge \bar{q}_i,$$

and therefore $q_i \vee (q \wedge \bar{q}_i)$ is not a superdivisor. This fact together with B implies that $q_i \geq q \wedge \bar{q}_i$, and hence $q \wedge \bar{q}_i = q \wedge q_i \wedge \bar{q}_i = a$.

We are now ready to complete the proof of (1). We say that an irreducible element q *replaces* q_i if $a = q \wedge \bar{q}_i$; similarly, q replaces r_j if $a = q \wedge \bar{r}_j$. Let i be a given positive integer not exceeding n. Renumbering, if necessary, we may assume that each $r_1, \ldots, r_k$ replaces q_i, while each $r_{k+1}, \ldots, r_n$ does not. According to E, there are superdivisors $s_{k+1}, \ldots, s_n$ such that $r_j \geq s_j \wedge \bar{q}_i$ for each $j = k + 1, \ldots, n$. Now suppose that q_i replaces none of the elements

$r_1, \ldots, r_k$. Again by E, there are superdivisors $t_1, \ldots, t_k$ such that $q_i \geq t_j \wedge \bar{r}_j$ for each $j = 1, \ldots, k$, and this fact and D yield that

$$q_i \geq t \wedge r_{k+1} \wedge \cdots \wedge r_n$$

for some superdivisor t. Moreover,

$$r_{k+1} \wedge \cdots \wedge r_n \geq s_{k+1} \wedge \cdots \wedge s_n \wedge \bar{q}_i = s \wedge \bar{q}_i,$$

where $s = s_{k+1} \wedge \cdots \wedge s_n$ is a superdivisor, and therefore $q_i \geq t \wedge s \wedge \bar{q}_i$. But this implies that

$$t \wedge s \wedge \bar{q}_i = t \wedge s \wedge \bar{q}_i \wedge q_i = a,$$

and as $t \wedge s$ is a superdivisor, we infer that $\bar{q}_i = a$, contrary to hypothesis. Thus there is some $j \leq k$ such that q_i replaces r_j, and (1) follows.

(2) is an easy consequence of (1). Starting with the finite decompositions $a = q_1 \wedge \cdots \wedge q_n = r_1 \wedge \cdots \wedge r_n$, we apply (1) to the element q_1, obtaining r_{j_1} such that $a = r_{j_1} \wedge \bar{q}_1 = q_1 \wedge \bar{r}_{j_1}$. Again we apply (1) to the element q_2 and the finite decompositions

$$a = q_1 \wedge \cdots \wedge q_n = q_1 \wedge \bigwedge_{j \neq j_1} r_j.$$

Since $q_1 \wedge \bar{q}_2 \neq a$, application of (1) to these decompositions yields an element $r_{j_2} \neq r_{j_1}$ such that

$$a = r_{j_2} \wedge \bar{q}_2 = q_2 \wedge q_1 \wedge \bigwedge_{j \neq j_1, j_2} r_j.$$

Continuing in this way we obtain a permutation $j_1, \ldots, j_n$ of the integers $1, \ldots, n$ such that, for each $k \leq n$,

$$a = r_{j_k} \wedge \bar{q}_k = q_k \wedge \cdots \wedge q_1 \wedge \bigwedge_{j \neq j_1, \cdots, j_k} r_j.$$

Thus (2) holds, and the proof is complete.

Having completed the proof of 5.3, it might be well to offer some slight motivation for the notion of superdivisor. When the sublattice $1/a$ is atomic, the exchange properties of the irredundant decompositions of a are closely related to the structure of the sublattice u_a/a, where $u_a = \bigvee \{p \mid p \succ a\}$, as we will see in the next two chapters. Moreover, in this case it is clear that s is a superdivisor if and only if $s \geq u_a$. So in essence the notion of superdivisor abstracts for the nonatomic case the role of the element u_a in the atomic case.

One might be tempted to conjecture that, under the hypotheses of 5.3, the r_j's can be renumbered in such a way that simultaneously each q_i replaces r_i and r_i replaces q_i. This, however, is in general impossible, as an examination Fig. 3-7 will reveal.

6

INFINITE DECOMPOSITIONS
EXISTENCE

In requiring decompositions to be finite, the lattices in which a decomposition theory can be developed are essentially limited to those satisfying the ascending chain condition. This, of course, excludes a great many lattices for which a decomposition theory would seem appropriate, e.g., most lattices of congruence relations. Therefore, to obtain a theory as comprehensive as possible, we now turn to the consideration of infinite decompositions.

In this connection the concept of irreducible element needs to be generalized. We say that an element q in a complete lattice L is *completely irreducible* if, for every subset S of L, $q = \bigwedge S$ implies that $q \in S$.

Certainly every completely irreducible element is irreducible. Indeed, if q is completely irreducible and $v = \bigwedge\{x \mid x > q\}$, then $v \succ q$, and $x \geq v$ whenever $x > q$. In particular, if the lattice L is strongly atomic, then for a given element $x \in L$ the following three statements are equivalent: $1/x$ contains a single atom, x is completely irreducible, and x is irreducible. So when dealing with a strongly atomic lattice we need not distinguish between irreducible and completely irreducible elements.

If a is an element of the lattice L, then a representation $a = \bigwedge Q$ of a as the meet of a set Q of completely irreducible elements of L is called a *decomposition* of a. The decomposition $a = \bigwedge Q$ is *irredundant* if $\bigwedge(Q - q) \neq a$ for all $q \in Q$.

Our first existence theorem is now the following.

6.1: *Every element of a compactly generated lattice has a decomposition.*

And to establish this, it is enough to prove:

6.2: *If a, b are elements of a compactly generated lattice L and $a \not\geq b$, then there exists a completely irreducible element $q \in L$ such that $q \geq a$ and $q \not\geq b$.*

43

PROOF: Since L is compactly generated and $a \not\geq b$, there exists a compact element c such that $c \leq b$ and $c \not\leq a$. Let

$$P = \{x \in L \mid x \geq a, x \not\geq c\}.$$

Then $a \in P$, and for each $x \in P$, $x \not\geq b$. Suppose C is a chain of elements in P. If $\bigvee C \geq c$, then the compactness of c implies that there is a finite subset $C' \subseteq C$ such that $\bigvee C' \geq c$. But C' is a finite chain, so that if x_0 is the largest element in C', we have $\bigvee C' = x_0 \geq c$, contrary to $x_0 \in P$. Thus $\bigvee C \in P$, and P contains a maximal element q by Zorn's lemma. Now let S be a subset of L such that $q = \bigwedge S$. Inasmuch as $q \not\geq c$, there must be some element $s \in S$ such that $s \not\geq c$, and as $s \geq q$, the maximality of q implies that $q = s$. Consequently q is completely irreducible.

Unlike the finite situation, the existence of decompositions does not imply the existence of irredundant decompositions. Consider, for example, the lattice L consisting of the rational numbers $1, 1/2, 1/3, \ldots, 0$, with the natural ordering. L is an infinite chain in which the ascending chain condition holds, each positive number in L is completely irreducible, 0 is the meet of any infinite set of positive numbers, but 0 is not the meet of any finite set of positive numbers; so the element 0 has many decompositions but no irredundant decomposition.

This situation is somewhat clarified by the following observation:

6.3: *If every element of a modular compactly generated lattice L has an irredundant decomposition, then L is strongly atomic.*

PROOF: Let 1 denote the greatest element of L. Pick any element $a \in L$ with $a < 1$, and let $a = \bigwedge Q$ be an irredundant decomposition. Choose any $q \in Q$, let v be the unique element covering q, and set $s = \bigwedge(Q - q)$. Then $s > s \wedge q = a$, and therefore $s \vee q \geq v$. Applying modularity,

$$q \vee (v \wedge s) = v \wedge (q \vee s) = v \succ q,$$

whence $v \wedge s \succ v \wedge s \wedge q = s \wedge q = a$. Thus every element less than 1 is covered by at least one element.

Suppose $b > a$. An application of upper continuity and Zorn's lemma yields the existence of an element $u \geq a$ which is maximal with respect to the property that $b \wedge u = a$. And as $u < 1$, the remarks of the preceding paragraph yield an element $r \succ u$, and the maximality of u implies that $b \wedge r > a$. Therefore $(b \wedge r) \vee u = r \succ u$, and hence $b \wedge r \succ b \wedge r \wedge u = a$. Thus b/a contains an atom, and L is strongly atomic.

Our principal existence theorem shows that strong atomicity in a general compactly generated lattice is also sufficient.

6.4: *If a compactly generated lattice L is strongly atomic, then every element of L has an irredundant decomposition.*[1]

PROOF: Let a be an element of L different from the greatest element of L, and let $p \in L$ be such that $p \succ a$. Then by 6.2 there is a completely irreducible element $q \geq a$ such that $q \not\geq p$; i.e., $q \wedge p = a$. Consequently, to prove the theorem, it suffices to prove the following: *Every element of a compactly generated lattice L has an irredundant decomposition if and only if for each element $a \in L$ distinct from the greatest element of L there is a completely irreducible element q and an element $x > a$ such that $a = q \wedge x$.*

The necessity is clear. To prove the sufficiency, let $a \in L$ be an element distinct from the greatest element of L. Let W be the set of all ordered pairs $\langle R, x \rangle$, where R is a set of completely irreducible elements of L, $x \in L$, and the following conditions are satisfied:

(1) $x \wedge \bigwedge R = a$.
(2) $x \wedge \bigwedge(R - q) > a$ for all $q \in R$.

Partially order W by defining $\langle R', x' \rangle \leq \langle R, x \rangle$ if

$$R' \subseteq R \qquad \text{and} \qquad x \wedge \bigwedge(R - R') \geq x'.$$

Now by assumption there is an element $x_0 > a$ and a completely irreducible element q such that $a = x_0 \wedge q$. Therefore $\langle \{q\}, x_0 \rangle \in W$, and W is nonempty.

Suppose $\langle R_i, x_i \rangle$ ($i \in I$) is a chain of elements in W. Set

$$\bar{R} = \bigcup_{i \in I} R_i, \qquad \bar{x} = \bigvee_{i \in I} x_i.$$

Then as the elements $x_i (i \in I)$ form a chain of L,

$$a \leq \bar{x} \wedge \bigwedge \bar{R} = (\bigwedge \bar{R}) \wedge \bigvee_{i \in I} x_i = \bigvee_{i \in I}(x_i \wedge \bigwedge \bar{R}) \leq \bigvee_{i \in I}(x_i \wedge \bigwedge R_i) = a;$$

i.e., $a = \bar{x} \wedge \bigwedge \bar{R}$. If $i \in I$ and q is any element of $\bar{R} - R_i$, then there is an index $h \in I$ such that $q \in R_h$ and $(R_h, x_h) > (R_i, x_i)$. Therefore

$$q \geq x_h \wedge \bigwedge(R_h - R_i) \geq x_i,$$

and it follows that $\bar{x} \wedge \bigwedge(\bar{R} - R_i) \geq x_i$. In particular, for every $q \in \bar{R}$, we have

$$\bar{x} \wedge \bigwedge(\bar{R} - q) = [\bar{x} \wedge \bigwedge(R - R_i)] \wedge \bigwedge(R_i - q) \geq x_i \wedge \bigwedge(R_i - q) > a,$$

where i is chosen such that $q \in R_i$. The foregoing calculations show that $\langle \bar{R}, \bar{x} \rangle \in W$ and that $\langle \bar{R}, \bar{x} \rangle$ is an upper bound of the chain $\langle R_i, x_i \rangle (i \in I)$. By Zorn's lemma, W contains a maximal element $\langle Q, y \rangle$.

[1] P. Crawley [19].

Since $\bigwedge(Q - q) > a$ for each $q \in Q$, to complete the proof we need to show that $\bigwedge Q = a$. Assume this is not the case. Then as $y \wedge \bigwedge Q = a$, there is an element $z \geq y$ which is maximal with respect to the property that $z \wedge \bigwedge Q = a$. z cannot be the greatest element of L, and therefore there is an element $t > z$ and a completely irreducible element r such that $t \wedge r = z$. If $Q_1 = Q \cup \{r\}$, we then have

$$t \wedge \bigwedge Q_1 = t \wedge r \wedge \bigwedge Q = z \wedge \bigwedge Q = a.$$

Moreover, for each $q \in Q$,

$$t \wedge \bigwedge(Q_1 - q) = z \wedge \bigwedge(Q - q) \geq y \wedge \bigwedge(Q - q) > a,$$

and the maximality of z implies that

$$t \wedge \bigwedge(Q_1 - r) = t \wedge \bigwedge Q > a.$$

Consequently $\langle Q_1, t \rangle \in W$. Also,

$$t \wedge \bigwedge(Q_1 - Q) = t \wedge r = z \geq y,$$

and therefore $\langle Q_1, t \rangle > \langle Q, y \rangle$. Since this is impossible, we conclude that $a = \bigwedge Q$, completing the proof.

In the proof of the preceding theorem, to establish the existence of an irredundant decomposition of an element a in the compactly generated lattice L, use was made of the fact that $1/x$ contains an atom for each $x \geq a$. If, however, we further assume that L is semimodular, then the existence of an irredundant decomposition follows just from the atomicity of $1/a$. To prove this we first need a few facts concerning independent sets of atoms.

Let L be a complete lattice with least element 0. A subset $A \subseteq L$ is said to be *independent* if, for all $a \in A$,

$$a \wedge \bigvee(A - a) = 0.$$

If L is upper continuous, then it follows from 2.4 that a subset A is independent if and only if every finite subset of A is independent. With this fact in hand, a straightforward application of Zorn's lemma yields the following: If B is a subset of an upper continuous lattice L and A is an independent subset of B, then A is contained in a maximal independent subset of B.

6.5: *If L is a complete semimodular lattice with least element 0 and u is the join of all the atoms of L, then an independent set A of atoms of L is a maximal independent set of atoms if and only if $\bigvee A = u$.*

PROOF: If $\bigvee A = u$, then certainly A is a maximal independent set of atoms. Assume then that A is maximal and that p is an atom of L. The maximality of A implies that either $\bigvee A \geq p$ or $p \vee \bigvee(A - a) \geq a$ for some $a \in A$. In the second case, $\bigvee(A - a) \not\geq p$, since otherwise we would have $\bigvee(A - a) \geq a$, contrary to the independence of A. Therefore $p \vee \bigvee(A - a) \succ \bigvee(A - a)$ by semimodularity. But

$$p \vee \bigvee(A - a) \geq a \vee \bigvee(A - a) = \bigvee A \succ \bigvee(A - a),$$

so it must be that $\bigvee A = p \vee \bigvee(A - a) \geq p$. Consequently $\bigvee A \geq p$ in either case, and it follows that $\bigvee A = u$.

6.6: *If L is a semimodular, compactly generated, atomic lattice with least element 0, A is an independent set of atoms of L, and $S_i(i \in I)$ is a collection of subsets of A which has an empty set-intersection, then $\bigwedge_{i \in I}\bigvee S_i = 0$.*

PROOF: If $\bigwedge_{i \in I}\bigvee S_i > 0$, then there is an atom p such that $\bigwedge_{i \in I}\bigvee S_i \geq p$. Consider a particular index $h \in I$. Then $\bigvee S_h \geq p$, and inasmuch as p is compact in L, there is a minimal finite subset $T \subseteq S_h$ such that $\bigvee T \geq p$. Pick any $a \in T$. The minimality of T implies that $\bigvee(T - a) \not\geq p$, and just as in the proof of 6.5, it follows that $p \vee \bigvee(T - a) = \bigvee T$. Now the S_i's have an empty set-intersection, and therefore there is an index $k \in I$ such that $a \notin S_k$. Thus

$$a \leq \bigvee T \leq p \vee \bigvee(T - a) \vee \bigvee S_k \leq \bigvee(T - a) \vee \bigvee S_k \leq \bigvee(A - a),$$

contrary to the independence of A.

The following two additional facts are noted for future use. Their proofs are left to the reader.

6.7: *If L is a semimodular, compactly generated, strongly atomic lattice with least element 0 and if A is an independent set of atoms of L, then the elements of L which are joins of subsets of A form a complete sublattice of L which is isomorphic to the Boolean algebra of all subsets of A.*

6.8: *If L is a semimodular lattice and the greatest element of L is the join of a finite independent set containing, say, n atoms, then L has dimension n.*

Now our final existence theorem:

6.9: *If a is an element of a semimodular compactly generated lattice L and the sublattice $1/a$ is atomic, then a has an irredundant decomposition.*[2]

PROOF: Let u_a be the join of all the atoms of $1/a$, and let A be a maximal independent set of these atoms. For each $p \in A$, set $s_p = \bigvee(A - p)$, and note that $u_a \succ s_p$. Consequently, for each $p \in A$, there is a completely irreducible

[2] R. P. Dilworth and P. Crawley [35].

element q_p such that $q_p \geq s_p$ and $q_p \not\geq u_a$; i.e., $q_p \wedge u_a = s_p$. Now if $p_0 \in A$, then

$$\bigwedge_{p \neq p_0} q_p \geq \bigwedge_{p \neq p_0} s_p \geq p_0 > a.$$

Moreover, if $\bigwedge_{p \in A} q_p > a$, then there is an element r such that $\bigwedge_{p \in A} q_p \geq r \succ a$. But this implies that

$$r \leq u_a \wedge \bigwedge_{p \in A} q_p = \bigwedge_{p \in A} u_a \wedge q_p = \bigwedge_{p \in A} s_p,$$

contrary to 6.6. Thus $a = \bigwedge_{p \in A} q_p$ is an irredundant decomposition of a.

At present it is not known whether the assumption of semimodularity is needed in Theorem 6.9; we conjecture that it is. We do know that modularity cannot be dropped from the statement of 6.3. Figure 6-1 represents a semi-modular lattice satisfying the ascending chain condition in which each element is uniquely the meet of at most two completely irreducible elements but which is not atomic. (The dots in Fig. 6-1 indicate that the diagram is continued indefinitely.)

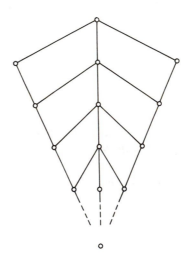

Fig. 6–1

7

INFINITE DECOMPOSITIONS
UNIQUENESS

Just as in the finite case, distributivity and modularity yield the anticipated uniqueness theorems for irredundant decompositions.

7.1: *An element in a complete distributive lattice has at most one irredundant decomposition.*

7.2: *If an element a in a complete modular lattice L has two decompositions $a = \bigwedge Q = \bigwedge Q'$, then for each $q \in Q$ there exists $q' \in Q'$ such that $a = q' \wedge \bigwedge(Q - q)$. Moreover, this resulting decomposition is irredundant if the decomposition $a = \bigwedge Q$ is irredundant.*

The proof of 7.2 is essentially identical to the proof of 5.2. Theorem 7.1, however, must be handled differently from 5.1. Suppose that a is an element of a complete distributive lattice L and a has irredundant decompositions $a = \bigwedge Q = \bigwedge Q'$. Pick an element $q \in Q$. Let v be the unique element covering q, and let $s = \bigwedge(Q - q)$. Then, as we saw in the proof of 6.3, $p = v \wedge s \succ a$. Now there must be an element $q' \in Q'$ such that $q' \not\geq p$. If v' is the unique element covering q', then it follows that $q' \vee p = v'$ and $q \vee p = v$. Consequently if $q \neq q'$, then either $q \vee q' \geq v$ or $q \vee q' \geq v'$, so that, under any circumstances, we would have $q \vee q' \geq p$. But this is impossible since it yields that

$$p = p \wedge (q \vee q') = (p \wedge q) \vee (p \wedge q') = a.$$

Therefore $q = q'$, and we conclude that $Q = Q'$.

Unlike the finite case, and in spite of 7.2, it is not true that two irredundant decompositions of an element in a complete modular lattice have the same cardinality, as the following example shows. Let A_n be an additive group of order 2 for each positive integer n, and let G be the complete direct sum of the A_n's; i.e. G consists of all functions f on the positive integers such that $f(n) \in A_n$, with addition defined componentwise. G is then an (additive) abelian group in which each element has order at most 2. Consequently, if

L is the lattice of subgroups of G, then L is modular, compactly generated, and strongly atomic. For each positive integer n, let Q_n be the subgroup of G consisting of those functions f for which $f(n)$ is the zero element of A_n. Each Q_n has index 2 in G, and therefore each Q_n is a completely irreducible element of L. Moreover, if 0 is the least element of L, then it follows that $0 = \bigwedge_n Q_n$ is an irredundant decomposition of 0. Now we can consider G as a vector space over the field of integers modulo 2, and accordingly G has a basis f_i ($i \in I$). And as G has cardinality $2^{\aleph_0}$, the number of these basis elements must also be $2^{\aleph_0}$. For each index $i \in I$, let Q'_i be that subgroup of G generated by the basis elements f_h ($h \neq i$). Again, each Q'_i has index 2 in G and therefore is completely irreducible in L, and $0 = \bigwedge_{i \in I} Q'_i$ is an irredundant decomposition of 0. Thus 0 has two irredundant decompositions with different cardinalities.

We will say that a complete lattice L has *unique irredundant decompositions* if every element of L has exactly one irredundant decomposition. We say that a complete lattice L has *replaceable irredundant decompositions* if each element of L has at least one irredundant decomposition, and whenever $a = \bigwedge Q = \bigwedge Q'$ are two irredundant decompositions of an element $a \in L$, for each $q \in Q$ there exists $q' \in Q'$ such that $a = q' \wedge \bigwedge(Q - q)$, and this resulting decomposition is irredundant.

Most of this chapter is devoted to describing those compactly generated strongly atomic lattices with unique irredundant decompositions and those with replaceable irredundant decompositions. The starting point for this is the following additional bit of notation and terminology. Let L be a compactly generated strongly atomic lattice. For each $a \in L$, let u_a denote the join of all those elements covering a. We say that the lattice L is *locally distributive* if u_a/a is distributive for each $a \in L$; similarly, L is *locally modular* if u_a/a is modular for each $a \in L$.

In view of 3.7, *every locally modular, compactly generated, strongly atomic lattice is semimodular*. These lattices also have the following technical, but useful, property.

7.3: *If a, b, p_1, p_2 are elements of a locally modular, compactly generated, strongly atomic lattice L, and if $p_1, p_2 \succ a$, $b \wedge (p_1 \vee p_2) = a$ and $p_1 \vee b = p_2 \vee b$, then $p_1 = p_2$.*

PROOF: Suppose the assumptions of 7.3 hold but $p_1 \neq p_2$. Let

$$T = \{x \in L \mid x \vee p_1 \not\geq p_2, \quad b \wedge (p_1 \vee p_2 \vee x) = x\}.$$

T is nonempty since $a \in T$. If C is a chain of elements in L, then

$$b \wedge (p_1 \vee p_2 \vee \bigvee C) = \bigvee_{x \in C} b \wedge (p_1 \vee p_2 \vee x) = \bigvee C,$$

and the compactness of p_2 in b/a implies that $p_1 \vee \bigvee C \not\geq p_2$. Hence $\bigvee C \in T$, and by Zorn's lemma T contains a maximal element w. Since $w \in T$, we have

$w \vee p_1 \neq w \vee p_2$, and this implies that $b > w$. Moreover, this last inequality yields that $w \not\geq p_1, p_2$, and therefore $w \vee p_1, w \vee p_2 \succ w$ by semimodularity. Furthermore, as L is strongly atomic, there exists $p \in L$ such that $b \geq p \succ w = b \wedge (p_1 \vee p_2 \vee w)$. And as $p_1 \vee p_2 \vee w \not\geq p$, it follows that

$$p_1 \vee p_2 \vee p \succ p_1 \vee p_2 \vee w \succ p_1 \vee w, p_2 \vee w \succ w.$$

Thus the local modularity of L implies that $p_1 \vee p_2 \vee p/w$ is a modular lattice of dimension 3. The sublattice $p_1 \vee p_2 \vee p/p$ is therefore of dimension 2, and since

$$p_1 \vee p_2 \vee p > b \wedge (p_1 \vee p_2 \vee p) \geq p,$$

we infer that either $p_1 \vee p_2 \vee p \succ b \wedge (p_1 \vee p_2 \vee p)$ or $b \wedge (p_1 \vee p_2 \vee p) = p$. If the first alternative holds, then the lower semimodularity of $p_1 \vee p_2 \vee p/w$ implies that

$$b \wedge (p_1 \vee p_2 \vee p) \wedge (p_1 \vee p_2 \vee w) = b \wedge (p_1 \vee p_2 \vee w) \succ w,$$

contrary to $w \in T$. The second alternative, together with the observation that $p \vee p_1 \not\geq p_2$, implies that $p \in T$, contrary to the maximality of w. Hence we must have $p_1 = p_2$.

Notice that the foregoing lemma shows the following: *If a is an element of a locally modular, compactly generated, strongly atomic lattice L, and if q is an irreducible element of L for which $q \geq a$ and $q \not\geq u_a$, then $u_a \succ q \wedge u_a$.* For if u_a does not cover $q \wedge u_a$, then it follows from 4.5 that there are two distinct elements p_1, p_2 such that $u_a \geq p_1, p_2 \succ q \wedge u_a$, and as q is irreducible and hence covered by a unique element, $p_1 \vee q = p_2 \vee q \succ q$, contrary to 7.3.

7.4: *A compactly generated strongly atomic lattice L has unique irredundant decompositions if and only if L is locally distributive.*[1]

PROOF: We will first show that L has unique irredundant decompositions if and only if L satisfies the following two conditions:

(1) L is semimodular.
(2) If $a, p, x, y \in L, x, y \geq a$, and $p \succ a$, then $p \wedge (x \vee y) = (p \wedge x) \vee (p \wedge y)$.

Suppose that L satisfies (1) and (2), and suppose that $a = \wedge Q = \wedge Q'$ are two irredundant decompositions of an element $a \in L$. Pick any element $q \in Q$. Then there is an element $p \in L$ such that $\wedge (Q - q) \geq p \succ a$, and there must be some element $q' \in Q'$ such that $q' \not\geq p$. It now follows, just as in the proof of 7.2, that $q = q'$, and we infer that $Q = Q'$.

Conversely, suppose that L has unique irredundant decompositions. Pick

[1] R. P. Dilworth and P. Crawley [35].

elements $x, p \in L$ such that $p \succ x \wedge p = a$. If $x \vee p$ does not cover x, then there is an element y such that $x \vee p > y > x$. By 6.2 there exist irreducible elements q_1 and q_2 such that $q_1 \geq x, q_1 \not\geq y, q_2 \geq y$, and $q_2 \not\geq x \vee p$. Observe that $q_1 \wedge p = q_2 \wedge p = a$. Consequently there are maximal elements w_1, $w_2 \geq p$ such that $q_1 \wedge w_1 = q_2 \wedge w_2 = a$. If $w_1 = \bigwedge R_1$ and $w_2 = \bigwedge R_2$ are irredundant decompositions of w_1 and w_2, respectively, then $a = q_1 \wedge \bigwedge R_1 = q_2 \wedge \bigwedge R_2$. Moreover, these decompositions are irredundant, for $\bigwedge R_1$, $\bigwedge R_2 \geq p > a$, and the maximality of w_1 and w_2 implies that $q_1 \wedge \bigwedge(R - r_1)$, $q_2 \wedge \bigwedge(R_2 - r_2) > a$ for every $r_1 \in R$ and $r_2 \in R_2$. They are also distinct, since $q_1 \neq q_2$ and $q_1 \notin R_2$. This contradiction shows that $x \vee p$ must cover x, and therefore (1) holds.

Now suppose that $x, y, p, a \in L$ are such that $x, y \geq a, p \succ a$, and x, $y \not\geq p$. Again by 6.2 there exist irreducible elements q_x and q_y such that $q_x \geq x, q_y \geq y$, and $q_x \wedge p = q_y \wedge p = a$. Hence if $w_1, w_2 \geq p$ are maximal elements such that $q_x \wedge w_1 = q_y \wedge w_2 = a$ and if $w_1 = \bigwedge R_1$ and $w_2 = \bigwedge R_2$ are irredundant decompositions of w_1 and w_2, then $a = q_x \wedge \bigwedge R_1 = q_y \wedge \bigwedge R_2$ are irredundant decompositions of a. By assumption, they must be identical, and as $q_x \notin R_2$, we have $q_x = q_y$. Therefore $q_x \geq x \vee y$, and it follows that $x \vee y \not\geq p$. Consequently (2) must hold.

It remains to show that L is locally distributive if and only if it satisfies (1) and (2). Suppose then that L satisfies (1) and (2). Note that (2) in conjunction with 2.4 implies that, for every $a \in L$, the set of all atoms of $1/a$ is an independent subset of $1/a$. Therefore, in view of 6.7 to show that L is locally distributive, we need only show that, for every $a \in L$, each element of u_a/a is a join of elements covering a. Consider a particular element $a \in L$. Let $x \in u_a/a$, and let b be the join in the sublattice u_a/a of all elements p for which $x \geq p \succ a$. If $x > b$, then there is an element r such that $x \geq r \succ b$. By (1), if $p \succ a$ and $p \not\leq b$, then $p \vee b \succ b$. Moreover, $r \neq p \vee b$ for every $p \succ a$. Consequently

$$r \leq u_a = \bigvee\{p \vee b \mid p \succ a\} \leq \bigvee\{s \mid s \succ b, s \neq r\},$$

contrary to the fact that all the atoms of $1/b$ are independent. Thus $x = b$, and every element of u_a/a is a join of elements covering a.

Finally, suppose that L is locally distributive. As we noted above, L is therefore semimodular. Suppose further that $a, p \in L$ with $p \succ a$ but $p \wedge (x \vee y) \neq (p \wedge x) \vee (p \wedge y)$ for some $x, y \geq a$. By 6.2 there is an irreducible element $q \geq x$ such that $q \not\geq p$. Since $p \leq x \vee y$ and $q \not\geq p$, it follows that $q \not\geq y$; i.e., $y > q \wedge y = b$. Note also that the semimodularity of L implies that $p \vee b \succ b$. If s is such that $y \geq s \succ b$, then $q \not\geq s$, and $p \vee b \neq s$ since $y \not\geq p$. Set $z = q \wedge u_b$. By the remark following the proof of 7.3, $u_b \succ z$. This together with the observation that $z \not\geq p \vee b, s$, yields that

$$z \wedge s = z \wedge (p \vee b) = b \qquad \text{and} \qquad z \vee s = z \vee (p \vee b) = u_b,$$

contrary to the distributivity of u_b/b. We infer that L must satisfy (2), and the proof of 7.4 is complete.

There are several alternative formulations of local distributivity. The reader may verify that *in a compactly generated strongly atomic lattice L the following three conditions are equivalent:* (1) *L is locally distributive,* (2) *L is semimodular and every modular sublattice of L is distributive, and* (3) *for every set of four distinct elements a*, p_1, p_2, $p_3 \in L$ *for which* p_1, p_2, $p_3 \succ a$, *the sublattice* $p_1 \vee p_2 \vee p_3/a$ *is an eight-element Boolean algebra.*

7.5: *A compactly generated strongly atomic lattice L has replaceable irredundant decompositions if and only if L satisfies the following condition:*

(∗)   *For all x*, $y \in L$, *if the sublattice* $x \vee y/x$ *has exactly one atom, then the sublattice* $y/x \wedge y$ *has exactly one atom.*[2]

PROOF: We make the proof of 7.5 in three steps, beginning with the following statement.

A. The lattice L has replaceable irredundant decompositions if and only if, for all $a, p_1, p_2 \in L$ and every irreducible element q, the condition $p_1, p_2 \succ a = q \wedge (p_1 \vee p_2)$ implies that $p_1 = p_2$.

For suppose L satisfies the conditions of A, and suppose that $a = \bigwedge Q = \bigwedge Q'$ are two irredundant decompositions of $a \in L$. Pick any $q \in Q$. Then by hypothesis, there is a unique element $p \in L$ such that $\bigwedge (Q - q) \geq p \succ a$. If an element $q' \in Q'$ is picked such that $q' \not\geq p$, then the strong atomicity of L implies that $a = q' \wedge \bigwedge(Q - q)$. Suppose this decomposition is not irredundant. Then there is some element $q_1 \in Q - q$ such that $a = q' \wedge \bigwedge(Q - \{q, q_1\})$. Again the hypothesis of A yields that there is a unique element p_1 such that $\bigwedge(Q - \{q, q_1\}) \geq p_1 \succ a$, and inasmuch as $\bigwedge(Q - \{q, q_1\}) \geq \bigwedge(Q - q) \geq p$, we must have $p_1 = p$. As before, the strong atomicity of L and the fact that $q \not\geq p$ imply that $q \wedge \bigwedge(Q - \{q, q_1\}) = \bigwedge(Q - q_1) = a$, contrary to the irredundance of the decomposition $a = \bigwedge Q$. Hence the decomposition $a = q' \wedge \bigwedge(Q - q)$ is irredundant, and we infer that L has replaceable irredundant decompositions.

Suppose the lattice L has replaceable irredundant decompositions. Let a, $p_1, p_2 \in L$ be such that $p_1, p_2 \succ a$, and let q be an irreducible element with $q \wedge (p_1 \vee p_2) = a$. Then there is an element $w \geq p_1 \vee p_2$ which is maximal with respect to the property that $q \wedge w = a$. If $w = \bigwedge R$ is an irredundant decomposition of w, then the maximality of w implies that $a = q \wedge \bigwedge R$ is an irredundant decomposition of a. Now if $p_1 \neq p_2$, then by 6.2 there is an irreducible element $q_1 \geq p_1$ such that $q_1 \not\geq p_2$. And as $q_1 \wedge p_2 = a$, there is a maximal element $w_1 \geq p_2$ such that $q_1 \wedge w_1 = a$. Once again, if $w_1 = \bigwedge R_1$ is an irredundant decomposition of w_1, then $a = q_1 \wedge \bigwedge R_1$ is an irredundant decomposition of a. But $q_1 \wedge \bigwedge R \geq p_1 > a$, and $q' \wedge \bigwedge R \geq p_2 > a$ for

[2] P. Crawley [19].

every $q' \in R_1$, and this, of course, contradicts the assumption that L has replaceable irredundant decompositions. Thus $p_1 = p_2$.

B. If L has replaceable irredundant decompositions, then the sublattice x/y has replaceable irredundant decompositions for every pair of elements $x > y$ in L.

Suppose r is an irreducible element of the sublattice x/y and $x \geq p_1, p_2$ $\succ r \wedge (p_1 \vee p_2) = y$. If $r = \wedge Q$ is a decomposition of r in the larger lattice L, then

$$r = x \wedge r = x \wedge \wedge Q = \bigwedge_{q \in Q} x \wedge q,$$

and as r is irreducible in x/y it follows that $r = x \wedge q$ for some irreducible element $q \in Q$. Hence

$$q \wedge (p_1 \vee p_2) = x \wedge q \wedge (p_1 \vee p_2) = r \wedge (p_1 \vee p_2) = y,$$

and as L has replaceable irredundant decompositions, we infer from A that $p_1 = p_2$. Consequently x/y has replaceable irredundant decompositions.

Now if L satisfies condition $(*)$, $a \in L$, q is an irreducible element in L, and $p_1, p_2 \succ a$ are such that $a = q \wedge (p_1 \vee p_2)$, then the irreducibility of q implies that $p_1 \vee p_2 \vee q/q$ contains a unique atom, and therefore $p_1 \vee p_2/a$ contains a unique atom. This means that $p_1 = p_2$, and hence by A the lattice L has replaceable irredundant decompositions. On the other hand, if L has replaceable irredundant decompositions, then according to B so does every quotient sublattice of L. Consequently, if $x, y \in L$ and $x \vee y/x$ contains a single atom, then x is irreducible in the sublattice $x \vee y/x \wedge y$, and it follows by A that $y/x \wedge y$ contains a single atom. Thus L satisfies $(*)$, as required.

Let us define a lattice L to be a *point lattice* if, for every pair of elements $x > y$ in L, x is the join of elements covering y. Observe that in a point lattice condition $(*)$ is equivalent to lower semimodularity. This observation plays a part in the proof of our next theorem.

7.6: *A semimodular, compactly generated, strongly atomic lattice L has replaceable irredundant decompositions if and only if L is locally modular.*[3]

PROOF: The fact that L satisfies $(*)$ if it is locally modular is immediate from 7.3. To prove the converse, assume that L satisfies $(*)$, and let $a \in L$. Suppose we know that every element of u_a/a is the join of elements covering a. Then if $u_a \geq x > y \geq a$, we have

$$x = \bigvee \{p \vee y \mid x \geq p \succ a, y \not\geq p\},$$

and as $p \vee y \succ y$ whenever $y \not\geq p \succ a$, it follows that u_a/a is a point lattice.

[3] R. P. Dilworth and P. Crawley [35].

Consequently 3.6 in conjunction with the observation above yields that u_a/a is modular. To complete the proof, therefore, we need only show that every element of u_a/a is a join of elements covering a. Moreover, inasmuch as u_a/a is compactly generated, it suffices to prove this for the compact elements of u_a/a. Let c be a compact element in u_a/a. Then there is a finite independent set $\{p_1, \ldots, p_n\}$ of atoms of u_a/a, which contains a minimal number of elements, such that

$$b = p_1 \vee \cdots \vee p_n \geq c.$$

The sublattice b/a is a finite dimensional semimodular lattice, and therefore if $b > c$, there is an element t such that $b \succ t \geq c$. The dimension of t/a is less than the dimension of b/a, and therefore, in view of 6.8 and the minimality of the set $\{p_1, \ldots, p_n\}$, t is not a join of elements covering a. Thus if

$$t_1 = \vee\{p \mid t \geq p \succ a\},$$

then b/t_1 has dimension at least 2, and there must be two distinct atoms s_1 and s_2 in b/a such that $t_1 \not\geq s_1$, s_2, and $t_1 \vee s_1 \not\geq s_2$. Now $s_1 \vee s_2 \vee t = b \succ t$, and hence by condition (∗) we must have $t \wedge (s_1 \vee s_2) > a$. Consequently $s_1 \vee s_2 \succ t \wedge (s_1 \vee s_2) \succ a$, since the sublattice $s_1 \vee s_2/a$ has dimension 2. This last relation, together with the definitions of t_1 and s_1, yields that $t_1 \geq t \wedge (s_1 \vee s_2)$ and $t \wedge (s_1 \vee s_2) \neq s_1$, and these imply that

$$t_1 \vee s_1 \geq s_1 \vee (t \wedge (s_1 \vee s_2)) = s_1 \vee s_2 \geq s_2,$$

a contradiction. Hence $c = p_1 \vee \cdots \vee p_n$, concluding the proof.

When a compactly generated strongly atomic lattice L satisfies either the descending chain condition or the ascending chain condition, then for any element $a \in L$, all the irredundant decompositions of a are finite. Consequently if the lattice L further has replaceable irredundant decompositions, then L has the *Kurosh-Ore property*: For each element $a \in L$, the number of irreducible elements in any irredundant decomposition of a is unique.

7.7: *If L is a semimodular compactly generated lattice satisfying the descending chain condition, then L has the Kurosh-Ore property if and only if it is locally modular.* [4]

PROOF: The sufficiency of local modularity follows from the preceding theorem. If L is not locally modular, then by the same result L does not have replaceable irredundant decompositions, and so by 7.5 there are three distinct elements $a, p_1, p_2 \in L$ and an irreducible element $q \in L$ such that

$$p_1, p_2 \succ a = q \wedge (p_1 \vee p_2).$$

Since L satisfies the descending chain condition, any maximal independent set of atoms of u_a/a is necessarily finite, and as the set $\{p_1, p_2\}$ is independent, this

---

[4] R. P. Dilworth [29].

set is contained in some finite maximal independent set $\{p_1, p_2, p_3, \ldots, p_n\}$ of elements covering a. For each $k = 1, \ldots, n$, set $s_k = \bigvee_{i \neq k} p_i$, and as in the proof of 6.9, choose an irreducible element q_k such that $q_k \wedge u_a = s_k$. Then

$$a = q_1 \wedge q_2 \wedge q_3 \wedge \cdots \wedge q_n = q \wedge q_3 \wedge \cdots \wedge q_n,$$

and the left-hand decomposition is irredundant. As the left-hand decomposition also involves the greater number of irreducible elements, L does not have the Kurosh-Ore property.

The results of the last two chapters deal rather satisfactorily with the questions of existence and uniqueness of irredundant decompositions in compactly generated lattices. The major inadequacy with this theory, of course, is that it does not extend beyond the strongly atomic case. In this regard it remains an important unsolved problem to modify the concept of "irredundant decomposition" in such a way that, at least, the existence of these new "irredundant decompositions" can be proved for each element in a general compactly generated lattice, and distributivity implies their uniqueness.

In a semimodular finite dimensional lattice, the Kurosh-Ore property is equivalent to the lattice having replaceable irredundant decompositions. If the assumption of semimodularity is dropped, however, this no longer holds. Figure 7-1 represents a finite lattice which has the Kurosh-Ore property but which does not have replaceable irredundant decompositions. At this time no necessary and sufficient conditions for an arbitrary finite lattice to have the Kurosh-Ore property are known.

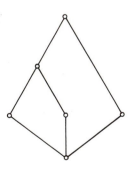

Fig. 7-1

8

DIRECT DECOMPOSITIONS

Independent sets have arisen significantly at several points in the preceding two chapters. They arise very naturally in other contexts also. For example, choosing a basis in a vector space V amounts to choosing a maximal independent set of atoms in the lattice of all subspaces of V. More generally, the representations of an operator group G as a direct product correspond to independent subsets of the lattice of all admissible normal subgroups of G whose join is G. There is another relevant feature to this example. If A and B are two admissible normal subgroups of G having a common complement in the lattice of admissible normal subgroups, then the second isomorphism theorem yields that A and B are isomorphic. Consequently, if the operator group G is represented in two ways as a direct product of admissible normal subgroups and if a subgroup in the first direct product can be replaced by a subgroup in the second, then these two subgroups are isomorphic.

With the foregoing example in mind, we now study certain representations of a lattice element as an independent join, with the hope of obtaining replacement theorems analogous to 7.2. As we will see, under suitable conditions this hope can be realized.

Throughout this chapter, the least element of a lattice will be denoted by 0. If a is an element of a complete lattice L and $A = \{a_i \mid i \in I\}$ is a subset of L, we say that a is a *direct join* of A, and we write

$$a = \dot{\bigvee} A \qquad \text{or} \qquad a = \dot{\bigvee_{i \in I}} a_i,$$

if A is independent and $a = \bigvee A$. The direct join of finitely many elements $a_1, \ldots, a_n$ is also written $a_1 \dot{\bigvee} \cdots \dot{\bigvee} a_n$. An element b is called a *direct factor* of a if $a = b \dot{\bigvee} x$ for some element x. The element a is *indecomposable* if $a \neq 0$ and the only direct factors of a are itself and 0.

We have already remarked that in an upper continuous lattice a subset A is independent if and only if every finite subset of A is independent. The following lemmas list some additional properties of independent sets in modular lattices. The reader can supply the proofs.

8.1: *If A is an independent subset of a complete modular lattice L and, for each $a \in A$, B_a is an independent subset of L such that $a \geq \bigvee B_a$, then the set-union of the subsets $B_a (a \in A)$ is independent.*

8.2: *If A is an independent subset of an upper continuous modular lattice L, then the elements of L which are joins of subsets of A form a complete sub-lattice of L which is isomorphic to the Boolean algebra of all subsets of A.*

8.3: *If a, x, y are elements of a modular lattice L, $x \vee y = x \dot\vee y$, and $x \leq a \leq x \dot\vee y$, then $a = x \dot\vee (a \wedge y)$.*

8.4: *If a, x, y, z are elements of a modular lattice L and $a = x \dot\vee y = x \dot\vee z$, then the quotient sublattices a/x, $y/0$, and $z/0$ are isomorphic.*

The principal results of this section are the following three theorems.[1]

8.5: *If a is an element of a modular compactly generated lattice L and*
$$a = x \dot\vee y = \dot\bigvee B,$$
where x is finite dimensional and indecomposable, then there exist an element $b \in B$ and elements e_1 and e_2 such that $b = e_1 \dot\vee e_2$ and
$$a = e_1 \dot\vee y = x \dot\vee e_2 \dot\vee \dot\bigvee(B - b).$$

8.6: *If a is an element of a modular compactly generated lattice L and a is a direct join of finite dimensional elements, then every direct factor of a is a direct join of finite dimensional elements.*

8.7: *If a is an element of a modular compactly generated lattice L and*
$$a = \dot\bigvee_{i \in I} a_i = \dot\bigvee_{j \in J} b_j,$$
where each a_i and each b_j is finite dimensional and indecomposable, then there is a one-to-one mapping φ of I onto J such that, for each $i \in I$,
$$a = a_i \dot\vee \dot\bigvee_{j \neq \varphi(i)} b_j.$$

Our proofs of these three theorems begin with the theorem of O. Ore[2]:

If a is an element of a finite dimensional modular lattice F and
$$a = a_1 \dot\vee \cdots \dot\vee a_m = b_1 \dot\vee \cdots \dot\vee b_n,$$

[1] P. Crawley [20].
[2] O. Ore [75]; the formulation and proof given here are essentially due to G. Birkhoff [12].

where each a_i and each b_j is indecomposable, then for each $h = 1, \ldots, m$ there exists an integer k such that

$$a = a_1 \; \dot{\vee} \; \cdots \; \dot{\vee} \; a_{h-1} \; \dot{\vee} \; b_k \; \dot{\vee} \; a_{h+1} \; \dot{\vee} \; \cdots \; \dot{\vee} \; a_m$$
$$= b_1 \; \dot{\vee} \; \cdots \; \dot{\vee} \; b_{k-1} \; \dot{\vee} \; a_h \; \dot{\vee} \; b_{k+1} \; \dot{\vee} \; \cdots \; \dot{\vee} \; b_n.$$

To prove Ore's theorem, let δ be the dimension function of the finite dimensional modular lattice F, and for each integer $i = 1, \ldots, m$ and each $j = 1, \ldots, n$ set

$$\bar{a}_i = a_1 \vee \cdots \vee a_{i-1} \vee a_{i+1} \vee \cdots \vee a_m,$$
$$\bar{b}_j = b_1 \vee \cdots \vee b_{j-1} \vee b_{j+1} \vee \cdots \vee b_n.$$

The proof proceeds by induction on the integer $\delta(a)$.

CASE 1: There is an integer k such that $a_h \vee \bar{b}_k = \bar{a}_h \vee b_k = a$. Under these circumstances,

$$\delta(a_h) = \delta(a) - \delta(\bar{b}_k) + \delta(a_h \wedge \bar{b}_k)$$
$$= \delta(b_k) + \delta(a_h \wedge \bar{b}_k) \geq \delta(b_k),$$

and similarly $\delta(b_k) \geq \delta(a_h)$. Thus $\delta(a_h) = \delta(b_k)$, and it follows that $\delta(a_h \wedge \bar{b}_k) = \delta(\bar{a}_h \wedge b_k) = 0$. This gives $a_h \wedge \bar{b}_k = \bar{a}_h \wedge b_k = 0$, and we conclude that $a = a_h \; \dot{\vee} \; \bar{b}_k = b_k \; \dot{\vee} \; \bar{a}_h$.

CASE 2: $a_h \vee \bar{b}_j < a$ for some j, say $j = 1$. For each j, set $d_j = a_h \vee \bar{b}_j$ and

$$q_j = d_j \wedge b_j = (a_h \vee \bar{b}_j) \wedge b_j.$$

Then $d_j \leq a$ and $b_j \geq q_j$ for each $j = 1, \ldots, n$. Also $b_1 > q_1$, for otherwise $a_h \vee \bar{b}_1 \geq b_1 \vee \bar{b}_1 = a$, contrary to assumption. The q_j's are independent since the b_j's are independent, and therefore

$$c = q_1 \vee \cdots \vee q_n = q_1 \; \dot{\vee} \; \cdots \; \dot{\vee} \; q_n.$$

Consequently, as $\delta(b_1) > \delta(q_1)$,

$$\delta(c) = \delta(q_1) + \cdots + \delta(q_n) < \delta(b_1) + \cdots + \delta(b_n) = \delta(a).$$

For each $r = 1, \ldots, n$, set

$$u_r = \bigvee_{j=1}^{r} q_j, \qquad v_r = \bigvee_{j=1}^{r} b_j, \qquad w_r = \bigwedge_{j=1}^{r} d_j.$$

We will show (by induction on r) that $u_r = v_r \wedge w_r$ for each $r = 1, \ldots, n$. This is clear for $r = 1$. If $u_r = v_r \wedge w_r$, then $u_{r+1} = u_r \vee q_{r+1} = (v_r \wedge w_r) \vee (b_{r+1} \wedge d_{r+1})$, and as $d_{r+1} \geq v_r \geq v_r \wedge w_r$ and $b_{r+1} \leq w_r$, two applications of modularity yield

$$u_{r+1} = (v_r \wedge w_r) \vee (d_{r+1} \wedge b_{r+1})$$
$$= d_{r+1} \wedge [(v_r \wedge w_r) \vee b_{r+1}] = d_{r+1} \wedge [(v_r \vee b_{r+1}) \wedge w_r]$$
$$= v_{r+1} \wedge w_{r+1}.$$

In particular,

$$c = u_n = v_n \wedge w_n = w_n = d_1 \wedge \cdots \wedge d_n \geq a_h,$$

and from 8.3 we infer that

$$c = a_h \dot\vee (c \wedge \bar{a}_h) = q_1 \dot\vee \cdots \dot\vee q_n.$$

Now by induction the conclusion of Ore's theorem holds for c, and therefore there is some integer k and some indecomposable direct factor e of q_k such that $c = e \dot\vee (c \wedge \bar{a}_h)$. This implies that $e \wedge \bar{a}_h = e \wedge c \wedge \bar{a}_h = 0$ and that

$$e \vee \bar{a}_h = e \vee (c \wedge \bar{a}_h) \vee \bar{a}_h = c \vee \bar{a}_h = c \vee a_h \vee \bar{a}_h = a.$$

Thus $a = e \dot\vee \bar{a}_h$. Application of 8.3 yields that $b_k = e \dot\vee (b_k \wedge \bar{a}_h)$, and since b_k is indecomposable and $e \neq 0$, we infer that $e = b_k$. This last equality gives us that $a = b_k \dot\vee \bar{a}_h$ and

$$b_k = e \leq q_k \leq a_h \vee \bar{b}_k,$$

so that $a_h \vee \bar{b}_k = a_h \vee \bar{b}_k \vee b_k = a$. Case 1 now applies, and we conclude that

$$a = b_k \dot\vee \bar{a}_h = a_h \dot\vee \bar{b}_k.$$

CASE 3: $a_h \vee \bar{b}_j = a$ and $\bar{a}_h \vee b_j < a$ for all j. We show that this, the only remaining case, does not occur. Assuming it does, by reversing the roles of the a_i's and b_j's, we can apply case 2 to the element b_n to obtain an integer $i \neq h$, say $i = m$, such that

$$a = a_m \dot\vee \bar{a}_m = \bar{b}_n \dot\vee a_m.$$

Therefore, in view of 3.4, the mapping

$$x \longrightarrow (x \vee a_m) \wedge \bar{a}_m, \qquad x \in \bar{b}_n/0,$$

is an isomorphism of the sublattice $\bar{b}_n/0$ onto the sublattice $\bar{a}_m/0$; and if we set $b'_j = (b_j \vee a_m) \wedge \bar{a}_m (j = 1, \ldots, n-1)$, this isomorphism yields that

$$\bar{a}_m = a_1 \dot\vee \cdots \dot\vee a_{m-1} = b'_1 \dot\vee \cdots \dot\vee b'_{n-1}.$$

By induction, Ore's theorem holds for $\bar{a}_m$, and hence there is some integer k such that

$$\bar{a}_m = a_1 \dot\vee \cdots \dot\vee a_{h-1} \dot\vee b'_k \dot\vee a_{h+1} \dot\vee \cdots \dot\vee a_{m-1}.$$

Moreover,

$$b_k \vee \bar{a}_h \geq b_k \vee a_m = (b_k \vee a_m) \wedge (\bar{a}_m \vee a_m)$$
$$= [(b_k \vee a_m) \wedge \bar{a}_m] \vee a_m = b'_k \vee a_m,$$

and we infer that

$$b_k \vee \bar{a}_h \geq \bar{a}_h \vee b'_k \vee a_m = \bar{a}_m \vee a_m = a,$$

a contradiction. Consequently case 3 cannot occur, and the proof of Ore's theorem is complete.

PROOF OF 8.5: Suppose a, x, y are elements of a modular compactly generated lattice L, B is a subset of L, x is finite dimensional and indecomposable, and

$$a = x \mathbin{\dot{\vee}} y = \dot{\bigvee} B.$$

Since x is compact, there is a finite subset $\{b_1, \ldots, b_n\} \subseteq B$ such that $x \leq b_1 \vee \cdots \vee b_n$. For each $j = 1, \ldots, n$, set

$$\bar{b}_j = b_1 \vee \cdots \vee b_{j-1} \vee b_{j+1} \vee \cdots \vee b_n$$

and

$$q_j = (x \vee \bar{b}_j) \wedge b_j.$$

Then it follows as in the proof of Ore's theorem that

$$x \leq c = q_1 \vee \cdots \vee q_n = q_1 \mathbin{\dot{\vee}} \cdots \mathbin{\dot{\vee}} q_n.$$

Also, $q_j \wedge \bar{b}_j = (x \vee \bar{b}_j) \wedge b_j \wedge \bar{b}_j = 0$, and

$$q_j \vee \bar{b}_j = [(x \vee \bar{b}_j) \wedge b_j] \vee \bar{b}_j = (x \vee \bar{b}_j) \wedge (b_j \vee \bar{b}_j) = x \vee \bar{b}_j,$$

so that

$$q_j/0 = q_j/q_j \wedge \bar{b}_j \cong q_j \vee \bar{b}_j/\bar{b}_j = x \vee \bar{b}_j/\bar{b}_j \cong x/x \wedge \bar{b}_j.$$

Consequently each q_j is finite dimensional, and the dimension of $q_j/0$ does not exceed the dimension of $x/0$. In particular c is finite dimensional. Further, 8.3 yields that

$$c = x \mathbin{\dot{\vee}} (c \wedge y) = q_1 \mathbin{\dot{\vee}} \cdots \mathbin{\dot{\vee}} q_n.$$

Now x is indecomposable and the dimension of each $q_j/0$ is at most the dimension of $x/0$. Therefore it follows from Ore's theorem that there exists an integer k, say $k = 1$, such that

$$c = q_1 \mathbin{\dot{\vee}} (c \wedge y) = x \mathbin{\dot{\vee}} q_2 \mathbin{\dot{\vee}} \cdots \mathbin{\dot{\vee}} q_n.$$

This implies that $q_1 \wedge y = q_1 \wedge c \wedge y = 0$ and

$$q_1 \vee y = q_1 \vee (c \wedge y) \vee y = c \vee y = c \vee x \vee y = a;$$

i.e. $a = q_1 \mathbin{\dot{\vee}} y$. Thus $b_1 = q_1 \mathbin{\dot{\vee}} (b_1 \wedge y)$ by 8.3. Moreover, with $b_1^* = \dot{\bigvee}(B - b_1)$, and noting that $q_2 \vee \cdots \vee q_n \leq b_2 \vee \cdots \vee b_n \leq b_1^*$, we have

$$x \vee [(b_1 \wedge y) \vee b_1^*] = x \vee q_2 \vee \cdots \vee q_n \vee (b_1 \wedge y) \vee b_1^*$$
$$= c \vee (b_1 \wedge y) \vee b_1^* = c \vee b_1 \vee b_1^* = a.$$

And as

$$x/x \wedge [(b_1 \wedge y) \vee b_1^*] \cong a/(b_1 \wedge y) \vee b_1^* \cong q_1/0 \cong x/0$$

by 8.4, the finite dimensionality of $x/0$ implies that $x \wedge [(b_1 \wedge y) \vee b_1^*] = 0$. Consequently

$$a = q_1 \mathbin{\dot{\vee}} y = x \mathbin{\dot{\vee}} (b_1 \wedge y) \mathbin{\dot{\vee}} b_1^*,$$

and the proof of 8.5 is complete.

Inasmuch as each finite dimensional element is the direct join of finitely many indecomposable elements, repeated application of 8.5 yields the following special case: *If a is an element in a modular compactly generated lattice, and*

$$a = x \dot{\vee} y = b \dot{\vee} e,$$

where x is finite dimensional, then there exist elements $b' \leq b$ and $e' \leq e$ such that $a = x \dot{\vee} b' \dot{\vee} e'$.

PROOF OF 8.6: Assume that a is an element of a modular compactly generated lattice L, A is a set of finite dimensional elements of L, and

$$a = \dot{\vee}A.$$

First we show that if $a = b \dot{\vee} e$, then b and e are both direct joins of elements which are joins of countably many compact elements. To this end, consider the collection $\mathcal{P}$ of all subsets P of L which satisfy the following conditions:

(1) $\bigvee P = \dot{\vee}P = \dot{\vee}K$ for some subset $K \in A$.
(2) $x = (x \wedge b) \dot{\vee} (x \wedge e)$ for all $x \in P$.
(3) For each $x \in P$, $x \wedge b$ and $x \wedge e$ are both joins of countably many compact elements.

$\mathcal{P}$ is nonempty since the null set is in $\mathcal{P}$. Moreover, the set-union of any chain of sets in $\mathcal{P}$ also belongs to $\mathcal{P}$, and therefore $\mathcal{P}$ contains a maximal element Q by Zorn's lemma. Set

$$q = \dot{\vee}Q = \bigvee M, \qquad u = \dot{\underset{x \in Q}{\vee}} (x \wedge b), \qquad v = \dot{\underset{x \in Q}{\vee}} (x \wedge e),$$

where $M \subseteq A$. Then it follows from (2) that $q = u \dot{\vee} v$, and it follows from (1) that $a = q \dot{\vee} w = u \dot{\vee} v \dot{\vee} w$, where $w = \bigvee(A - M)$. Furthermore, if $b' = b \wedge (w \vee v)$ and $e' = e \wedge (w \vee v)$, then 8.3 yields that $b = b' \dot{\vee} u$ and $e = e' \dot{\vee} v$, whence

$$a = b' \dot{\vee} e' \dot{\vee} q.$$

Suppose $q < a$. Then there is some element $s_0 \in A - M$. Since s_0 is compact and the lattice L is compactly generated, there are compact elements $c_1 \leq b'$ and $d_1 \leq e'$ such that

$$s_0 \leq c_1 \vee d_1 \vee q.$$

$c_1 \vee d_1$ is compact, and hence there is a finite subset $S_1 \subseteq A$ such that

$$c_1 \vee d_1 \leq \bigvee S_1.$$

Again $\bigvee S_1$ is compact, and so there are compact elements $c_2 \leq b'$ and $d_2 \leq e'$ such that

$$\bigvee S_1 \leq c_2 \vee d_2 \vee q.$$

Continuing in this way we obtain a sequence $\{s_0\}, S_1, S_2, \ldots, S_n, \ldots$ of finite subsets of A and two sequences of compact elements $c_1, c_2, \ldots, c_n, \ldots \leq b'$

and $d_1, d_2, \ldots, d_n, \ldots \leq e'$ such that, for $n = 1, 2, \ldots$,

$$c_n \vee d_n \leq \bigvee S_n \leq c_{n+1} \vee d_{n+1} \vee q.$$

Set

$$b^* = \bigvee_{n<\infty} c_n, \qquad e^* = \bigvee_{n<\infty} d_n, \qquad M^* = M \cup \{s_0\} \cup \bigcup_{n<\infty} S_n.$$

Then $b^* \leq b'$ and $e^* \leq e'$, and it is clear that

$$x^* = b^* \vee e^* = b^* \mathbin{\dot\vee} e^*$$

and that

$$x^* \vee q = x^* \mathbin{\dot\vee} q = \mathbin{\dot\bigvee} M^*.$$

But this implies that $Q \cup \{x^*\}$ is a member of $\mathcal{P}$ that is greater than Q. And since this contradicts the maximality of Q, we must have $q = a$. It follows that $b = u$ and $e = v$, and therefore b and e are direct joins of elements which are joins of countably many elements.

Next we observe the following: If b is a direct factor of a and c is a compact element for which $b \geq c$, then there is a finite dimensional direct factor v of b such that $v \geq c$. To prove this, write $a = b \mathbin{\dot\vee} e$. Since c is compact, there is a finite subset $F \subseteq A$ such that $f = \bigvee F \geq c$. Note that f is finite dimensional. Therefore, applying the remark following the proof of 8.5 to the direct joins $a = f \mathbin{\dot\vee} \mathbin{\dot\bigvee}(A - F) = b \mathbin{\dot\vee} e$, we obtain elements $b' \leq b$ and $e' \leq e$ such that $a = f \mathbin{\dot\vee} b' \mathbin{\dot\vee} e'$. Set

$$v = b \wedge (e' \vee f) \qquad \text{and} \qquad w = e \wedge (b' \vee f).$$

Then $b = v \mathbin{\dot\vee} b'$ and $e = w \mathbin{\dot\vee} e'$. These equations also imply that $v \vee w/0 \cong f/0$, so that v is finite dimensional. Moreover, $v \geq b \wedge f \geq c$.

In view of what we have shown so far, to complete the proof of 8.6, it suffices to show that if b is a direct factor of a and b is the join of countably many compact elements, then b is a direct join of finite dimensional elements. Write

$$b = \bigvee_{n<\infty} c_n,$$

where each c_n is compact. From the preceding paragraph we infer that elements v_1 and w_1 exist such that v_1 is finite dimensional, $v_1 \geq c_1$, and

$$b = v_1 \mathbin{\dot\vee} w_1.$$

Since c_2 is compact, there is a compact element $d_1 \leq w_1$ such that $c_2 \leq v_1 \vee d_1$. Now w_1 is a direct factor of a_1, and again applying the observation of the preceding paragraph, we obtain elements v_2 and w_2 such that v_2 is finite dimensional, $v_2 \geq d_1$, and $w_1 = v_2 \mathbin{\dot\vee} w_2$. Thus $c_2 \leq v_1 \vee v_2$, and

$$b = v_1 \mathbin{\dot\vee} v_2 \mathbin{\dot\vee} w_2.$$

Continuing this process, we obtain a sequence of finite dimensional elements

$v_1, v_2, \ldots, v_n \ldots \leq b$ such that, for each $n = 1, 2, \ldots,$

$$c_n \leq v_1 \vee \cdots \vee v_n = v_1 \dot{\vee} \cdots \dot{\vee} v_n.$$

It follows that $b = \dot{\mathsf{V}}_{n<\infty} v_n$, completing the proof of 8.6.

PROOF OF 8.7: The concept of an ascending well-ordered chain was defined in Chap. 1. For the purpose of this proof, let us define a binary relation $\leq$ in a set X to be a *well-ordering* of X if the set X together with the relation $\leq$ is an ascending well-ordered chain.

Let a be an element of a modular compactly generated lattice L, and suppose that

$$a = \dot{\mathsf{V}}_{i \in I} a_i = \dot{\mathsf{V}}_{j \in J} b_j,$$

where each a_i and each b_j is finite dimensional and indecomposable. We will prove: *There exist a well-ordering $\leq$ of the index set I and a one-to-one mapping φ of I onto J such that, for each $h \in I$,*

$$a = \dot{\mathsf{V}}_{i \leq h} b_{\varphi(i)} \vee \dot{\mathsf{V}}_{i > h} a_i = a_h \vee \dot{\mathsf{V}}_{j \neq \varphi(h)} b_j.$$

To begin, let $\mathcal{P}$ the collection of all ordered triples $\langle H, \leq, \psi \rangle$, where $H \subseteq I$, $\leq$ is a well-ordering of H, ψ is a one-to-one mapping of H to J, and such that the following conditions hold:

(1) For each $h \in H$,

$$a = \dot{\mathsf{V}}_{i \in H, i \leq h} b_{\psi(i)} \vee \dot{\mathsf{V}}_{i \in H, i > h} a_i \dot{\vee} \dot{\mathsf{V}}_{i \in I - H} a_i$$
$$= a_h \vee \dot{\mathsf{V}}_{j \neq \psi(h)} b_j.$$

(2) $\mathsf{V}_{i \in H} a_i \leq \mathsf{V}_{i \in H} b_{\psi(i)}.$

Partially order $\mathcal{P}$ by defining $\langle H, \leq, \psi \rangle \leq \langle H', \leq', \psi' \rangle$ if either $H = H'$ or

$$H = \{i \in H' \,|\, i <' h\}$$

for some $h \in H'$, the restriction of $\leq'$ to H coincides with $\leq$, and the restriction of ψ' to H coincides with ψ. Note that $\mathcal{P}$ is nonempty since it contains the triple consisting of the empty set, the empty relation, and the empty mapping.

If $\langle H_\sigma, \leq^\sigma, \psi_\sigma \rangle$, $(\sigma \in \Sigma)$ is a chain of elements in $\mathcal{P}$, define $\bar{H}$ to be the set-union of the sets $H_\sigma (\sigma \in \Sigma)$, define $\leq^-$ to be the set-union of the relations $\leq^\sigma$ $(\sigma \in \Sigma)$, and define $\bar{\psi}$ to be the set-union of the functions $\psi_\sigma (\sigma \in \Sigma)$. (Here, of course, we are considering relations and functions as sets of ordered pairs.) It is then easily checked that $\langle \bar{H}, \leq^-, \bar{\psi} \rangle \in \mathcal{P}$ and that $(\bar{H}, \leq^-, \bar{\psi})$ is an upper bound of the chain $\langle H_\sigma, \leq^\sigma, \psi_\sigma \rangle$ $(\sigma \in \Sigma)$. Thus Zorn's lemma yields that $\mathcal{P}$ contains a maximal element $\langle M, \leq, \varphi \rangle$.

Now

$$\{b_{\varphi(i)} \mid i \in M\} \cup \{a_i \mid i \in I - M\}$$

is an independent subset of the lattice L, since by (1) all its finite subsets are independent. This fact together with (2) yields that

$$a = \bigvee_{j \in J} b_j = \bigvee_{i \in M} b_{\varphi(i)} \vee \bigvee_{i \in I-M} a_i.$$

Notice that the foregoing formula shows that $M = I$ if and only if $\varphi(M) = J$. Consequently, to complete the proof, it is enough to show that $M = I$. Suppose that $M \neq I$. Then $\varphi(M) \neq J$, and there is an element $j_0 \in J - \varphi(M)$. Applying 8.5 to the element b_{j_0} and the preceding direct joins, we obtain an element $i_0 \in I - M$ such that

$$a = a_{i_0} \vee \bigvee_{j \neq j_0} b_j = b_{j_0} \vee \bigvee_{j \in M} b_{\varphi(i)} \vee \bigvee_{i \notin M, i \neq i_0} a_i.$$

The element a_{i_0} is compact, and hence there is a finite subset $J_0 \subseteq J$ such that

$$a_{i_0} \leq \bigvee_{j \in J_0} b_j.$$

Let M_0 be the set-union of M and $\{i_0\}$, and let $\{j_1, \ldots, j_r\}$ denote the set of those elements in J_0 which are different from j_0 and not contained in $\varphi(M)$. Then applying 8.5 successively to the elements $b_{j_1}, \ldots, b_{j_r}$, it follows that distinct indices $i_1, \ldots, i_r \in I - M_0$ exist such that, for each $n = 1, \ldots, r$,

$$(3) \quad a = a_{i_n} \vee \bigvee_{j \neq j_n} b_j$$

$$= b_{j_n} \vee \cdots \vee b_{j_0} \vee \bigvee_{i \in M} b_{\varphi(i)} \vee \bigvee_{i \notin M, i \neq i_0, \cdots, i_n} a_i.$$

Again the element $a_{i_1} \vee \cdots \vee a_{i_r}$ is compact, and there exists a finite subset $J_1 \subseteq J$ such that

$$a_{i_1} \vee \cdots \vee a_{i_r} \leq \bigvee_{j \in J_1} b_j.$$

Let M_1 denote the set-union of M and $\{i_0, \ldots, i_r\}$, and let $\{j_{r+1}, \ldots, j_s\}$ denote the set of those elements in J_1 which are not contained in either $\varphi(M)$ or $\{j_0, \ldots, j_r\}$. As before, repeated application of 8.5 to the elements $b_{j_{r+1}}, \ldots, b_{j_s}$ yields the existence of distinct elements $i_{r+1}, \ldots, i_s \in I - M$, such that (3) holds for each $n = r + 1, \ldots, s$. By continuing this process, we obtain two sequences of distinct indices $i_0, i_1, \ldots, i_n, \ldots \in I - M$ and $j_0, j_1, \ldots, j_n, \ldots \in J - \varphi(M)$ (both of which might be finite with an equal number of terms) such that (3) holds for each $n = 0, 1, 2, \ldots$, and such that

$$\bigvee_{n \geq 0} a_{i_n} \leq \bigvee_{n \geq 0} b_{j_n} \vee \bigvee_{i \in M} b_{\varphi(i)}.$$

Set $M^* = M \cup \{i_0, i_1, \ldots, i_n, \ldots\}$. Define the well-ordering $\leq^*$ of M^* by the following rules: if $i, i' \in M$, then $i \leq^* i'$ if and only if $i \leq i'$ in M, and, for every $i \in M$,

$$i <^* i_0 <^* i_1 <^* \cdots <^* i_n <^* \cdots.$$

Define the mapping φ^* by $\varphi^*(i) = \varphi(i)$ for every $i \in M$, and $\varphi^*(i_n) = j_n$ for each $n = 0, 1, 2, \ldots$. Then it is clear that $\langle M^*, \leq^*, \varphi^* \rangle \in \mathcal{P}$ and that $\langle M^*, \leq^*, \varphi^* \rangle$ is greater than $\langle M, \leq, \varphi \rangle$. This contradiction forces the equality of M and I, completing the proof of 8.7.

It is impossible to simply drop the assumptions of finite dimensionality in the above results. The lattice of subgroups of a free abelian group of rank 2 shows that in general Ore's theorem fails for lattices satisfying only the ascending chain condition. (The examination of this lattice is left to the reader.) For an example of a modular compactly generated lattice satisfying the descending chain condition in which Ore's theorem fails, consider an additively written abelian group G isomorphic to the direct sum of two copies of $Z(3)$ and four copies of $Z(3^\infty)$. Here, as usual, $Z(3)$ denotes the three-element cyclic group, and $Z(3^\infty)$ denotes the group of rational numbers whose denominators are powers of 3, under addition modulo 1. Pick subgroups Q, R, S, T, U, and V such that $Q \cong R \cong Z(3)$ and $S \cong T \cong U \cong V \cong Z(3^\infty)$ and such that in the lattice of subgroups of G,

$$G = Q \ \dot\vee \ R \ \dot\vee \ S \ \dot\vee \ T \ \dot\vee \ U \ \dot\vee \ V.$$

Let q and r generate Q and R, respectively, and let S, T, U, and V be generated by the sequences $\{s_n\}, \{t_n\}, \{u_n\}$, and $\{v_n\}$, respectively, where

$$3s_1 = 0 \quad \text{and} \quad 3s_{n+1} = s_n \quad (n = 1, 2, \ldots),$$

with analogous relations holding for the t_n's, u_n's, and v_n's. Set

$$A = Q \vee S \vee T \quad \text{and} \quad B = R \vee U \vee V.$$

Let C be the subgroup of G generated by the elements

$$q + r, s_1, s_2 + u_1, s_3 + u_2, \ldots, v_1, v_2 + t_1, v_3 + t_2, \ldots,$$

and let D be the subgroup generated by the elements

$$q + 2r, u_1, u_2 + s_1, u_3 + s_2, \ldots, t_1, t_2 + v_1, t_3 + v_2, \ldots.$$

Then with these definitions it follows that

$$G = A \ \dot\vee \ B = C \ \dot\vee \ D,$$

$$A \wedge C, \ A \wedge D, \ B \wedge C, \ B \wedge D \neq \{0\},$$

and the join of any two of the subgroups A, B, C, or D equals G. Now let L be the set consisting of all subgroups $X \leq S \vee T \vee U \vee V$; all subgroups of the form $A \vee X, B \vee X, C \vee X$, or $D \vee X$ with $X \leq S \vee T \vee U \vee V$; and the group G. It is easily checked that L is a complete sublattice of the lattice of subgroups of G. In particular, L is a modular compactly generated lattice satisfying the descending chain condition. Moreover, in L, the subgroups A, B, C, and D are indecomposable. Thus Ore's theorem fails in L for the direct joins $G = A \ \dot\vee \ B = C \ \dot\vee \ D$.

One aspect of the theory of direct decompositions that we have not touched upon, except in the finite dimensional case, is that of existence. This is not just an oversight. The theory developed in this chapter suffers substantially because, at this time, there is no known necessary and sufficient condition for an element in a modular compactly generated lattice to be a direct join of finite dimensional elements. There is not even a useful sufficient such condition.

Finally, it is not surprising that distributivity yields the strongest type of uniqueness theorem for direct decompositions, as our concluding result demonstrates. (The reader can provide its proof.)

8.8: *If a is an element of a complete distributive lattice L and*

$$a = \dot{\bigvee}B = \dot{\bigvee}C,$$

then $b = \dot{\bigvee}_{c \in C}(b \wedge c)$ for each $b \in B$.

9

IDEALS

At this point we describe a simple technique for constructing a compactly generated lattice which contains a given lattice as a sublattice and which satisfies every lattice identity satisfied by the given lattice.

Let L be an arbitrary lattice. A subset A of L is called an *ideal* of L if

(1) $a, b \in A$ implies $a \vee b \in A$.
(2) $a \in A$, $x \in L$, and $x \leq a$ imply $x \in A$.

Every lattice has at least two ideals, the empty set and L itself. Moreover, for each $a \in L$, the subset

$$a/0 = \{x \in L \mid x \leq a\}$$

is an ideal of L; we refer to ideals of this type as *principal ideals*. Notice that *every nonempty ideal of L is principal if and only if L satisfies the ascending chain condition*. (Proof?)

The collection of all the ideals of the lattice L, together with the relation of set-inclusion, is a partially ordered set which we will denote by $\mathcal{I}(L)$.

9.1:   *For every lattice L, $\mathcal{I}(L)$ is a compactly generated lattice, the mapping*

$$a \longrightarrow a/0$$

is an isomorphism of L to $\mathcal{I}(L)$, and $\mathcal{I}(L)$ satisfies every lattice identity that L satisfies.[1]

PROOF: First, let $\mathfrak{A}$ be a set of ideals of the lattice L. Then the set-intersection of the ideals in $\mathfrak{A}$ is again an ideal of L, and therefore in $\mathcal{I}(L)$,

$$\bigwedge \mathfrak{A} = \bigcap \mathfrak{A}.$$

Set

$$J_{\mathfrak{A}} = \{x \in L \mid x \leq \bigvee F \text{ some } F \in \mathfrak{B}\},$$

[1] G. Birkhoff [12], pp. 79–80.

where $\mathfrak{B}$ is the set of all finite subsets of $\bigcup\mathfrak{A}$. Then $J_{\mathfrak{A}}$ is an ideal of L, and any ideal of L that includes every ideal in $\mathfrak{A}$ necessarily includes $J_{\mathfrak{A}}$. Thus, in $\mathscr{I}(L)$,

$$\bigvee\mathfrak{A} = J_{\mathfrak{A}}.$$

$\mathscr{I}(L)$ is therefore a complete lattice. The preceding formula also shows that every principal ideal of L is compact in $\mathscr{I}(L)$, and as $A = \bigvee_{a \in A} a/0$ for each $A \in \mathscr{I}(L)$, we infer that $\mathscr{I}(L)$ is compactly generated.

When specialized to two ideals $A, B \in \mathscr{I}(L)$, the formulas for the meet and join of a set of ideals yield

$$A \wedge B = A \cap B = \{x \in L \,|\, x \le a \wedge b \text{ for some } a \in A \text{ and } b \in B\},$$

$$A \vee B = \{x \in L \,|\, x \le a \vee b \text{ for some } a \in A \text{ and } b \in B\}.$$

In particular, if A and B are principal ideals, say $A = a/0$ and $B = b/0$, then we have

$$a/0 \wedge b/0 = (a \wedge b)/0 \qquad \text{and} \qquad a/0 \vee b/0 = (a \vee b)/0.$$

These formulas imply that the mapping $a \longrightarrow a/0$ is an isomorphism.

To show that $\mathscr{I}(L)$ satisfies every lattice identity that L satisfies, it is sufficient to prove: If p is a lattice polynomial over the set $Z = \{z_1, \ldots, z_n\}$, and if $A_1, \ldots, A_n$ is a sequence of ideals of L, then $p(A_1, \ldots, A_n) = J_p$, where

$$J_p = \{x \in L \,|\, x \le p(a_1, \ldots, a_n) \text{ for some } a_i \in A_i\}.$$

For the proof of this statement, we will assume that the sequence of ideals $A_1, \ldots, A_n$ is fixed, and we will proceed by induction on the rank of the polynomial p. Note that the statement is trivial in case p has rank 1. Suppose $p = (p_1 \vee p_2)$. By the induction we then infer that

$$p(A_1, \ldots, A_n) = p_1(A_1, \ldots, A_n) \vee p_2(A_1, \ldots, A_n) = J_{p_1} \vee J_{p_2}.$$

If $x \in J_{p_1} \vee J_{p_2}$, then from the formula above for the join of two ideals we obtain that

$$x \le p_1(a_1, \ldots, a_n) \vee p_2(b_1, \ldots, b_n),$$

where $a_i, b_i \in A_i$. Now for any lattice polynomial q over Z and any two sequences of elements $d_1, \ldots, d_n$ and $e_1, \ldots, e_n$ with each $d_i \le e_i$, it is true that $q(d_1, \ldots, d_n) \le q(e_1, \ldots, e_n)$. (Proof?) Consequently

$$x \le p_1(a_1 \vee b_1, \ldots, a_n \vee b_n) \vee p_2(a_1 \vee b_1, \ldots, a_n \vee b_n)$$
$$= p(a_1 \vee b_1, \ldots, a_n \vee b_n),$$

so that $x \in J_p$. Thus $J_{p_1} \vee J_{p_2} \subseteq J_p$. It is easy to see that $J_p \subseteq J_{p_1} \vee J_{p_2}$, whence $J_p = J_{p_1} \vee J_{p_2}$. A similar argument handles the case $p = (p_1 \wedge p_2)$, and therefore the proof of 9.1 is complete.

If $\mathscr{I}_0(L)$ denotes the set of all nonempty ideals of the lattice L, then $\mathscr{I}_0(L)$ is a sublattice of $\mathscr{I}(L)$, and the mapping $a \longrightarrow a/0$ is an isomorphism of L to $\mathscr{I}_0(L)$. Furthermore $\mathscr{I}_0(L)$ is a complete sublattice of $\mathscr{I}(L)$ if the lattice L has a least element. It is easy to determine the atoms of $\mathfrak{I}_0(L)$. The reader can show that *an ideal $A \in \mathfrak{I}_0(L)$ is an atom of $\mathfrak{I}_0(L)$ if and only if $A = p/0$ for some atom p in L.* One further observation will be of use later on: *If K is a compactly generated lattice and the compact elements of K form a sublattice L, then $K \cong \mathfrak{I}_0(L)$.* (Proof?)

An ideal of the dual of the lattice L is called a *filter* of L, and the dual $\mathfrak{F}(L)$ of the lattice of all ideals of the dual lattice of L is referred to as the *lattice of filters* of L. Alternatively, a subset D of L is a filter of L if

(1') $a, b \in D$ implies $a \wedge b \in D$.

(2') $a \in D$, $x \in L$, and $x \geq a$ imply $x \in D$.

The lattice $\mathfrak{F}(L)$ consists of the set of all filters of L together with the relation $\leq$ defined by

$$D \leq E \quad \text{if} \quad D \supseteq E.$$

We can now apply Theorem 9.1 to obtain: *For every lattice L, $\mathfrak{F}(L)$ is a complete lattice, the dual of $\mathfrak{F}(L)$ is compactly generated, the mapping $a \rightarrow 1/a$ is an isomorphism of L to $\mathfrak{F}(L)$, and $\mathfrak{F}(L)$ satisfies every lattice identity that L satisfies.* Also, a straightforward application of Zorn's lemma yields that $\mathfrak{F}(L)$ *is atomic if the lattice L has a least element.*

Theorem 9.1 is an example of an *embedding theorem*; it establishes the existence of a lattice with certain desired properties having a sublattice isomorphic to a given lattice. We will encounter a number of results of this type in subsequent chapters, and to facilitate their description, it is helpful to introduce some additional terminology.

Let P and Q be partially ordered sets. A one-to-one mapping φ of P to Q is defined to be a *weak embedding* if both φ and its inverse are order-preserving. The map φ is an *embedding* if it preserves finite meets and joins, i.e., if it satisfies the following condition and its dual: If X is any finite subset of P such that $\bigvee X$ exists, then $\bigvee_{x \in X} \varphi(x)$ exists in Q and $\varphi(\bigvee X) = \bigvee_{x \in X} \varphi(x)$. φ is a *strong embedding* if it preserves arbitrary meets and joins: If X is any subset of P such that $\bigvee X$ exists, then $\bigvee_{x \in X} \varphi(x)$ exists in Q and $\varphi(\bigvee X) = \bigvee_{x \in X} \varphi(x)$; and dually.

Further we say that P is *weakly embedded, embedded,* or *strongly embedded* in Q if there exists, respectively, a weak embedding, an embedding, or a strong embedding of P to Q. Note that when P and Q are lattices, an embedding is simply an isomorphism, and to say that P is embedded in Q is the same as saying that P is isomorphic with a sublattice of Q.

Theorem 9.1 shows that any lattice is embedded in its lattice of ideals. But this is not a strong embedding; arbitrary meets are preserved, but joins are not. A strong embedding is obtainable, however, if we take a suitable subset of the lattice of all ideals and appropriately redefine joins. The reader should observe that the construction to follow is just the abstraction to partially ordered sets of the familiar construction of the real numbers from the rationals with the completion by cuts.

Again let P be any partially ordered set. For any subset $S \subseteq P$ let S^* denote the set of all upper bounds of S, let S_* denote the set of all lower bounds of S, and let

$$S^v = (S^*)_*.$$

It is easy to check that the map $S \longrightarrow S^v$ is a closure operator, i.e., that $S \subseteq S^v$, $S \subseteq T$ implies $S^v \subseteq T^v$, and $(S^v)^v = S^v$, and that

$$\{a\}^v = \{x \in P \mid x \le a\} \qquad \text{for each } a \in P.$$

Consequently if K_v denotes the collection of all those subsets $S \subseteq P$ for which $S = S^v$, partially ordered by set-inclusion, then K_v *is a complete lattice, and the map* $a \longrightarrow \{a\}^v$ *is a strong embedding of P to K_v*. The lattice K_v is usually referred to as the *normal completion* of P. The normal completion is a minimal completion in the sense that *if φ is a weak embedding of P to a complete lattice L, then φ extends to a weak embedding of K_v to L.* (Proofs of the preceding assertions are left as exercises.)

The foregoing results allow us to make two statements about a lattice L: The lattice L can be embedded in a complete lattice that satisfies every identity that L satisfies, and L can be strongly embedded in a complete lattice. These two statements cannot be combined, unfortunately, for *there exists a distributive lattice that cannot be strongly embedded in a complete modular lattice.*[2] To construct such a distributive lattice, choose an infinite set u, and choose three infinite disjoint subsets a, b, $c \subseteq u$ such that $a \cup b \cup c = u$. Select two infinite sequences $\{d_n\}_{n<\infty}$ and $\{e_n\}_{n<\infty}$ of subsets of c such that

$$c \supset d_1 \supset d_2 \supset d_3 \supset \cdots, \qquad c \supset e_1 \supset e_2 \supset e_3 \supset \cdots,$$

and such that, for each $k = 1, 2, \ldots$,

$$c = d_k \cup e_k, \qquad d_k \cap e_k \nsubseteq \bigcap_{n<\infty} d_n, \qquad d_k \cap e_k \nsubseteq \bigcap_{n<\infty} e_n.$$

Define two more sequences $\{s_n\}_{n<\infty}$ and $\{t_n\}_{n<\infty}$ by

$$s_n = a \cup d_n \qquad \text{and} \qquad t_n = b \cup e_n,$$

and observe that $s_n \cap (t_n \cup c) = d_n$ and $t_n \cap c = e_n$ for each $n = 1, 2, \ldots$. Now let L_1 be the collection of all the subsets d_n, e_n, s_n, and t_n $(n = 1, 2, \ldots)$; all subsets of the form $d_n \cap e_m$ $(n, m = 1, 2, \ldots)$; and the sets u, $a \cup c$ $b \cup c$, c, and the null set $\varnothing$, and notice that L_1 is closed under finite set-unions and finite set-intersections. Let L be the collection of all subsets of u of the form

$$x \cup f,$$

where $x \in L_1$ and f is a finite subset of $a \cup b$. L is then also closed under finite

(2) P. Crawley [21].

set-unions and finite set-intersections, and consequently L is a distributive lattice containing L_1 as a sublattice. Observe that the empty set $\varnothing$ is the only element of L which is included in $\bigcap_{n<\infty} d_n$ and the only element included in $\bigcap_{n<\infty} e_n$. Therefore in L,

$$\varnothing = \bigwedge_{n<\infty} d_n = \bigwedge_{n<\infty} e_n.$$

Moreover, if $A = \{x \mid x \subseteq a,\ x\ \textit{finite}\}$ and $B = \{x \mid x \subseteq b,\ x\ \textit{finite}\}$, then u is the only element of L which includes every set in A or B, and hence in L,

$$u = \bigvee(A \cup B).$$

Finally, suppose that K is a complete lattice and φ is a strong embedding of L to K. Set

$$\bar{a} = \bigvee_{x \in A} \varphi(x), \qquad \bar{b} = \bigvee_{x \in B} \varphi(x), \qquad \bar{c} = \varphi(c).$$

It follows that $\bar{a} \vee \bar{b} = \bar{a} \vee \bar{b} \vee \bar{c} = \varphi(u)$, and as

$$\bar{b} \wedge \bar{c} \le \varphi(t_n) \wedge \varphi(c) = \varphi(t_n \cap c) = \varphi(e_n),$$

$$\bar{a} \wedge (\bar{b} \vee \bar{c}) \le \varphi(s_n) \wedge \big(\varphi(t_n) \vee \varphi(c)\big) = \varphi\big(s_n \cap (t_n \cup c)\big) = \varphi(d_n)$$

for each $n = 1, 2, \ldots$, we infer that

$$\bar{b} \wedge \bar{c} \le \bigwedge_{n<\infty} \varphi(e_n) = \varphi(\varnothing),$$

$$\varphi(\varnothing) \le \bar{a} \wedge \bar{b} \le \bar{a} \wedge (\bar{b} \vee \bar{c}) \le \bigwedge_{n<\infty} \varphi(d_n) = \varphi(\varnothing).$$

Thus $\bar{b} \ne \bar{b} \vee \bar{c}$, and $\{\bar{a}, \bar{b}, \bar{b} \vee \bar{c}, \varphi(u), \varphi(\varnothing)\}$ is a five-element nonmodular sublattice of K. Hence K is nonmodular, and the distributive lattice L has the required properties.

In one important instance the normal completion does preserve much of the structure of the lattice: *The normal completion of a Boolean algebra is again a Boolean algebra.*[3] (The proof is a challenging exercise.)

[3] V. Glivenko [42], M. H. Stone [79].

10

CONGRUENCE RELATIONS

A binary relation θ in a lattice L is a *congruence relation* if

(1) θ is an equivalence relation.

(2)   For all a, b, $c \in L$, $a\,\theta\,b$ implies $a \vee c\,\theta\,b \vee c$ and $a \wedge c\,\theta\,b \wedge c$.

If the lattice L has at least two elements, then it has at least two congruences relations, the relations 1 and 0 defined in L by

$$a\ 1\ b \text{ for all } a \text{ and } b,$$
$$a\ 0\ b \text{ if and only if } a = b.$$

Since it is an equivalence relation, a congruence relation θ partitions the lattice L into a set of disjoint θ-*classes*; the θ-class to which an element $a \in L$ belongs will be denoted by $a\theta$; i.e.,

$$a\theta = \{x \in L \,|\, x\,\theta\,a\}.$$

For any two elements a, $b \in L$, write

$$a\theta \vee b\theta = (a \vee b)\theta \quad \text{and} \quad a\theta \wedge b\theta = (a \wedge b)\theta.$$

These formulas define two binary operations in the set of all θ-classes, since by property (2), $a\,\theta\,a'$ and $b\,\theta\,b'$ imply that $a \vee b\,\theta\,a' \vee b'$ and that $a \wedge b\,\theta\,a' \wedge b'$. Moreover, the set

$$L/\theta = \{a\theta \,|\, a \in L\}$$

together with these binary operations is a lattice, which we call the *factor lattice of L by* θ. The mapping f_θ defined by

$$f_\theta(a) = a\theta \quad (a \in L)$$

is a homomorphism of L onto L/θ, and we call this homomorphism the *natural homomorphism belonging* to θ.

On the other hand, if h is a homomorphism of the lattice L onto a lattice K and if the relation θ_h is defined in L by the rule

$$a\,\theta_h\,b \text{ if } h(a) = h(b),$$

then θ_h is a congruence relation, and there is an isomorphism g of L/θ_h onto K with the property that $h = gf_{\theta_h}$, where f_{θ_h} is the natural homomorphism belonging to θ_h. We call θ_h the *congruence relation belonging* to h.

If the lattice L satisfies a given lattice identity, then certainly L/θ also satisfies this identity for each congruence relation θ in L. Further, if L is (relatively) complemented, then so is L/θ. Again, if L satisfies a chain condition, then L/θ also satisfies this chain condition. On the other hand, completeness and atomicity are not always preserved under congruence relations. For example, if L is the Boolean algebra of all subsets of an infinite set and θ is that relation defined in L by the rule $x \, \theta \, y$ if x and y differ by at most a finite number of elements, then θ is a congruence relation in L, and L/θ is neither complete nor atomic. (Proof?) Semimodularity also is not always preserved, except in the presence of both chain conditions. To show this, we first need a little lemma: *If θ is a congruence relation in a lattice L, $x \prec y$ in L, and $x\theta \ne y\theta$, then $x\theta \prec y\theta$ in L/θ.* For if

$$x\theta < z\theta \le y\theta$$

for some $z \in L$, then $x \le w = y \wedge (x \vee z) \le y$, and $z \, \theta \, w$. Therefore $x \ne w$, so that $w = y$, whence $z\theta = y\theta$. Now: *If a semimodular lattice L satisfies the ascending and descending chain conditions, then L/θ is semimodular for each congruence relation θ in L.* For if a, b are elements of the lattice L, and

$$a\theta \succ a\theta \wedge b\theta = (a \wedge b)\theta,$$

let u be a minimal element in the set $\{x \in a/a \wedge b \,|\, a \, \theta \, x\}$, and let v be a maximal element in the set $\{y \in u/a \wedge b \,|\, y \, \theta \, a \wedge b\}$. Then $u \succ v$, and $v \vee b \, \theta \, (a \wedge b) \vee b = b$. Observe that $v \vee b \ge u$ implies that

$$a \, \theta \, u = u \wedge (v \vee b) \, \theta \, a \wedge b,$$

an impossibility. Consequently $v \vee b \not\ge u$, and it follows that $u \wedge (v \vee b) = v \prec u$. By semimodularity we infer that $u \vee (v \vee b) = u \vee b \succ v \vee b$. And inasmuch as $u \vee b \, \theta \, a \vee b$ and $v \vee b \, \theta \, b$, the lemma yields that $a\theta \vee b\theta = (a \vee b)\theta \succ b\theta$, completing the proof. (The reader may find it instructive to construct a semimodular lattice having a nonsemimodular homomorphic image.)

If congruence relations are considered as sets of ordered pairs, then the set of all congruence relations in a lattice L is partially ordered by set-inclusion. This partial order clearly coincides with the relation $\le$ defined in the set of all congruence relations in L by the rule

$$\theta \le \psi \text{ if } a \, \theta \, b \text{ implies } a \, \psi \, b.$$

For each lattice L, $\Theta(L)$ will denote the set of all congruence relations in L, together with the foregoing partial order. Notice that the congruence relations 1 and 0 defined in the second paragraph of this chapter are, respectively, the greatest element and least element of $\Theta(L)$. Any congruence relation in L that is different from 1 and 0 will be referred to as a *nontrivial congruence relation*.

10.1: *For every lattice L, $\Theta(L)$ is a distributive compactly generated lattice.*[1]

PROOF: Let Σ be a subset of $\Theta(L)$. Define the relation π in L by

$$a \,\pi\, b \text{ if } a \,\theta\, b \text{ for all } \theta \in \Sigma,$$

and define the relation σ in L by the rule: $a \,\sigma\, b$ if there exist a sequence $a = a_0, a_1, \ldots, a_n = b$ in L and congruence relations $\theta_1, \ldots, \theta_n \in \Sigma$ such that $a_{i-1} \,\theta_i\, a_i$ for each $i = 1, \ldots, n$. The reader can check that π and σ are congruence relations, that π is the meet in $\Theta(L)$ of the subset Σ, and that σ is the join of Σ. In particular, $\Theta(L)$ is a complete lattice.

At this point we make a useful definition. For each pair of elements a, b in a lattice L, we define

$$\theta_{a,b} = \bigwedge \{\theta \in \Theta(L) \,|\, a \,\theta\, b\};$$

that is, $\theta_{a,b}$ is the least congruence relation in L that identifies a and b.

Now for any congruence relation $\theta \in \Theta(L)$,

$$\theta = \bigvee \{\theta_{a,b} \,|\, a, b \in L, a \,\theta\, b\},$$

and consequently to show that $\Theta(L)$ is compactly generated, it is enough to show that $\theta_{a,b}$ is compact for every $a, b \in L$. Assume, therefore, that Σ is a subset of $\Theta(L)$ and $\theta_{a,b} \leq \bigvee \Sigma = \sigma$. Then $a \,\sigma\, b$, and consequently there exist a sequence $a = a_0, a_1, \ldots, a_n = b$ in L and congruence relations $\theta_1, \ldots, \theta_n \in \Sigma$ such that $a_{i-1} \,\theta_i\, a_i$ for each $i = 1, \ldots, n$. But this also means that $a(\theta_1 \vee \cdots \vee \theta_n)b$, whence $\theta_{a,b} \leq \theta_1 \vee \cdots \vee \theta_n$, and $\theta_{a,b}$ is compact.

Before taking up the distributivity of $\Theta(L)$, we need the following observation. If $a, b \in L, \theta \in \Theta(L)$ and $a \vee b \geq c \geq a \wedge b$, then $a \,\theta\, b$ implies that

$$a \vee b \,\theta\, b \vee b = b = b \wedge b \,\theta\, a \wedge b,$$

and $a \vee b \,\theta\, a \wedge b$ implies that

$$c = (a \vee b) \wedge c \,\theta\, (a \wedge b) \wedge c = a \wedge b.$$

Therefore two elements a, b belong to the same θ-class if and only if every element in the quotient sublattice $a \vee b / a \wedge b$ belongs to the same θ-class.

To show that $\Theta(L)$ is distributive, let $\theta \in \Theta(L)$ and let Σ be a subset of $\Theta(L)$. If $\sigma = \bigvee \Sigma$ and $\tau = \bigvee_{\varphi \in \Sigma} \theta \wedge \varphi$, then we certainly have $\theta \wedge \sigma \geq \tau$. Suppose $a(\theta \wedge \sigma)b$. Then $a \,\theta\, b$ and $a \,\sigma\, b$, and hence there exist a sequence $a = a_0, a_1, \ldots, a_n = b$ of elements in L and congruence relations $\varphi_1, \ldots, \varphi_n \in \Sigma$ such that $a_{i-1} \,\varphi_i\, a_i$ for each $i = 1, \ldots, n$. Set

$$c_i = (a \vee b) \wedge (a_i \vee a_{i+1} \vee \cdots \vee a_n) \qquad (i = 0, \ldots, n).$$

---

[1] N. Funayama and T. Nakayama [40].

We then have $a \vee b = c_0 \geq c_1 \geq \cdots \geq c_n = b$, and as $a \vee b \, \theta \, b$, this implies that $c_{i-1} \, \theta \, c_i$. But

$$c_{i-1} \, \varphi_i \, (a \vee b) \wedge (a_i \vee \cdots \vee a_n) = c_i$$

since $a_{i-1} \, \varphi_i \, a_i$, and therefore $c_{i-1}(\theta \wedge \varphi_i)c_i$ for each $i = 1, \ldots, n$. Thus $a \vee b \, \tau \, b$. By symmetry $a \vee b \, \tau \, a$, so that $a \, \tau \, b$. It follows that $\theta \wedge \sigma \leq \tau$, completing the proof of 10.1.

The foregoing proof actually shows that $\Theta(L)$ has the stronger property of infinite distributivity. This, however, is to be expected in view of our observation in Chap. 4 that every distributive upper continuous lattice is infinitely distributive.

As with other algebraic systems, the lattice of congruence relations of a factor lattice can be described in terms of the congruence relations in the original lattice: *If θ is a congruence relation in a lattice L, then there is an isomorphism f of the quotient sublattice $1/\theta$ of $\Theta(L)$ onto $\Theta(L/\theta)$ such that $L/\varphi \cong (L/\theta)/f(\varphi)$ for all $\varphi \in 1/\theta$.* (The proof of this important fact is left to the reader.)

Further progress requires a more penetrating look at lattice congruence relations. First, some definitions. The quotient sublattices of a lattice L will be referred to simply as *quotients*. A quotient c/d is a *subquotient* of a/b if $a \geq c \geq d \geq b$. We say that a quotient a/b is *proper* if $a > b$, and we call it *prime* if $a \succ b$.

Given two quotients a/b and c/d, we say that a/b is an *upper transpose* of c/d and c/d is a *lower transpose* of a/b if $b \vee c = a$ and $b \wedge c = d$. Notice that if s/t is an upper transpose of u/v and u/v is an upper transpose of x/y, then s/t is an upper transpose of x/y. A corresponding statement holds, of course, for lower transposes. For simplicity, a/b will be called a *transpose* of c/d if a/b is either an upper or lower transpose of c/d.

Two quotients a/b and c/d are *projective* if there is a finite sequence of quotients $a/b = x_0/y_0, x_1/y_1, \ldots, x_n/y_n = c/d$ such that each x_{i-1}/y_{i-1} is a transpose of x_i/y_i; specifically, under these circumstances we say that a/b and c/d are *projective in n steps*. More generally, a/b is said to be *weakly projective* into c/d if there is a finite sequence of quotients $a/b = x_0/y_0$, $x_1/y_1, \ldots, x_n/y_n = c/d$ such that each x_{i-1}/y_{i-1} is a subquotient of a transpose of x_i/y_i.

Later we will make use of the following observation. Let $a/b = x_0/y_0$, $x_1/y_1, \ldots, x_n/y_n = c/d$ be a sequence of quotients such that each x_{i-1}/y_{i-1} is a transpose of x_i/y_i. Define a quotient x_i/y_i in this sequence to be *superfluous* if either x_i/y_i is an upper transpose of x_{i-1}/y_{i-1} and a lower transpose of x_{i+1}/y_{i+1} or x_i/y_i is a lower transpose of x_{i-1}/y_{i-1} and an upper transpose of x_{i+1}/y_{i+1}. Then by deleting superfluous quotients in the sequence $a/b = x_0/y_0, x_1/y_1, \ldots, x_n/y_n = c/d$, we obtain a subsequence $a/b = u_0/v_0$,

$u_1/v_1, \ldots, u_m/v_m = c/d$ such that each u_{i-1}/v_{i-1} is a transpose of u_i/v_i, and such that no quotient in this subsequence is superfluous.

We say that a congruence relation θ *collapses* a quotient a/b if $a\,\theta\,b$. As we observed in the course of proving 10.1, a congruence is determined by those quotients it collapses. Our next theorem provides a description of the least congruence relation that collapses a given set of quotients.

10.2: *Let Q be a set of quotients of a lattice L. Define the relation θ_Q in L by the rule: $a\,\theta_Q\,b$ if there exists a finite sequence of elements $a \vee b = x_0 \geq x_1 \geq \cdots \geq x_n = a \wedge b$ in L such that each x_{i-1}/x_i is weakly projective into some quotient in Q. Then θ_Q is the least congruence relation that collapses the quotients in Q.*[2]

PROOF: Observe first that for every $\theta \in \Theta(L)$ and $a, b \in L$, $a \vee b\,\theta\,a$ implies that

$$b = b \wedge (a \vee b)\,\theta\,a \wedge b,$$

and, similarly, $b\,\theta\,a \wedge b$ implies that $a \vee b\,\theta\,a$; i.e., a congruence relation collapses a quotient if and only if it collapses every transpose of that quotient. This observation implies that if a congruence relation θ collapses a quotient c/d and a/b is weakly projective into c/d, then θ collapses a/b.

Now if θ is a congruence relation in L which collapses all the quotients in Q and if $a, b \in L$ are such that a finite chain $a \vee b = x_0 \geq x_1 \geq \cdots \geq x_n = a \wedge b$ exists with each x_{i-1}/x_i weakly projective into some quotient in Q, then

$$a \vee b = x_0\,\theta\,x_1\,\theta \cdots \theta\,x_n = a \wedge b,$$

and therefore $a\,\theta\,b$. Consequently to prove 9.2, it is enough to show that θ_Q is a congruence relation.

Certainly, $a\,\theta_Q\,a$ for each $a \in L$, since the quotient a/a is weakly projective into every quotient of L. Also, from the symmetry of the definition of θ_Q, we have that $a\,\theta_Q\,b$ implies $b\,\theta_Q\,a$.

Next we show that if c/d is a subquotient of a transpose a_1/b_1 of a/b and $a\,\theta_Q\,b$, then $c\,\theta_Q\,d$. Assume, therefore, that $a \vee b_1 = a_1, a \wedge b_1 = b$, and $a = x_0 \geq x_1 \geq \cdots \geq x_n = b$, where each x_{i-1}/x_i is weakly projective into a quotient in Q. Set

$$y_i = c \wedge (d \vee x_i) \qquad (i = 0, \ldots, n).$$

Then $c = y_0 \geq y_1 \geq \cdots \geq y_n = d$. Moreover, for each $i = 1, \ldots, n$, the quotient y_{i-1}/y_i is a transpose of $y_{i-1} \vee d \vee x_i/d \vee x_i$, which is a subquotient of $d \vee x_{i-1}/d \vee x_i$; $d \vee x_{i-1}/d \vee x_i$ is a transpose of $x_{i-1}/x_{i-1} \wedge (d \vee x_i)$ which is a subquotient of x_{i-1}/x_i; and x_{i-1}/x_i is weakly projective into some quotient in Q. Thus each y_{i-1}/y_i is weakly projective into some quotient in Q,

[2] R. P. Dilworth [33].

and hence $c\,\theta_\varrho\,d$. Duality yields the same conclusion in the case $a_1 \vee b = a$ and $a_1 \wedge b = b_1$.

Now suppose that $a\,\theta_\varrho\,c$ and $b\,\theta_\varrho\,c$. If $a \geq b \geq c$, then it follows directly from the definition that $a\,\theta_\varrho\,c$. In the general case, $a \vee b \vee c/a \vee b$ is a transpose of $b \vee c/(a \vee b) \wedge (b \vee c)$, which is a subquotient of $b \vee c/b \wedge c$, and since $b \vee c\,\theta_\varrho\,b \wedge c$, the result of the previous paragraph yields that $a \vee b \vee c\,\theta_\varrho\,a \vee b$. Dually, $a \wedge b \wedge c\,\theta_\varrho\,a \wedge b$. As $a \vee b\,\theta_\varrho\,a \wedge b$, it follows that $a \vee b \vee c\,\theta_\varrho\,a \wedge b \wedge c$, and another application of the result of the previous paragraph yields that $a \vee c\,\theta_\varrho\,a \wedge c$ and hence that $a\,\theta_\varrho\,c$.

Finally, if $a\,\theta_\varrho\,b$ and c is any element of L, then $a \vee b \vee c\,\theta_\varrho\,b \vee c$, since $a \vee b \vee c/b \vee c$ is a transpose of $a \vee b/(a \vee b) \wedge (b \vee c)$, which is a subquotient of $a \vee b/a \wedge b$. Similarly, $a \vee b \vee c\,\theta_\varrho\,a \vee c$, and therefore $a \vee c\,\theta_\varrho\,b \vee c$. Duality yields that $a \wedge c\,\theta_\varrho\,b \wedge c$, and the proof of 10.2 is complete.

In certain cases weak projectivities can be replaced by projectivities. In this connection, let us define a lattice L to have the *projectivity property* if whenever a quotient a/b is weakly projective into a quotient c/d, then a/b and a subquotient of c/d are projective.

10.3:   *Every modular lattice and every relatively complemented lattice has the projectivity property.*

The proof of this is left to the reader, as is the proof of the following theorem, which further simplifies projectivity in the distributive case.

10.4:   *If in a distributive lattice L two quotients a/b and c/d are projective, then there exists a quotient x/y that is a transpose of both a/b and c/d.*

In conjunction with 10.4, it should be observed that if $a > b \geq c > d$ in a lattice L, then a/b and c/d cannot have a common transpose in L. And this fact, together with 10.2, 10.3, and 10.4, yields the following useful property of distributive lattices: *If $a > b \geq c > d$ in a distributive lattice L, then $\theta_{a,b} \wedge \theta_{c,d} = 0$.*

With the foregoing results in hand, we can now investigate some of the relationships between properties of a lattice and properties of its congruence lattice. To begin with:

10.5:   *If a weakly atomic lattice L has the projectivity property, then $\Theta(L)$ is atomic. On the other hand, if a lattice L is distributive and $\Theta(L)$ is atomic, then L is weakly atomic.*

PROOF: Suppose first that L is a lattice having the projectivity property and that p/q is a prime quotient of L. If a proper quotient a/b is such that $\theta_{a,b} \leq$

$\theta_{p,q}$, then by 10.2 there is an element c with $a > c \geq b$ such that a/c is weakly projective into p/q. But L has the projectivity property and p/q is prime, so that a/c and p/q must be projective. Therefore $\theta_{p,q} = \theta_{a,c} \leq \theta_{a,b} \leq \theta_{p,q}$, and it follows that $\theta_{p,q}$ is an atom of $\Theta(L)$. Now if L is further weakly atomic, $\theta \in \Theta(L)$ and a/b is a proper quotient collapsed by θ, then there is a prime subquotient p/q of a/b, and $\theta \geq \theta_{p,q}$. Since $\theta_{p,q}$ is an atom of $\Theta(L)$, we conclude that $\Theta(L)$ is atomic.

Assume that L is a distributive lattice with the property that $\Theta(L)$ is atomic. If θ is an atom of $\Theta(L)$, then for some proper quotient p/q, $\theta = \theta_{p,q}$. Suppose p/q is not prime; i.e., $p > x > q$ for some $x \in L$. Then inasmuch as θ is an atom, $\theta = \theta_{p,q} = \theta_{p,x} = \theta_{x,q}$, contrary to the observation made following 10.4 that $\theta_{p,x} \wedge \theta_{x,q} = 0$. Thus p/q is a prime quotient. Now let a/b be any proper quotient of L. The atomicity of $\Theta(L)$ and the preceding remarks imply that $\theta_{a,b} \geq \theta_{p,q}$ for some prime quotient p/q. In particular, $p\,\theta_{a,b}\,q$, and hence by 10.2 and 10.3 there exists some subquotient c/d of a/b such that p/q and c/d are projective. By 3.4, projective quotients in any modular lattice are isomorphic, whence c/d is a prime quotient. We conclude that L is weakly atomic, completing the proof.

Let us define a proper quotient a/b of a lattice L to be *primitive* if for each proper quotient c/d weakly projective into a/b there exists a finite chain $a = e_0 > e_1 > \cdots > e_k = b$ such that each e_{i-1}/e_i is weakly projective into c/d. In view of 10.2, *a congruence relation θ in a lattice L is an atom of $\Theta(L)$ if and only if $\theta = \theta_{a,b}$ for some primitive quotient a/b*. Moreover, the essence of the first part of 10.5 is the fact that *every prime quotient in a lattice having the projectivity property is primitive*.

10.6:   *A lattice L has the property that $\Theta(L)$ is a Boolean algebra if and only if for each proper quotient a/b of L there exists a finite chain $a = c_0 > c_1 > \cdots > c_n = b$ such that each c_{i-1}/c_i is primitive.*[3]

PROOF: Suppose first that the lattice L is such that for every proper quotient a/b there exists a finite chain $a = c_0 > c_1 > \cdots > c_n = b$ with each c'_{i-1}/c_i primitive. Theorem 10.2 shows that

$$\theta_{a,b} = \theta_{c_0,c_1} \vee \cdots \vee \theta_{c_{n-1},c_n},$$

and as each θ_{c_{i-1},c_i} is an atom of $\Theta(L)$, it follows that every element of $\Theta(L)$ is a join of atoms. This, together with 4.3 and the fact that $\Theta(L)$ is a distributive compactly generated lattice, implies that $\Theta(L)$ is a Boolean algebra.

On the other hand, if $\Theta(L)$ is a Boolean algebra, then 4.3 shows that every element of $\Theta(L)$ is a join of atoms. In particular, if a/b is a proper quotient of L, then $\theta_{a,b}$ is the join of congruence relations θ_{x_j,y_j}, where each x_j/y_j is a

[3] P. Crawley [18]. Cf. T. Tanaka [81], G. Grätzer and E. T. Schmidt [44].

primitive quotient. Therefore by 10.2 there is a finite chain $a = c_0 > c_1 > \cdots$ $> c_n = b$ such that each c_{i-1}/c_i is weakly projective into some x_j/y_j. But any proper quotient which is weakly projective into a primitive quotient is itself primitive, and consequently each c_{i-1}/c_i is primitive.

10.7:   *If a lattice L has the projectivity property and if every quotient sub-lattice of L contains a finite maximal chain, then $\Theta(L)$ is a Boolean algebra.*

10.8:   *If L is a relatively complemented lattice satisfying the ascending chain condition, then $\Theta(L)$ is a Boolean algebra.*[4]

Theorem 10.7 is a direct consequence of 10.6. To prove 10.8, let L be a relatively complemented lattice satisfying the ascending chain condition, and let a/b be a proper quotient of L. By the inductive form of the chain condition, we may assume that if $a > x > b$, then there is a finite chain $a = c_0 > c_1 > \cdots > c_n = x$ such that each c_{i-1}/c_i is primitive. Choose an element w such that $a \succ w \geq b$, and pick a complement x of w in the sub-lattice a/b. Then since a/w is a prime quotient, it is primitive, and hence its transpose x/b is primitive. Therefore the conditions of 10.6 are satisfied, and $\Theta(L)$ is a Boolean algebra.

Theorem 10.6 has two further consequences. First: *If L is a weakly atomic modular lattice, then $\Theta(L)$ is a Boolean algebra if and only if every quotient sublattice of L is finite dimensional.*[5] The fact that $\Theta(L)$ is a Boolean algebra if every quotient sublattice of L is finite dimensional follows from 10.3 and 10.7. In view of 10.6, to prove the converse, it suffices to show that every primitive quotient in a weakly atomic modular lattice L is finite dimensional. Thus let a/b be a primitive quotient of L. Choose elements p, q such that $a \geq p \succ q \geq b$. Then the prime quotient p/q is trivially weakly projective into a/b, and hence there is a finite chain $a = e_0 > e_1 > \cdots > e_k = b$ such that each e_{i-1}/e_i and the prime quotient p/q are projective. This means that e_{i-1}/e_i is a prime quotient, and therefore a/b is finite dimensional.

The second result is obtained by combining the preceding one with 10.5: *If L is a distributive lattice, then $\Theta(L)$ is a Boolean algebra if and only if every quotient sublattice of L is finite dimensional.*[6]

When a lattice L has a least element 0, for each congruence relation $\theta \in \Theta(L)$, the set

$$K_\theta = \{x \in L \,|\, x \,\theta\, 0\}$$

is an ideal of L. In the presence of sufficient complements, this ideal deter-

[4] R. P. Dilworth [33].
[5] P. Crawley [18].
[6] J. Hashimoto [51].

mines the congruence relation. To be specific, if we define a lattice L to be *principally complemented* provided that the sublattice $a/0$ is complemented for each $a \in L$, then it is easy to show that *for any congruence relation θ in a principally complemented lattice L, θ is precisely the least congruence relation which collapses the quotients $x/0$ ($x \in K_\theta$).* Principally complemented lattices have a further property: *A congruence relation θ in a principally complemented lattice L is compact in $\Theta(L)$ if and only if $\theta = \theta_{a,0}$ for some $a \in L$.*

Define an ideal A of a lattice L to be a *distributive ideal* if, for all ideals $B, C \in \mathcal{I}(L)$,

$$A \vee (B \wedge C) = (A \vee B) \wedge (A \vee C).$$

Distributive ideals are exactly those ideals A for which the mapping $x \longrightarrow A \vee x/0$ is a homomorphism of L to $\mathcal{I}(L)$. Thus, *if A is a nonempty distributive ideal of a lattice L with a least element, then there is a congruence relation θ in L such that $K_\theta = A$.* And combining this with the results of the preceding paragraph, we obtain the following: *If L is a principally complemented distributive lattice, then $\Theta(L) \cong \mathcal{I}_0(L)$.*

In connection with the foregoing result, recall our observation in Chap. 9 that if K is a compactly generated lattice in which the collection L of compact elements forms a sublattice of K, then $K \cong \mathcal{I}_0(L)$. This fact together with the final result of the preceding paragraph yields half of the following theorem.

10.9.   *A lattice K has the property that $K \cong \Theta(L)$ for some distributive lattice L if and only if K is a compactly generated distributive lattice in which the compact elements form a principally complemented sublattice.*

PROOF: To complete the proof, we must show that if L is a distributive lattice, then the compact elements of $\Theta(L)$ form a principally complemented sublattice. The basis of the argument is the following lemma: If a/b and c/d are quotients in the distributive lattice L, then there exist elements $x, y \in L$ such that $a \geq x \geq y \geq b$ and such that a/x is projective to a subquotient of $1/c$, x/y is projective to a subquotient of c/d, and y/b is projective to a subquotient of $d/0$. For if we set

$$x = a \wedge (b \vee c) = b \vee (a \wedge c),$$

$$y = a \wedge (b \vee d) = b \vee (a \wedge d),$$

then a/x is a lower transpose of $a \vee c/b \vee c$, and y/b is an upper transpose of $a \wedge d/b \wedge d$. Furthermore, x/y is a lower transpose of $(a \wedge c) \vee b \vee d/b \vee d$, and by symmetry $c \wedge (d \vee a)/c \wedge (d \vee b)$ is also a lower transpose of $(a \wedge c) \vee b \vee d/b \vee d$, whence x/y and $c \wedge (d \vee a)/c \wedge (d \vee b)$ are projective.

With our lemma in hand, observe that if a/b and c/d are quotients in L, and x, y are those elements in L given by the lemma, then $\theta_{a,b} = \theta_{a,x} \vee \theta_{x,y} \vee \theta_{y,b}$, and the distributivity of $\Theta(L)$ together with the remark following 10.4

yields that $\theta_{a,b} \wedge \theta_{c,d} = \theta_{x,y}$. From this fact and the distributivity of $\Theta(L)$ it follows that the meet of any two compact congruence relations in $\Theta(L)$ is again a compact congruence relation.

Now suppose that $a \geq c \geq d \geq b$ in the lattice L. If $\psi = \theta_{a,c} \vee \theta_{d,b}$, then ψ is compact and ψ is a complement of $\theta_{c,d}$ in the sublattice $\theta_{a,b}/0$. Suppose next that φ is a compact congruence relation and $\varphi \leq \theta_{a,b}$. Then by 10.2 and 10.3 there are finitely many quotients $c_1/d_1, \ldots, c_k/d_k$ such that each is a subquotient of a/b, and $\varphi = \theta_{c_1,d_1} \vee \cdots \vee \theta_{c_k,d_k}$. Consequently if ψ_i is a complement of θ_{c_i,d_i} in the sublattice $\theta_{a,b}/0$, then $\sigma = \psi_1 \wedge \cdots \wedge \psi_k$ is a complement of φ in the sublattice $\theta_{a,b}/0$. Finally, let θ and φ be compact congruence relations with $\varphi \leq \theta$. Write $\theta = \theta_{a_1,b_1} \vee \cdots \vee \theta_{a_n,b_n}$, and, for each $i = 1, \ldots, n$, let σ_i be a complement of $\varphi \wedge \theta_{a_i,b_i}$ in the sublattice $\theta_{a_i,b_i}/0$. Then $\sigma_1 \vee \cdots \vee \sigma_n$ is a complement of φ in the sublattice $\theta/0$, and the proof is complete.

What about a characterization of the congruence lattice of an arbitrary lattice? We know that the congruence lattice of any lattice is distributive and compactly generated. Is it true that, conversely, each compactly generated distributive lattice is isomorphic to the lattice of congruence relations of some lattice? This important question remains unanswered. It does, however, have an affirmative answer in one significant special case.

10.10:   *If a distributive lattice K has the property that both K and its dual lattice are compactly generated, then there exists a lattice L such that $K \cong \Theta(L)$.*[7]

Before proving 10.10, we need some additional information about the lattices under consideration. Let P be any partially ordered set. Define a subset E of P to be an *o-ideal* of P if

$$e \in E, x \in P, \text{ and } x \leq e \text{ imply } x \in E.$$

The set-union and the set-intersection of any set of o-ideals of P is again an o-ideal, and thus if $\Theta(P)$ denotes the collection of all o-ideals of P partially ordered by set-inclusion, $\Theta(P)$ is a complete sublattice of the Boolean algebra of all subsets of P. Note also that inasmuch as a Boolean algebra is isomorphic to its dual lattice and a complete atomic Boolean algebra is compactly generated, a complete sublattice of a complete atomic Boolean algebra has the property that it and its dual lattice are compactly generated.

Now suppose that K is a distributive lattice, with least element 0, such that it and its dual lattice are compactly generated. Call an element $p \in K$ *completely join-irreducible* if, for every subset $S \subseteq K$, $p = \bigvee S$ implies $p \in S$. Then by the dual of 6.1, every element of K is the join of completely join-

[7] R. P. Dilworth (unpublished). G. Grätzer and E. T. Schmidt [45].

irreducible elements. Let P denote the set of all the completely join-irreducible elements of K which are greater than 0, partially ordered by the partial order of K. For each element $x \in K$, set

$$E_x = \{p \in P \,|\, p \leq x\}.$$

Each E_x is then an *o*-ideal of P. Moreover, the mapping $x \longrightarrow E_x$ of K into $\Theta(P)$ is one-to-one, and both the mapping and its inverse are order-preserving. Let $E \in \Theta(P)$ be any *o*-ideal, and set $e = \bigvee E$. If $p \in E_e$, then as L is infinitely distributive we have

$$p = p \wedge e = p \wedge \bigvee E = \bigvee_{s \in E} p \wedge s,$$

and since p is completely join-irreducible and E is an *o*-ideal, we infer that $p \in E$. Consequently $E = E_e$, and we conclude that the mapping $x \longrightarrow E_x$ is an isomorphism of K onto $\Theta(P)$.

   Summarizing, *for a lattice K the following conditions are equivalent:* (1) *K is distributive and both K and its dual lattice are compactly generated;* (2) *K is a compactly generated distributive lattice in which each element is a join of completely join-irreducible elements;* (3) *$K \cong \Theta(P)$ for some partially ordered set P; and* (4) *K is a complete sublattice of some complete atomic Boolean algebra.*

   We will need two other related observations. It follows from 10.2 that *if p/q is a prime quotient of a lattice L, then $\theta_{p,q}$ is a completely join-irreducible element of $\Theta(L)$.* Therefore if a quotient sublattice a/b of L has a finite maximal chain, then $\theta_{a,b}$ is a join of finitely many completely join-irreducible congruence relations. From this we infer that *if every quotient sublattice of the lattice L has a finite maximal chain, then the dual lattice of $\Theta(L)$ is compactly generated.*

PROOF OF 10.10: In view of the foregoing remarks, to prove 10.10, we need to show that for any partially ordered set P there is a lattice L such that $\Theta(L) \cong \Theta(P)$. In some sense the proof is based on the six-element lattice shown in Fig. 10-1. Observe that for this lattice, $0 < \theta_{a_0, 0} = \theta_{a_1, 0} < \theta_{b, 0} = 1$, and so the lattice of congruence relations is the three-element chain. In the construction

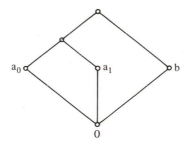

Fig. 10-1

to follow, a number of copies of this six-element lattice are "hooked together" to give the desired example.

Let P be a partially ordered set. For each $i = 0, 1$, let $P_i = \{p^i \mid p \in P\}$ be a set such that the mapping $p \to p^i$ of P onto P_i is one-to-one. Further, let P_0 and P_1 be chosen in such a way that

$$p^0 = p^1 \text{ if and only if } p \text{ is maximal in } P.$$

Let us also agree that superscripts are added modulo 2; i.e., if $i = 1$, then $p^{i+1} = p^0$.

Set $P_2 = P_0 \cup P_1$. Call a subset $u \subseteq P_2$ *closed* if

$$q^i, p^j \in u \text{ and } p < q \text{ in } P \text{ imply } p^{j+1} \in u.$$

Then the empty set is closed, and for each $p^i \in P_2$ the single-element set $\{p^i\}$ is closed. Throughout this proof we will identify the element p^i with the singleton $\{p^i\}$. Also, the set-intersection of any collection of closed subsets is again closed. Consequently for each subset $w \subseteq P_2$ there is a least closed subset $\bar{w}$ which contains w. Note that if w is finite, then $\bar{w}$ is finite.

Let L denote the system consisting of all finite closed subsets of P_2 partially ordered by set-inclusion. L is then a lattice in which meets and joins are given by the formulas

$$u \wedge v = u \cap v, \qquad u \vee v = \overline{u \cup v}.$$

L has a least element, the empty set, which we denote by 0. And L has the additional property that the quotient sublattice $u/0$ is finite for each $u \in L$. Therefore, by the remarks above, the dual lattice of $\Theta(L)$ is compactly generated, and consequently the proof will be completed if we show that the partially ordered set of nonzero completely join-irreducible elements of $\Theta(L)$ is isomorphic to P.

It is useful to show that L is principally complemented. Suppose $u, v \in L$ and $u \supseteq v$. Set $t = (u - v) - t_1$, where t_1 is the set of all elements $p^i \in u - v$ satisfying

there exists $q \in P$ such that $p < q$, $q^j \in u - v$, and $p^{i+1} \in v$.

If $p < q$ in P and $q^i, p^j \in t$, then as $q^i, p^j \in u$ and u is closed, we have $p^{j+1} \in u$. Moreover, inasmuch as $p^j \notin v$, it follows that $p^{j+1} \notin v$, and therefore $p^{j+1} \notin t_1$. Thus $p^{j+1} \in t$, and we infer that t is closed. Certainly $t \wedge v = 0$ and $t \vee v \subseteq u$. To show that $t \vee v = u$, suppose that $p^i \in u$ and $p^i \notin t \vee v$. The finiteness of u allows us to choose p^i in such a way that p is maximal in P with respect to the conditions $p^i \in u$ and $p^i \notin t \vee v$. Then $p^i \notin t \vee v$ implies that $p^i \in t_1$, and hence there exists $q \in P$ such that

$$p < q \text{ in } P, \, q^j \in u - v, \text{ and } p^{i+1} \in v.$$

The maximality of p yields that $q^j \in t \vee v$. But then $p < q$ and $q^j, p^{i+1} \in t \vee v$ imply that $p^i \in t \vee v$ since $t \vee v$ is closed. This contradiction shows that $t \vee v = u$, and we conclude that L is principally complemented.

Since each p^i is an atom of L, as remarked above $\theta_{p^i, 0}$ is a completely join-irreducible element of $\Theta(L)$. On the other hand, as L is principally complemented and every element of L is a join of finitely many p^i, it follows that a congruence relation $\theta \in \Theta(L)$ is the join of the congruence relations $\theta_{p^i, 0}(p^i \ \theta \ 0)$. Thus if θ is completely join-irreducible, then $\theta = \theta_{p^i, 0}$ for some p^i. The nonzero completely join-irreducible congruence relations of L therefore are precisely the congruence relations $\theta_{p^i, 0}$.

Let $p \in P$. If $p^0 \neq p^1$, then there exists $q \in P$ with $p < q$. The elements p^0, p^1, q^0 are atoms of L, and we have that $p^{i+1} \subseteq p^i \vee q^0$, while $q^0 \nsubseteq \{p^0, p^1\} = p^0 \vee p^1$. This means that p^0, p^1, q^0 generate a six-element sublattice of L isomorphic to the lattice diagrammed at the beginning of the proof (Fig. 10-1). In particular, for each $p \in P$,

$$\theta_{p^0, 0} = \theta_{p^1, 0}.$$

For the remainder of the proof we will denote the congruence relation $\theta_{p^i, 0}$ simply by θ_p.

Let r be an element of P. Define

$$A_r = \{u \in L \,|\, p^i \in u \text{ implies } p \leq r\}.$$

A_r is then an ideal of L, and $r^0, r^1 \in A_r$. A_r also has the following property: If $u \in A_r$ and $v, w \in L$, then there is an element $u^* \in A_r$ such that $u \subseteq u^*$ and $u^* \vee z = u^* \cup z$ for any closed subset $z \subseteq v \cup w$. Indeed, if we set

$$u^* = \{p^i, p^{i+1} \,|\, p^i \in u\} \cup \{p^i, p^{i+1} \,|\, p^i \in v \cup w \text{ and } p \leq r\},$$

then it is easily checked that u^* has the required properties. Now suppose that B and C are any ideals of L. If $t \in (A_r \vee B) \wedge (A_r \vee C)$, then there are elements $u \in A_r$, $v \in B$, and $w \in C$ such that $t \subseteq (u \vee v) \wedge (u \vee w)$. By the foregoing results there is an element $u^* \in A_r$ such that $u^* \supseteq u$ and $u^* \vee z = u^* \cup z$ for any closed subset $z \subseteq v \cup w$, and therefore

$$t \subseteq (u^* \vee v) \wedge (u^* \vee w) = (u^* \cup v) \cap (u^* \cup w)$$
$$= u^* \cup (v \cap w) = u^* \vee (v \wedge w) \in A_r \vee (B \wedge C).$$

It follows that $A_r \vee (B \wedge C) = (A_r \vee B) \wedge (A_r \vee C)$, and consequently A_r is a distributive ideal.

Finally, suppose $\theta \in \Theta(L)$ is such that $r^i \ \theta \ 0$, and suppose $p \in P$ is such that $p < r$. Then p^0, p^1, r^i generate a six-element sublattice of L isomorphic to the lattice in Fig. 10-1. Therefore $r^i \ \theta \ 0$ implies $p^0 \ \theta \ 0$ and $p^1 \ \theta \ 0$. But each element in A_r is the join of finitely many p^j such that $p \leq r$, and hence $u \ \theta \ 0$ for every $u \in A_r$. This fact and the fact that A_r is a distributive ideal yield that

$$K_{\theta_r} = \{u \in L \,|\, u \ \theta_r \ 0\} = A_r.$$

The preceding formula shows that the map $r \to \theta_r$ of P onto the partially ordered set of all nonzero join-irreducible elements of $\Theta(L)$ is one-to-one and that both the map and its inverse are order-preserving. Consequently $\Theta(P) \cong \Theta(L)$, and the proof of 10.10 is complete.

We hasten to point out that not every lattice of congruence relations has the property that its dual lattice is compactly generated. For example, consider the distributive lattice L consisting of an infinite ascending chain $0 = a_0 < a_1 < a_2 < \cdots$ and a greatest element 1. Let θ be the least congruence relation that collapses the quotients $a_i/0$ $(i = 1, 2, \ldots)$, and for each $i = 1, 2, \ldots$, let φ_i be the least congruence relation that collapses the quotient $1/a_i$. Then $\varphi_1 > \varphi_2 > \varphi_3 > \cdots$, and $\theta \vee \varphi_i = 1$ for all i. But $\theta \neq 1$ and $\bigwedge_i \varphi_i = 0$, so that the dual lattice of $\Theta(L)$ is not even upper continuous.

On the other hand, every finite lattice is certainly compactly generated, and therefore 10.10 yields that *each finite distributive lattice is isomorphic to the lattice of congruence relations of some finite lattice.*

Theorem 10.9 shows that the meet of two compact congruence relations in a distributive lattice is again a compact congruence relation. But this is not generally true. Observe that the lattice in Fig. 10-2 is distributive and that it and its dual lattice are compactly generated. Consequently by 10.10 there is a lattice L having the lattice of Fig. 10-2 as its congruence lattice, and it is clear that L has two compact congruence relations whose meet is not compact.

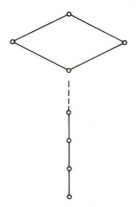

Fig. 10-2

11

STRUCTURE THEORY

The decomposition theory of Chaps. 6 and 7 and the properties of congruence lattices derived in the preceding chapter now enable us to develop a structure theory for lattices. Accordingly, the present section seeks theorems concerning the existence of certain subdirect representations and, in some cases, accompanying uniqueness theorems.

Let $M_i (i \in I)$ be a family of lattices. By *the direct product* of the lattices $M_i (i \in I)$ we mean the system $\mathsf{X}_{i \in I} M_i$ consisting of the set of all functions x defined on I such that $x(i) \in M_i$ for all $i \in I$, together with the binary relation $\leq$ defined in this set of functions by the rule

$$x \leq y \quad \text{if} \quad x(i) \leq y(i) \quad \text{for all } i \in I.$$

$\mathsf{X}_{i \in I} M_i$ is certainly a lattice. And, for each $i \in I$, M_i is both isomorphic to a sublattice of $\mathsf{X}_{i \in I} M_i$ and a homomorphic image of $\mathsf{X}_{i \in I} M_i$. In fact, if the function π_i on $\mathsf{X}_{i \in I} M_i$ to M_i is defined by the rule

$$\pi_i(x) = x(i) \qquad \text{all } x \in \mathsf{X}_{i \in I} M_i,$$

then π_i is a homomorphism of $\mathsf{X}_{i \in I} M_i$ onto M_i. We refer to this homomorphism π_i as the *i*th *projection* of $\mathsf{X}_{i \in I} M_i$.

The reader may verify that $\mathsf{X}_{i \in I} M_i$ satisfies a given lattice identity if and only if each M_i satisfies this identity. $\mathsf{X}_{i \in I} M_i$ is complete if and only if each M_i is complete. Moreover, if any of the following phrases is substituted for the word *complete* in the preceding sentence, the resulting statement remains true: compactly generated, atomic, strongly atomic, weakly atomic, complemented, relatively complemented, semimodular, lower semimodular.

By a *subdirect representation* of a lattice L we will mean an ordered pair $\langle M_i (i \in I), f \rangle$, where $M_i (i \in I)$ is a family of lattices and f is an isomorphism of L to $\mathsf{X}_{i \in I} M_i$ such that the mapping

$$f_i = \pi_i f$$

is onto for each $i \in I$. This mapping f_i, which is a homomorphism of L onto M_i, will be referred to as the *i*th *f-projection*. We say that a lattice L is *a* *subdirect product* of lattices $M_i(i \in I)$ if there exists a subdirect representation of L of the form $\langle M_i(i \in I), f \rangle$.

11.1: *If $\langle M_i(i \in I), f \rangle$ is a subdirect representation of a lattice L and if θ_i is the congruence relation belonging to the ith f-projection f_i, then in $\Theta(L)$,*

$$0 = \bigwedge_{i \in I} \theta_i.$$

Conversely, if $\theta_i(i \in I)$ is a family of congruence relations in the lattice L such that $0 = \bigwedge_{i \in I} \theta_i$, then there is a subdirect representation $\langle L/\theta_i(i \in I), f \rangle$ of L such that, for each $i \in I$, the ith f-projection is just the natural homomorphism belonging to θ_i.

PROOF: We will outline the proof of the second part; the reader may supply the proof of the first. Form $X_{i \in I} L/\theta_i$. Define the function f on the lattice L to $X_{i \in I} L/\theta_i$ by the rule ·

$$f(a)(i) = a\theta_i \qquad \text{all } i \in I.$$

(Keep in mind that $f(a)$ is a function with domain I.) This function f is then an isomorphism with the required properties.

It can happen that a lattice L containing more than one element has only trivial subdirect representations in the sense that for every subdirect representation $\langle M_i(i \in I), f \rangle$ of L there is at least one index $i \in I$ such that the ith f-projection f_i is an isomorphism. Such lattices are said to be *subdirectly irreducible*. Of use to us are the alternative formulations of this concept. The reader can show that *for a lattice L the following conditions are equivalent*: (1) *L is subdirectly irreducible;* (2) *the least element of $\Theta(L)$ is completely irreducible;* (3) *$\Theta(L)$ is an atomic lattice having a single atom;* and (4) *there exist two distinct elements $a, b \in L$ such that $a \theta b$ for every nontrivial congruence relation θ in L.* As a consequence, the factor lattice L/θ is subdirectly irreducible if and only if the congruence relation θ is completely irreducible in $\Theta(L)$. And 11.1 and 6.1 combined with this fact yield our first existence theorem.

11.2: *Every lattice is a subdirect product of subdirectly irreducible lattices.*[1]

The distributive subdirectly irreducible lattices are particularly easy to describe. For if $a > b > c$ in a distributive lattice L, then $\theta_{a,b} \wedge \theta_{b,c} = 0$, and L cannot be subdirectly irreducible. Therefore *a distributive lattice L is subdirectly irreducible if and only if L is a two-element chain.* Since the direct product of two-element chains is a complete atomic Boolean algebra, we infer from 11.2 that

[1] G. Birkhoff [11].

11.3: *Every distributive lattice can be embedded in a complete atomic Boolean algebra.*[2]

The foregoing result shows in particular that a finite distributive lattice can be embedded in a direct product of finitely many finite chains. Surprisingly enough, there is a neat description of the least number of chains needed for such a representation: *If L is a finite distributive lattice, if k_a denotes the number of elements covering the element $a \in L$, and if k is the largest of the integers $k_a (a \in L)$, then L is isomorphic to a sublattice of the direct product of k chains, and k is the least such number.*[3] That k is the least such number is a consequence of the following fact: If a is an element in a direct product of m chains, then the quotient sublattice $1/a$ contains at most m atoms. We leave the verification of this fact as an exercise for the reader. To prove the rest of the statement, let P be the set of all irreducible elements of L partially ordered by the restriction to P of the partial order of L. Pick $k + 1$ elements $q_1, \ldots, q_{k+1} \in P$, and consider the element $a = q_1 \wedge \cdots \wedge q_{k+1} \in L$. The sublattice $1/a$ contains at most k atoms, and therefore the unique irredundant decomposition of a involves at most k irreducible elements. Consequently the decomposition $a = q_1 \wedge \cdots \wedge q_{k+1}$ is not irredundant, and there is some q_t such that

$$q_t \geq a = q_1 \wedge \cdots \wedge q_{t-1} \wedge q_{t+1} \wedge \cdots \wedge q_{k+1}.$$

Since L is distributive and q_t is irreducible, it follows that there is some q_s such that $q_t = q_t \vee q_s \geq q_s$. Thus every set of $k + 1$ elements of P contains a comparable pair. By 1.1, P is the set-union of k chains $C'_1, \ldots, C'_k$. Set $C_i = C'_i \cup \{1\}$, where 1 is the largest element of L. For each element $a \in L$ define the element $x_a \in X_{i \leq k} C_i$ by the rule: $x_a(i)$ is the least element of the chain C_i such that $x_a(i) \geq a$. Then, since the element a has a decomposition, we must have that

$$a = x_a(1) \wedge \cdots \wedge x_a(k),$$

and it follows that the mapping $a \longrightarrow x_a$ of L to $X_{i \leq k} C_i$ is one-to-one. The reader can complete the proof by showing that this mapping is also a homomorphism.

As one would expect, there is no corresponding uniqueness theorem associated with 11.2. To obtain a uniqueness theorem, the class of subdirect representations considered must be suitably restricted. Let $\langle M_i (i \in I), f \rangle$ be a subdirect representation of the lattice L. For each index $k \in I$, define the mapping f_k^* of L to $X_{i \neq k} M_i$ by the rule

$$f_k^*(a)(i) = f(a)(i) \qquad \text{all } i \neq k.$$

[2] G. Birkhoff [7].
[3] R. P. Dilworth [32].

In other words, for each $a \in L$, $f_k^*(a)$ is just the restriction of $f(a)$ to $I - k$. Then if none of the mappings $f_k^*(k \in I)$ is an isomorphism, we say that the subdirect representation $\langle M_i(i \in I), f \rangle$ is *irredundant*. The next result characterizes irredundant subdirect representations internally. (Proof?)

11.4: *If $\langle M_i(i \in I), f \rangle$ is a subdirect representation of a lattice L and if θ_i is the congruence relation belonging to the ith f-projection f_i, then the subdirect representation $\langle M_i(i \in I), f \rangle$ is irredundant if and only if, for each index $k \in I$, $0 \neq \bigwedge_{i \neq k} \theta_i$.*

And combining 11.4 with 7.1, we obtain the following strong uniqueness theorem.

11.5: *If $\langle M_i(i \in I), f \rangle$ and $\langle N_j(j \in J), g \rangle$ are two irredundant subdirect representations of a lattice L such that each M_i and each N_j is subdirectly irreducible, then there is a one-to-one mapping φ of I onto J and for each $i \in I$ there is an isomorphism h_i of M_i onto $N_{\varphi(i)}$ such that $g_{\varphi(i)} = h_i f_i$ for all $i \in I$.*

A preliminary existence theorem for irredundant representations is obtained by applying 6.9 to the lattice of congruence relations: If $\Theta(L)$ is atomic, then the lattice L is an irredundant subdirect product of subdirectly irreducible lattices. This, together with 10.5, provides part of the proof of the following general result.

11.6: *A weakly atomic lattice having the projectivity property is an irredundant subdirect product of subdirectly irreducible weakly atomic lattices each having the projectivity property.*

PROOF: First we prove that *if a lattice L has the projectivity property and $\theta \in \Theta(L)$, then L/θ also has the projectivity property*. And to prove this it suffices to show that if in L/θ, $x\theta/y\theta$ is a subquotient of $u\theta/v\theta$, and $u\theta/v\theta$ is a lower transpose of $s\theta/t\theta$, then $x\theta/y\theta$ is projective to a subquotient of $s\theta/t\theta$. Set

$$x' = (x \wedge u) \vee (u \wedge t), \qquad y' = (y \vee (u \wedge t)) \wedge x',$$
$$v' = u \wedge t, \qquad\qquad s' = u \vee t.$$

Then it is clear that $s' \theta s$, $v' \theta v$, $x' \theta x$, and $y' \theta y$. Moreover, $u \geq x' \geq y' \geq v'$, so that x'/y' is weakly projective into s'/t. Therefore as L has the projectivity property, x'/y' is projective to a subquotient of s'/t, and passing to L/θ, we obtain that $x\theta/y\theta = x'\theta/y'\theta$ is projective to a subquotient of $s'\theta/t\theta = s\theta/t\theta$.

It remains to show that if θ *is a completely irreducible congruence relation in a weakly atomic lattice L having the projectivity property and if there is some prime quotient p/q not collapsed by θ, then L/θ is weakly atomic*. Let $a > b$ be elements in L such that $a\theta > b\theta$. Then as θ is completely irreducible in $\Theta(L)$, $\theta_{p,q}$ is an atom of $\Theta(L)$ and $\theta \not\geq \theta_{p,q}$, it follows that $\theta \vee \theta_{p,q}$ is the unique element in $\Theta(L)$ covering θ. Consequently, as $\theta \not\geq \theta_{a,b}$, we must have that $\theta \vee \theta_{a,b} \geq \theta \vee \theta_{p,q} \geq \theta_{p,q}$. This inequality together with the fact that $\theta \wedge \theta_{p,q} = 0$ yields that $\theta_{a,b} \geq \theta_{p,q}$. Therefore p/q is projective to a subquotient of a/b, and since L is weakly atomic and has the projectivity property, it follows that there is a prime subquotient u/v of a/b such that u/v and p/q projective. Thus $u\theta \neq v\theta$, and as $u \succ v$ in L, we conclude that $a\theta \geq u\theta \succ v\theta \geq b\theta$, completing the proof.

Inasmuch as the lattice of ideals of a modular lattice is weakly atomic and modular, 11.5 and 11.6 yield that *for any modular lattice L, the lattice of ideals of L is uniquely an irredundant subdirect product of subdirectly irreducible weakly atomic modular lattices.*

A satisfactory description exists of those subdirectly irreducible lattices in the class of all weakly atomic lattices having the projectivity property: *A weakly atomic lattice L having the projectivity property is subdirectly irreducible if and only if any two prime quotients of L are projective.* If the lattice further satisfies chain conditions, even more can be said. For if a lattice L has the projectivity property and satisfies the ascending and descending chain conditions, then L is subdirectly irreducible if and only if $\Theta(L)$ has a single atom, and as $\Theta(L)$ is necessarily a finite Boolean algebra by 10.7, we infer that L is subdirectly irreducible if and only if $\Theta(L)$ is a two-element chain.

Let us define a lattice L to be a *simple* if L has no nontrivial congruence relations, i.e., if $\Theta(L)$ is a two-element chain. Then combining the observation made at the end of the preceding paragraph with 11.6, we obtain the following theorem: *If a lattice L has the projectivity property and satisfies the ascending and descending chain conditions, then L is a subdirect product of finitely many simple lattices.*

Of course a subdirect representation $\langle M_i(i \in I), f \rangle$ of a lattice L is most satisfactory when the isomorphism f is onto and L is actually isomorphic to $\mathsf{X}_{i \in I} M_i$. Subdirect representations of this type will be referred to as *direct representations*, and when $L \cong \mathsf{X}_{i \in I} M_i$, we say that L is *a direct product of* the lattices $M_i(i \in I)$. If L is not a direct product of two lattices having more than one element, then we say that L is *indecomposable*; that is, L is indecomposable if whenever $L \cong \mathsf{X}_{i \in I} M_i$, there is an index $h \in I$ for which $M_h \cong L$ and each $M_i(i \neq h)$ is a one-element lattice. It should be apparent that each simple lattice is subdirectly irreducible and that each subdirectly irreducible lattice is indecomposable.

In at least one important instance the subdirect representation provided by 11.6 is actually direct, as the remainder of this chapter is devoted to showing.

Relevant to direct representations is the concept of permutable congruence relations. We say that two congruence relations θ and φ in a lattice L *permute* if whenever $a, b, c \in L$, $a \, \theta \, b$ and $b \, \varphi \, c$, then there is an element

$d \in L$ such that $a \varphi d$ and $d \theta c$. Notice that θ and φ permute if and only if whenever $a(\theta \vee \varphi)b$ there is an element c such that $a \theta c$ and $c \varphi b$.

A second relevant concept is that of a consistent family of congruence relations. We define a family of congruence relations $\theta_i (i \in I)$ in a lattice L to be *consistent* if for every indexed family of elements $a_i (i \in I)$ in L such that

$$a_i(\bar{\theta}_i \vee \bar{\theta}_j)a_j$$

for all $i, j \in I$, where $\bar{\theta}_i = \bigwedge_{k \neq i} \theta_k$, there is an element $a \in L$ such that $a \theta_i a_i$ for all $i \in I$. Consistency is not unrelated to permutability; the reader should note that if $\theta_1, \ldots, \theta_n$ are finitely many congruence relations in a lattice L any two of which permute, then $\theta_1, \ldots, \theta_n$ are consistent.

Direct representations are now internally characterized as follows.

11.7:   *If $\langle M_i(i \in I), f \rangle$ is a direct representation of a lattice L and if θ_i is the congruence relation belonging to ith f-projection f_i, then the following conditions hold:*

(1) *$0 = \bigwedge_{i \in I} \theta_i$.*
(2) *For all $i \in I$, $\theta_i \vee \bar{\theta}_i = 1$, where $\bar{\theta}_i = \bigwedge_{k \neq i} \theta_k$.*
(3) *For all $i \in I$, θ_i and $\bar{\theta}_i$ permute.*
(4) *The congruence relations $\theta_i(i \in I)$ are consistent.*

Conversely, if $\theta_i(i \in I)$ is a family of congruence relations in L such that conditions (1)–(4) are satisfied, then there is a direct representation $\langle L/\theta_i(i \in I), f \rangle$ such that, for each $i \in I$, the ith f-projection is just the natural homomorphism belonging to θ_i.[4]

PROOF: Again we outline the proof of the second part, and leave the proof of the first to the reader. By 11.1, $\langle L/\theta_i(i \in I), f \rangle$ is a subdirect representation of L, so all we need to show is that f is onto, i.e., if $a_i(i \in I)$ is a family of elements in L, then there is an element $a \in L$ such $a \theta_i a_i$ for all $i \in I$. Pick any element $b \in L$. Then for every $i \in I$, $a_i(\theta_i \vee \bar{\theta}_i)b$, and therefore there is an element b_i such that $a_i \theta_i b_i$ and $b_i \bar{\theta}_i a$. Observe that $b_i(\bar{\theta}_i \vee \bar{\theta}_j)b_j$ for any $i, j \in I$. Consequently by the consistency assumption there is an element $a \in L$ such that $a \theta_i b_i$ and hence $a \theta_i a_i$ for all $i \in I$.

The reader can use the preceding theorem in conjunction with 8.8 to derive the following isomorphic refinement theorem for direct representations.[5]

11.8:   *If L is a lattice and $L \cong \mathsf{X}_{i \in I} M_i \cong \mathsf{X}_{j \in J} N_j$, then there exist lattices*

[4] J. Hashimoto [52].
[5] J. Hashimoto [50].

$K_{ij}(i \in I, j \in J)$ such that for each $i \in I$ and each $j \in J$,

$$M_i \cong \mathsf{X}_{j \in J} K_{ij} \quad \text{and} \quad N_j \cong \mathsf{X}_{i \in I} K_{ij}.$$

11.9: *If a lattice L is complete, and if $\theta_i (i \in I)$ is a family of congruence relations in L satisfying conditions (1)–(3) of 11.7, then L is a direct product of the lattices $L/\theta_i (i \in I)$.*[6]

PROOF: The lattice L is a subdirect product of the lattices $L/\theta_i (i \in I)$, and, as in the proof of 11.7, we need only show that for a given family of elements $a_i (i \in I)$ in L there is an element $a \in L$ such that $a \, \theta_i \, a_i$ for all $i \in I$. To prove this, let 0 be the least element of L, and observe that as $0(\theta_i \vee \bar{\theta}_i) a_i$ and θ_i and $\bar{\theta}_i$ permute, there is an element b_i such that $0 \leq b_i \leq a_i$, and

$$0 \, \bar{\theta}_i \, b_i \, \theta_i \, a_i.$$

Set $a = \bigvee_{i \in I} b_i$. Then there exist elements $c_i (i \in I)$ in L such that $b_i \leq c_i \leq a$ and

$$b_i \, \theta_i \, c_i \, \bar{\theta}_i \, a.$$

Now $b_i \, \bar{\theta}_i \, 0$ implies that $b_i \, \theta_j \, 0$ for all $j \neq i$. Therefore, for all $i, j \in I$,

$$b_i \, \theta_i \, (b_i \vee b_j) \, \theta_i \, (c_i \vee b_j) \, \bar{\theta}_i \, (a \vee b_j) = a,$$

and thus

$$(c_i \vee b_j) \, \theta_i \, b_i \, \theta_i \, c_i \quad \text{and} \quad (c_i \vee b_j) \, \bar{\theta}_i \, a \, \bar{\theta}_i \, c_i.$$

Consequently, for all $i, j \in I$, we must have $(c_i \vee b_j)(\theta_i \wedge \bar{\theta}_i) c_i$, which implies that $c_i = c_i \vee b_j \geq b_j$. This inequality yields that $c_i \geq a$, so that $c_i = a$ for all $i \in I$. It follows that $a \, \theta_i \, b_i \, \theta_i \, a_i$ and hence that $a \, \theta_i \, a_i$ for all $i \in I$, completing the proof.

We are now in a position to state the result we are seeking.

11.10: *A complete, weakly atomic, relatively complemented lattice is a direct product of subdirectly irreducible lattices.*[7]

PROOF: The proof begins with the following observation: *Any two congruence relations in a relatively complemented lattice permute.* For suppose that θ and φ are congruence relations in a relatively complemented lattice L, and suppose that $a, b, c \in L$ are such that $a \, \theta \, b$ and $b \, \varphi \, c$. Let a_1 be a complement of $a \vee b$ in the sublattice $a \vee b \vee c/a$, and let c_1 be a complement of $b \vee c$ in $a \vee b \vee c/c$. Set $d = a_1 \wedge c_1$. Then $a \vee b = (a \vee b \vee b) \, \varphi \, (a \vee b \vee c)$, and as a_1/a is a transpose of $a \vee b \vee c/a \vee b$, we must have $a_1 \, \varphi \, a$. Similarly, $c_1 \, \theta \, c$. Also, $a \vee b \, \theta \, a$ and $a \vee b/a$ is a transpose of $a \vee b \vee c/a_1$, so that

---

[6] J. Hashimoto [52].
[7] J. Hashimoto [52].

$(a \vee b \vee c) \, \theta \, a_1$. And as $a \vee b \vee c \geq a_1 \vee c_1 \geq a_1$, we infer that $a_1 \vee c_1$ $\theta \, a_1$. Thus $c \, \theta \, c_1 \, \theta \, (a_1 \wedge c_1) = d$. Similarly, $a \, \varphi \, d$.

Continuing with the proof of 11.10, let L be a complete, weakly atomic, relatively complemented lattice, and let $\theta_i (i \in I)$ be the unique family of completely irreducible congruence relations in L such that L is an irredundant subdirect product of the lattices $L/\theta_i (i \in I)$, as guaranteed by 11.6. In view of 11.9 and the result of the preceding paragraph, to complete the proof we need to show that, for each $i \in I$, $\theta_i \vee \bar{\theta}_i = 1$, where $\bar{\theta}_i = \bigwedge_{k \neq i} \theta_k$.

Consider a particular θ_i. Then as θ_i is a completely irreducible element in an irredundant decomposition of the least element of $\Theta(L)$ and L is weakly atomic, there exists a prime quotient p/q of L such that θ_i is maximal in $\Theta(L)$ with respect to the property $\theta_i \not\geq \theta_{p,q}$. Define the relation φ_i in L by the following rule: $a \, \varphi_i \, b$ if and only if every prime quotient of $a \vee b/a \wedge b$ is projective to p/q. The reader can check that φ_i is a congruence relation. Clearly $\theta_i \wedge \varphi_i = 0$. We further assert that $\theta_i \vee \varphi_i = 1$. To see this, consider a pair of elements $b \geq a$ in L. Set $S = \{x \in L \, | \, a \leq x \leq b \text{ and } x \, \theta_i \, a\}$, and set $c = \bigvee S$. Suppose a subquotient r/s of c/a is projective to p/q. If t is a complement of r in c/s, then there must be some element $x \in S$ such that $t < t \vee x \leq c$. $t \vee x/t$ is weakly projective to p/q, and therefore $t \vee x/t$ and p/q are projective, so that $x/x \wedge t$ and p/q are projective. But $x/x \wedge t$ is a subquotient of x/a, contrary to $x \, \theta_i \, a$ and $p\theta_i \neq q\theta_i$. Hence no subquotient of c/a is projective to p/q, and this fact together with the maximal property of θ_i implies that $c \, \theta_i \, a$, i.e., that c is the largest element of S.

Now suppose that there is a prime subquotient r/s of b/c which is not projective to p/q. Then, as above, it follows that $r \, \theta_i \, s$, and if t is a complement of s in r/c, we must have $t \, \theta_i \, c$, so that $t \, \theta_i \, a$, contrary to the fact that c is the largest element in S. Thus every prime quotient of b/c is projective to p/q, and consequently $b \, \varphi_i \, c$. Hence $b(\theta_i \vee \varphi_i)a$, and we conclude that $\theta_i \vee \varphi_i = 1$, as asserted. Therefore θ_i and φ_i are complements in $\Theta(L)$, and it follows that the sublattice $1/\varphi_i$ is isomorphic to the sublattice $\theta_i/0$. And as $\Theta(L)$ is atomic, $1/\varphi_i$ is atomic. Consequently 6.9 guarantees that φ_i has an irredundant decomposition in $\Theta(L)$, say $\varphi_i = \bigwedge \Sigma$. But then $0 = \theta_i \wedge \bigwedge \Sigma$ is an irredundant decomposition of 0, and as irredundant decompositions in $\Theta(L)$ are unique, we conclude that $\varphi_i = \bigwedge \Sigma = \bigwedge_{k \neq i} \theta_k = \bar{\theta}_i$. Hence $\theta_i \vee \bar{\theta}_i = 1$, and the proof of 11.10 is complete.

Again, a somewhat stronger theorem is obtained in the presence of a chain condition. For if a complete relatively complemented lattice L satisfies the ascending chain condition, then 10.8 assures us that $\Theta(L)$ is a Boolean algebra, and therefore if L is further subdirectly irreducible, it is simple. Thus *a complete relatively complemented lattice satisfying the ascending chain condition is a direct product of finitely many simple lattices.*[8] (The reader should derive this result more simply from 10.8 and 11.7 directly.)

[8] R. Dilworth [33].

It should be observed that the word "complete" cannot be dropped from the hypotheses of 11.10. If L is the lattice of all finite subsets of some infinite set, then L is certainly weakly atomic and relatively complemented, besides being distributive. Consequently, if L were a direct product of subdirectly irreducible lattices, it would have to be isomorphic to a direct product of two-element chains, an impossibility since L is not complete.

12

REPRESENTATIONS
BY
EQUIVALENCE RELATIONS

An important class of complete relatively complemented lattices arises out of equivalence relations. Let U be any set. Let U^2 denote the set of all ordered pairs $\langle u, v \rangle$ with $u, v \in U$. As subsets of U^2 the equivalence relations in U are partially ordered by set-inclusion. And if we denote by $\Pi(U)$ the set of all equivalence relations in U together with this partial order, then $\Pi(U)$ is a complete lattice in which the meet and join of a collection Σ of equivalence relations are given by the following rules: $u(\bigwedge\Sigma)v$ if $u R v$ for all $R \in \Sigma$; and $u(\bigvee\Sigma)v$ if there is a finite sequence of elements $u = u_0, u_1, \ldots, u_n = v$ in U and equivalence relations $R_1, \ldots, R_n \in \Sigma$ such that $u_{i-1} R_i u_i$ for each $i = 1, \ldots, n$. We will refer to $\Pi(U)$ as a *partition lattice*.

As a matter of fact, $\Pi(U)$ *is a simple, compactly generated, atomic, relatively complemented, semimodular lattice*.[1] To prove this statement, observe first that an equivalence relation R is an atom of $\Pi(U)$ if and only if each equivalence class of R, with one exception, contains a single element and the exceptional class contains exactly two distinct elements. This makes it clear that each element in $\Pi(U)$ is a join of atoms and that each atom is compact, whence $\Pi(U)$ is compactly generated and atomic. Next observe that if $R \in \Pi(U)$, then the quotient sublattice $1/R$ is isomorphic to $\Pi(V)$, where V is the set of equivalence classes of R. Consequently, to show that $\Pi(U)$ is semimodular, it suffices to show that if $R, S \in \Pi(U)$, R is an atom, and $R \nsubseteq S$, then $R \vee S \succ S$. In this situation there is a unique pair of distinct elements $u, v \in U$ such that $u R v$, and $u S v$ does not hold. Therefore the equivalence classes of $R \vee S$ are the equivalence classes of S that contain neither u nor v and the set-union of the equivalence class of S that contains u with that equivalence class of S containing v. From this description of $R \vee S$ it should be apparent that $R \vee S \succ S$. Now in view of the fact that $\Pi(U)$ is semimodular and each of its elements is a join of atoms, 4.1 shows that $\Pi(U)$ is relatively complemented. So it remains to show that $\Pi(U)$ is

[1] O. Ore [76].

simple. Under any circumstances the reader can check that if R and S are distinct equivalence relations that are both covered by the greatest element of $\Pi(U)$, then there exists $T \in \Pi(U)$ such that R, S, and T generate a five-element modular nondistributive sublattice, and this implies that any two prime quotients in $\Pi(U)$ are projective. (Proof?) In particular, if U is finite, then $\Pi(U)$ is simple. If U is infinite, write U as the set-union of two infinite disjoint subsets U_1 and U_2 having the same cardinality, and let f be a one-to-one map of U_1 onto U_2. Let R be that equivalence relation whose equivalence classes are U_1 and U_2, let S be that equivalence relation whose equivalence classes are the two-element sets $\{u, f(u)\}$ $(u \in U_1)$, and, for each $i = 1$, 2, let T_i be that equivalence relation whose only equivalence class containing more than one member is U_i. We then have that R is covered by the greatest element of $\Pi(U)$, T_1 and T_2 are complements in the sublattice $R/0$, and R, T_1, and T_2 are complements of S in $\Pi(U)$. It follows that each $1/T_i$ is projective to $1/R$. And therefore if θ is any congruence relation in $\Pi(U)$ that collapses at least one nontrivial quotient, then θ collapses $1/R$ and hence collapses each $1/T_i$, and as $T_1 \wedge T_2$ is the least element of $\Pi(U)$, we conclude that θ collapses every quotient of $\Pi(U)$. Thus $\Pi(U)$ is simple.

It is useful to introduce a new operation. If X and Y are subsets of U^2, then the *relative product* $X ; Y$ is defined to be the set of all ordered pairs $\langle u, v \rangle$ such that $\langle u, w \rangle \in X$ and $\langle w, v \rangle \in Y$ for some $w \in U$. The relative product of two equivalence relations R, $S \in \Pi(U)$ is usually not an equivalence relation; when it is, it coincides with the join of R and S in $\Pi(U)$. Also, the assertion that $R ; S$ is an equivalence relation is equivalent to the formula

$$R ; S = S ; R ;$$

i.e., $R ; S$ is an equivalence relation if and only if R and S *permute*. In general, for two equivalence relations R, $S \in \Pi(U)$, the join $R \vee S$ is the set-union of the increasing sequence

$$R ; S \subseteq R ; S ; R \subseteq R ; S ; R ; S \subseteq \cdots.$$

The importance of these lattices of equivalence relations stems from the fact that every lattice can be embedded in some $\Pi(U)$, a theorem we will derive in this chapter. Actually our concern here is not just with embedding a lattice in some $\Pi(U)$, but with embedding the lattice in such a way that when forming joins the sequences of relative products are constant from the first, second, or third term on. Thus the following definitions. By a *representation* of a lattice L we mean an ordered pair $\langle U, F \rangle$, where U is a set and F is an embedding of L to $\Pi(U)$; we say that $\langle U, F \rangle$ is

  (1)   *Of type* 1 if $F(x) \vee F(y) = F(x) ; F(y)$ for all x, $y \in L$.
  (2)   *Of type* 2 if $F(x) \vee F(y) = F(x) ; F(y) ; F(x)$ for all x, $y \in L$.
  (3)   *Of type* 3 if $F(x) \vee F(y) = F(x) ; F(y) ; F(x) ; F(y)$ for all $x, y \in L$.

For example, the lattice of all normal subgroups of a group G has a representation of type 1; we set $U = G$, and for each normal subgroup H we define $F(H)$ to be the set of all ordered pairs $\langle u, v \rangle$, where $uv^{-1} \in H$.

The first theorem of this chapter neatly characterizes those lattices having a representation of type 2.

12.1:   *A lattice L has a representation of type* 2 *if and only if L is modular.*[2]

PROOF: Suppose that $\langle U, F \rangle$ is a representation of the lattice L of type 2. Let a, b, c be elements of L with $a \geq b$. If $u, v \in U$ and $u \, F(a \wedge (b \vee c)) \, v$, then

$$u \, F(b \vee c) \, v \qquad \text{and} \qquad u \, F(a) \, v.$$

Now $\langle U, F \rangle$ is of type 2, and hence there exist $p, q \in U$ such that

$$u \, F(b) \, p, \qquad p \, F(c) \, q, \qquad q \, F(b) \, v.$$

And as $F(b) \subseteq F(a)$, we have that $p \, F(a) \, u$, $u \, F(a) \, v$, and $v \, F(a) \, q$, so that $p \, F(a) \, q$. Thus $p \, F(a \wedge c) \, q$. This fact, together with the formulas $u \, F(b) \, p$ and $q \, F(b) \, v$, yields that $u \, F(b \vee (a \wedge c)) \, v$. It follows that $F(a \wedge (b \vee c)) \subseteq F(b \vee (a \wedge c))$ and hence that $a \wedge (b \vee c) \leq b \vee (a \wedge c)$, giving the modularity of L.

The proof of the converse is made in several steps and requires the following definitions. By a *weak representation* of a lattice L we mean an ordered pair $\langle U, F \rangle$, where U is a set and F is a one-to-one mapping of L into $\Pi(U)$ with the property that

$$F(x \wedge y) = F(x) \wedge F(y) \qquad \text{for all } x, y \in L.$$

If $\langle U, F \rangle$ and $\langle V, G \rangle$ are two weak representations of the lattice L, we say that $\langle V, G \rangle$ is an *extension of* $\langle U, F \rangle$ if $U \subseteq V$ and

$$G(x) \cap U^2 = F(x) \qquad \text{for all } x \in L.$$

A. Any lattice L has a weak representation $\langle U, F \rangle$ that satisfies the following condition:

(∗) If $u, v \in U$ and $u \neq v$, then the set $\{x \in L \,|\, u \, F(x) \, v\}$ is either empty or has a least element.

To prove this, associate with each element $a \in L$ an element a^* in such a way that $a^* \notin L$ and the map $a \longrightarrow a^*$ is one-to-one. Let

$$U = L \cup \{a^* \,|\, a \in L\},$$

and for each element $x \in L$ define $F(x)$ to be that equivalence relation in U whose equivalence classes are the sets

$$\{a, a^*\}$$

---

[2] B. Jónsson [54].

for $a \leq x$, and the sets

$$\{a\}, \{a^*\}$$

for $a \not\leq x$. It is easy to check that $\langle U, F \rangle$ is a weak representation of L. Moreover, if u, v are distinct elements of U, and if the set

$$A = \{x \in L \,|\, u \, F(x) \, v\}$$

is nonempty, then $\langle u, v \rangle = \langle a, a^* \rangle$ or $\langle u, v \rangle = \langle a^*, a \rangle$ for some $a \in L$. Hence $A = \{x \in L \,|\, x \geq a\}$, so that a is the least element of A, and condition (∗) is satisfied.

B. Suppose L is a modular lattice and $\langle U, F \rangle$ is a weak representation of L satisfying condition (∗). If $a, b \in L$ and $p \, F(a \vee b) \, q$, then there exists an extension $\langle V, G \rangle$ of $\langle U, F \rangle$ such that $\langle V, G \rangle$ satisfies condition (∗) and

$$\langle p, q \rangle \in G(a) \,;\, G(b) \,;\, G(a).$$

In proving this statement we can assume that p and q are distinct elements of U. Take two distinct elements r and s which do not belong to U, and set

$$V = U \cup \{r, s\}.$$

Invoking condition (∗), pick the least element d in the set

$$\{x \in L \,|\, p \, F(x) \, q\},$$

and let

$$a' = a \vee d, \qquad b' = a' \wedge b.$$

Then as $d \leq a \vee b$, and hence that $a \leq a' \leq a \vee b$, it follows by modularity that

$$a' = a \vee b'.$$

(This is the only place where modularity is used in the proof of 13.1!)

In defining $G(x)$ we consider four cases.

If $a' \leq x$, then $p \, F(x) \, q$, so that p and q belong to the same $F(x)$ equivalence class. In this case $G(x)$ is that equivalence relation in V whose equivalence classes are the $F(x)$ equivalence classes that do not contain p and q and the set obtained by adjoining r and s to that $F(x)$ equivalence class containing p and q.

If $a \leq x$ and $b' \not\leq x$, then $d \not\leq x$, and hence p and q belong to different $F(x)$ equivalence classes. In this case the $G(x)$ equivalence classes are the $F(x)$ equivalence classes not containing p or q, the set obtained by adjoining r to the $F(x)$ equivalence class containing p, and the set obtained by adding s to the $F(x)$ equivalence class containing q.

If $a \not\leq x$ and $b' \leq x$, then the $G(x)$ equivalence classes are the $F(x)$ equivalence classes and the set $\{r, s\}$.

If $a \not\leq x$ and $b' \not\leq x$, then the $G(x)$ equivalence classes are the $F(x)$ equivalence classes and the sets $\{r\}$ and $\{s\}$.

These conditions certainly define a mapping G of L to $\Pi(V)$. Furthermore, if $u, v \in U$ and $x \in L$, then the following four statements hold:

(1) $u\,G(x)\,v$ if and only if $u\,F(x)\,v$.
(2) $u\,G(x)\,r$ if and only if $u\,F(x)\,p$ and $a \leq x$.
(3) $u\,G(x)\,s$ if and only if $u\,F(x)\,q$ and $a \leq x$.
(4) $r\,G(x)\,s$ if and only if $b' \leq x$.

Condition (1) yields that

$$G(x) \cap U^2 = F(x) \qquad \text{for all } x \in L,$$

and as F is one-to-one, the function G is also one-to-one. Using (1)–(4), it is easily seen that $G(x \wedge y) = G(x) \wedge G(y)$ for all $x, y \in L$. Consequently $\langle V, G \rangle$ is a weak representation of L and an extension of $\langle U, F \rangle$.

Next we need to show that $\langle V, G \rangle$ satisfies (∗). If u and v are distinct elements of U, then the set

$$\{x \in L \mid u\,G(x)\,v\} = \{x \in L \mid u\,F(x)\,v\}$$

is either empty or has a least element, since F satisfies (∗). If $u \in U$ and if the set

$$A = \{x \in L \mid u\,G(x)\,r\}$$

is nonempty, then it follows from (2) that the set $\{x \in L \mid u\,F(x)\,p\}$ is nonempty and hence has a least element c. And again using (2), we infer that $a \vee c$ is the least element of A. Similarly, if $u \in U$, then the set $\{x \in L \mid u\,G(x)\,s\}$ is either empty or has a least element. The set

$$\{x \in L \mid r\,G(x)\,s\} = \{x \in L \mid x \geq b'\}$$

has the least element b'. Therefore $\langle V, G \rangle$ satisfies condition (∗).

Finally, as $p\,G(a)\,r$, $r\,G(b)\,s$, and $s\,G(a)\,q$, we conclude that $\langle p, q \rangle \in G(a); G(b); G(a)$, completing the proof of B.

The next lemma is entirely set-theoretical, and its proof is left to the reader.

C. Suppose L is a lattice and λ is a limit ordinal, and suppose with each ordinal number $\xi < \lambda$ there is associated a weak representation $\langle U_\xi, F_\xi \rangle$ of L such that $\langle U_\eta, F_\eta \rangle$ is an extension of $\langle U_\xi, F_\xi \rangle$ whenever $\xi < \eta < \lambda$. If

$$U_\lambda = \bigcup_{\xi < \lambda} U_\xi \quad \text{and} \quad F_\lambda(x) = \bigcup_{\xi < \lambda} F_\xi(x) \qquad \text{for } x \in L,$$

then $\langle U_\lambda, F_\lambda \rangle$ is a weak representation of L and an extension of each $\langle U_\xi, F_\xi \rangle$ $(\xi < \lambda)$. Moreover, if each $\langle U_\xi, F_\xi \rangle$ satisfies (∗), then $\langle U_\lambda, F_\lambda \rangle$ also satisfies (∗).

D. If L is a modular lattice and $\langle U, F \rangle$ is a weak representation of L satisfying (∗), then there exists an extension $\langle V, G \rangle$ of $\langle U, F \rangle$ such that $\langle V, G \rangle$

satisfies (∗) and

$$F(a \vee b) \subseteq G(a); G(b); G(a) \qquad \text{for all } a, b \in L.$$

Letting K denote the set of all ordered quadruples $\langle p, q, a, b \rangle$, where $a, b \in L$ and $p\, F(a \vee b)\, q$, arrange the members of K into a (possibly transfinite) sequence

$$\langle p_0, q_0, a_0, b_0 \rangle, \langle p_1, q_1, a_1, b_1 \rangle, \ldots, \langle p_\xi, q_\xi, a_\xi, b_\xi \rangle, \ldots, (\xi < \lambda),$$

and use B and C to obtain a sequence

$$\langle U_0, F_0 \rangle, \langle U_1, F_1 \rangle, \ldots, \langle U_\xi, F_\xi \rangle, \ldots, (\xi \leq \lambda)$$

of weak representations of L with the following properties:

(1) $U_0 = U$ and $F_0 = F$.

(2) If $\xi < \lambda$, then $\langle U_{\xi+1}, F_{\xi+1} \rangle$ is an extension of $\langle U_\xi, F_\xi \rangle$ and $\langle p_\xi, q_\xi \rangle \in F_{\xi+1}(a_\xi); F_{\xi+1}(b_\xi); F_{\xi+1}(a_\xi)$.

(3) If $\xi \leq \lambda$ is a limit ordinal, then

$$U_\xi = \bigcup_{\eta < \xi} U_\eta \qquad \text{and} \qquad F_\xi(x) = \bigcup_{\eta < \xi} F_\eta(x) \qquad \text{all } x \in L$$

(4) $\langle U_\xi, F_\xi \rangle$ satisfies (∗) for all $\xi \leq \lambda$.

Set $V = U_\lambda$ and $G = F_\lambda$. Then if $a, b \in L$ and $p\, F(a \vee b)\, q$, for some $\xi < \lambda$ we have $\langle p, q, a, b \rangle = \langle p_\xi, q_\xi, a_\xi, b_\xi \rangle$ and hence

$$\langle p, q \rangle \in F_{\xi+1}(a); F_{\xi+1}(b); F_{\xi+1}(a) \subseteq G(a); G(b); G(a).$$

Consequently $F(a \vee b) \subseteq G(a); G(b); G(a)$ for all $a, b \in L$.

The proof of 12.1 is now easily completed, for if L is a modular lattice, it follows by A and D that there exists an infinite sequence

$$\langle U_0, F_0 \rangle, \langle U_1, F_1 \rangle, \ldots, \langle U_n, F_n \rangle, \ldots$$

of weak representations of L such that each $\langle U_n, F_n \rangle$ satisfies (∗), and $\langle U_{n+1}, F_{n+1} \rangle$ is an extension of $\langle U_n, F_n \rangle$ with the property that

$$F_n(a \vee b) \subseteq F_{n+1}(a); F_{n+1}(b); F_{n+1}(a) \qquad \text{for all } a, b \in L.$$

If

$$V = \bigcup_{n < \infty} U_n \qquad \text{and} \qquad G(x) = \bigcup_{n < \infty} F_n(x) \qquad \text{for } x \in L,$$

then C assures us that $\langle V, G \rangle$ is a weak representation of L. Furthermore, for any $a, b \in L$,

$$G(a \vee b) = \bigcup_{n < \infty} F_n(a \vee b) \subseteq \bigcup_{n < \infty} F_{n+1}(a); F_{n+1}(b); F_{n+1}(a)$$

$$\subseteq G(a); G(b); G(a) \subseteq G(a) \vee G(b) \subseteq G(a \vee b),$$

so that $G(a \vee b) = G(a); G(b); G(a)$. Consequently $\langle V, G \rangle$ is a representation of L of type 2, and the proof of 12.1 is complete.

Representations of type 3 are sufficient for the representation of arbitrary lattices.

12.2:   *Every lattice has a representation of type* 3.[3]

PROOF: In the proof of the preceding theorem the assumption of modularity was used only once, in the proof of part B. We will modify that part, but otherwise use the same reasoning to prove 12.2. The modified version of part B is the following:

B′. Suppose L is a lattice and $\langle U, F \rangle$ is a weak representation of L. If a, $b \in L$ and $p\, F(a \vee b)\, q$, then there exists an extension $\langle V, G \rangle$ of $\langle U, F \rangle$ such that

$$\langle p, q \rangle \in G(a); G(b); G(a); G(b).$$

To prove this, take three distinct elements r, s, t not belonging to U, and let

$$V = U \cup \{r, s, t\}.$$

As before, there are four cases to consider in defining $G(x)$.

If $a \leq x$ and $b \leq x$, then $p\, F(x)\, q$ so that p and q belong to the same $F(x)$ equivalence class. In this case the $G(x)$ equivalence classes are the $F(x)$ equivalence classes which do not contain p and q and the set obtained by adjoining r, s, and t to that $F(x)$ equivalence class containing p and q.

If $a \leq x$ and $b \not\leq x$, then the $G(x)$ equivalence classes are the $F(x)$ equivalence classes which do not contain p, the set obtained by adjoining r to that $F(x)$ equivalence class containing p, and the set $\{s, t\}$.

If $a \not\leq x$ and $b \leq x$, then the $G(x)$ equivalence classes are the $F(x)$ equivalence classes which do not contain q, the set obtained by adjoining t to that $F(x)$ equivalence class containing q, and the set $\{r, s\}$.

If $a \not\leq x$ and $b \not\leq x$, then the $G(x)$ equivalence classes are the $F(x)$ equivalence classes and the sets $\{r\}$, $\{s\}$, $\{t\}$.

These conditions again define a mapping G of L to $\Pi(V)$. Moreover, if $u, v \in U$, then the following seven statements hold:

(1) $u\, G(x)\, v$ if and only if $u\, F(x)\, v$,
(2) $u\, G(x)\, r$ if and only if $u\, F(x)\, p$ and $a \leq x$,
(3) $u\, G(x)\, s$ if and only if $u\, F(x)\, p$, $a \leq x$, and $b \leq x$,
(4) $u\, G(x)\, t$ if and only if $u\, F(x)\, q$ and $b \leq x$,
(5) $r\, G(x)\, s$ if and only if $b \leq x$,
(6) $r\, G(x)\, t$ if and only if $a \leq x$ and $b \leq x$,
(7) $s\, G(x)\, t$ if and only if $a \leq x$.

---

[3] That every lattice can be embedded in some lattice of equivalence relations was first proved by P. Whitman [90]. The stronger version given here is due to B. Jónsson [54].

And these conditions easily yield that $\langle V, G \rangle$ is a weak representation of L and an extension of $\langle U, F \rangle$. Finally, $p\,G(a)\,r$, $r\,G(b)\,s$, $s\,G(a)\,t$, and $t\,G(b)\,q$, so that $\langle p, q \rangle \in G(a); G(b); G(a); G(b)$.

Using B′ in place of B, we proceed as in the proof of part D of 12.1 to obtain

D′. If L is a lattice and $\langle U, F \rangle$ is a representation of L, then there is an extension $\langle V, G \rangle$ of $\langle U, F \rangle$ such that

$$F(a \vee b) \subseteq G(a); G(b); G(a); G(b) \qquad \text{all } a, b \in L.$$

The proof of 12.2 is now completed exactly as the proof of 12.1, using D′ in place of D.

Theorem 12.2 and its proof raise a question that has long remained unanswered. Notice that in the final step of the proof of 12.2 a representation $\langle V, G \rangle$ of the lattice L is obtained for which, in general, the set V is infinite. Consequently these techniques fail to handle the following important open question: Can any finite lattice be embedded in $\Pi(U)$ for some *finite* set U?

Theorem 12.2 also has an interesting corollary: *Any lattice can be embedded in the lattice of all subgroups of some group.*[4] It should be emphasized that this result is only an embedding theorem. There is at this time no known necessary and sufficient condition for a lattice to be isomorphic to the lattice of all subgroups of a group. A necessary condition, of course, is compact generation, but it is not sufficient; the reader might show, for example, that there is no group whose lattice of subgroups is isomorphic to the five-element nonmodular lattice. The proof of the corollary is left to the reader with this hint: Embed $\Pi(U)$ in the lattice of all subgroups of the group of all permutations of U.

It remains to describe those lattices having a representation of type 1. Unfortunately the only existing description of this class of lattices involves an infinite set of implications,[5] and it is not known if the class can be characterized by finitely many implications or by lattice identities. We will not give this description but content ourselves with obtaining an identity that is satisfied by every lattice having a representation of type 1.

Let us define a lattice L to be *Arguesian* provided that, for every $a_0, a_1, a_2, b_0, b_1, b_2 \in L$,

$$(a_0 \vee b_0) \wedge (a_1 \vee b_1) \wedge (a_2 \vee b_2) \le (a_0 \wedge (c \vee a_1)) \vee (b_0 \wedge (c \vee b_1)),$$

where

$$c = (a_0 \vee a_1) \wedge (b_0 \vee b_1) \wedge (((a_0 \vee a_2) \wedge (b_0 \vee b_2))$$
$$\vee ((a_1 \vee a_2) \wedge (b_1 \vee b_2))).$$

[4] P. Whitman [90].
[5] B. Jónsson [57].

The Arguesian condition is obviously equivalent to a lattice identity involving six variables, although it is easier to write it as the inequality above. In addition,

12.3:　*Every Arguesian lattice is modular.*[6]

On the other hand, modularity is not equivalent to the Arguesian property; in the next chapter we will give an example of a modular lattice which is not Arguesian.

12.4:　*If a lattice L has a representation of type* 1, *then L is Arguesian.*[7]

Consequently there are modular lattices which do not have representations of type 1. Another consequence of 12.4 is the fact that *for any operator group G, the lattice of all admissible normal subgroups of G is Arguesian.*

Modularity is easily derived from the Arguesian condition: assuming that a, b, and c are elements of the Arguesian lattice L with $a \geq b$, apply the Arguesian condition with

$$a_0 = b_1 = c, \qquad a_1 = a_2 = b_0 = b, \qquad b_2 = a.$$

(The proof of 12.4 is left to the reader.)

It would be a pleasant occurrence if the class of all Arguesian lattices were identical with the class of all those lattices having a representation of type 1. We (optimistically) conjecture that this is so.

[6] B. Jónsson [55].
[7] B. Jónsson [54].

13

COMPLEMENTED
MODULAR LATTICES

At several points in the preceding chapters we have developed some of the properties of relatively complemented lattices. In this chapter and in Chap. 15 we focus on complemented modular lattices and probe fairly deeply into their structure. These two chapters, in some sense, are complementary; here we are mainly concerned with atomic lattices, while in Chap. 15 our concern is with lattices having no atoms whatsoever. As a by-product of the main theorems derived in this chapter we get an answer, at least in the complemented case, to the question raised at the end of the last chapter; we will see that the classes of complemented Arguesian lattices and complemented lattices having a representation of type 1 coincide.

We begin with the following basic embedding theorem.

13.1: *Each complemented modular lattice L can be embedded in a compactly generated, complemented modular lattice K with the property that every lattice identity holding in L also holds in K.*[1]

PROOF: Let 0 and 1 denote the least and greatest elements of L, respectively. Form the lattice $\mathcal{F}(L)$ of all filters of L and the lattice $\mathcal{I}_0(\mathcal{F}(L))$ of all nonempty ideals of $\mathcal{F}(L)$. Since L has a least element, the lattice $\mathcal{F}(L)$ is atomic, and therefore $\mathcal{I}_0(\mathcal{F}(L))$ is also atomic. Let $\mathcal{A}$ denote the set of all atoms of $\mathcal{F}(L)$, and let A denote the least ideal in $\mathcal{I}_0(\mathcal{F}(L))$ such that $A \supseteq \mathcal{A}$. Then in $\mathcal{I}_0(\mathcal{F}(L))$, A is a join of atoms, and as $\mathcal{I}_0(\mathcal{F}(L))$ is compactly generated, we infer from 4.3 that the quotient sublattice

$$K = \{B \in \mathcal{I}_0(\mathcal{F}(L)) \mid B \leq A\}$$

of $\mathcal{I}_0(\mathcal{F}(L))$ is a compactly generated, complemented modular lattice. Moreover, the results of Chap. 9 guarantee that every lattice identity that holds in L also holds in K. We will complete the proof by showing that L is embedded in K.

[1] O. Frink [39], B. Jónsson [55].

For each $x \in L$ let $f(x)$ denote the least ideal in $\mathcal{I}_0(\mathcal{F}(L))$ that contains the set

$$\{P \in \mathcal{Q} \mid x \in P\}.$$

This defines a map f from L to K, and to complete the proof we will show that f is an isomorphism.

It is helpful to more fully describe the ideal $f(x)$. Note that a filter $F \in \mathcal{F}(L)$ is a member of $f(x)$ if and only if there are finitely many elements $P_1, \ldots, P_n \in \{P \in \mathcal{Q} \mid x \in P\}$ such that in $\mathcal{F}(L)$

$$F \le P_1 \vee \cdots \vee P_n.$$

This formula is equivalent to the formula $F \supseteq P_1 \cap \cdots \cap P_n$. [Keep in mind that the partial order of $\mathcal{F}(L)$ is the dual of set-inclusion, and join in $\mathcal{F}(L)$ coincides with set-intersection.] Therefore $x \in F$. In addition, since $\mathcal{F}(L)$ is modular, it follows from 4.3 that F is actually equal to the join of finitely many atoms of $\mathcal{F}(L)$, i.e., that F is the set-intersection of finitely many atoms of $\mathcal{F}(L)$. In summary, a filter $F \in \mathcal{F}(L)$ is a member of $f(x)$ if and only if $x \in F$ and F is the set intersection of finitely many elements in $\mathcal{Q}$. It follows easily from this statement that, for all $x, y \in L$, $f(x \wedge y) = f(x) \wedge f(y)$.

Next we prove that $f(x \vee y) = f(x) \vee f(y)$. In view of the fact that we at least have $f(x \vee y) \supseteq f(x) \vee f(y)$, it is enough to prove that if $P \in \mathcal{Q}$ and $x \vee y \in P$, then there exist $Q, R \in \mathcal{Q}$ such that $x \in Q$, $y \in R$, and $P \le Q \vee R$ in $\mathcal{F}(L)$. Notice that if either $x \in P$ or $y \in P$, then this condition clearly holds, so we can assume that $x \notin P$ and $y \notin P$. We can further assume that $x \wedge y = 0$, for if this is not the case, we simply choose a complement x' of $x \wedge y$ in the quotient sublattice $x/0$ of L, and observing that x' is also a complement of y in the sublattice $x \vee y/0$ and any filter containing x' also contains x, we proceed with x replaced by x'.

Consider then the filters P, $1/x$, $1/y$, $1/x \vee y \in \mathcal{F}(L)$. Since $x \vee y \in P$, in $\mathcal{F}(L)$ we have $P \le 1/x \vee y$. Therefore in $\mathcal{F}(L)$,

$$1/x \vee 1/y = 1/x \vee (1/y \vee P) = 1/x \vee y.$$

And as $1/x \wedge 1/y = 1/0$, the modularity of $\mathcal{F}(L)$ yields that

$$1/x \wedge (1/y \vee P) \ne 1/0.$$

Now the atomicity of $\mathcal{F}(L)$ ensures that there is an atom $Q \in \mathcal{Q}$ with

$$1/x \wedge (1/y \vee P) \ge Q.$$

In particular, $1/x \ge Q$, so that $x \in Q$, and $1/y \vee P \ge Q$. This last inequality implies that $1/y \vee P = 1/y \vee (P \vee Q)$, and since $1/y \wedge P = 1/0$, the modularity of $\mathcal{F}(L)$ again yields that $1/y \wedge (P \vee Q) \ne 1/0$. Therefore there is another atom $R \in \mathcal{Q}$ such that

$$1/y \wedge (P \vee Q) \ge R.$$

It follows that $y \in R$ and that $P \vee Q \ge R$. The atoms Q and R are in fact distinct since $x \in Q$, $y \in R$, and $x \wedge y = 0 \notin Q$. Consequently $Q \vee R \succ Q$, and as $P \vee Q \vee R = P \vee Q \succ Q$, we infer that

$$P \leq P \vee Q \vee R = Q \vee R,$$

the desired result.

Finally, suppose that $x > y$ in L. If y' is a complement of y in the quotient sublattice $x/0$, then $y' \neq 0$, and there is an atom $Q \in \mathcal{Q}$ such that $y' \in Q$. The element x also belongs to Q since $x \geq y'$, but $y \notin Q$, as otherwise $y \wedge y' = 0 \in Q$, an impossibility. Therefore $Q \in f(x)$ and $Q \notin f(y)$, whence $f(x) \neq f(y)$. Thus f is an isomorphism, and the proof of 13.1 is complete.

It is important to keep in mind that every compactly generated complemented modular lattice is strongly atomic (Theorem 4.3). And because of 11.10, this means that *every compactly generated, complemented, modular lattice is a direct product of subdirectly irreducible, compactly generated, complemented, modular lattices.* These subdirectly irreducible lattices will be the subject of concern for much of this chapter and hence deserve a shorter name; hereafter we will refer to a subdirectly irreducible, compactly generated, complemented, modular lattice as a *geomodular lattice*.[2]

The next result describes subdirect irreducibility in terms of the atoms.

13.2: *A complemented, atomic modular lattice L is subdirectly irreducible if and only if for each pair of distinct atoms $p_1, p_2 \in L$ there is an atom $p_3 \in L$, distinct from p_1 and p_2, such that $p_1 \vee p_2 \geq p_3$.*

PROOF: If the complemented, atomic modular lattice L satisfies the condition of 13.2, then for each pair of atoms $p_1, p_2 \in L$, the quotients $p_1/0$ and $p_2/0$ are projective. Consequently, if x/y and u/v are any two prime quotients of L, p_1 is a complement of y in $x/0$, and p_2 is a complement of v in $u/0$, then p_1 and p_2 are atoms, and inasmuch as $p_1/0$ and $p_2/0$ are projective, we infer that x/y and u/v are projective. Thus L is subdirectly irreducible.

Suppose for the moment that L is any modular lattice. It is useful to define a relation $\sim$ in the set of all atoms of L as follows: $p_1 \sim p_2$ if either $p_1 = p_2$ or there exists an atom $p_3 \in L$, distinct from p_1 and p_2, such that $p_3 \leq p_1 \vee p_2$. This relation $\sim$ is clearly reflexive and symmetric. To show that it is also transitive, assume that p_1, p_2, and p_3 are distinct atoms of L with $p_1 \sim p_2$ and $p_2 \sim p_3$. If these atoms are not independent, then $p_2 \leq p_1 \vee p_3$, so we can impose the additional assumption that p_1, p_2, and p_3 are independent elements. Let q_1 be an atom distinct from p_1 and p_2 with $q_1 \leq p_1 \vee p_2$, and let q_2 be an atom distinct from p_2 and p_3 with $q_2 \leq p_2 \vee p_3$. Notice that $q_1 \neq q_2$, as otherwise

$$p_1 \vee p_2 = q_1 \vee p_2 = q_2 \vee p_2 = p_2 \vee p_3,$$

---

[2] In the past the name "projective lattices" has been used for these lattices. However, the term "projective" now has a different meaning in the context of universal algebra.

contrary to our assumption that the p_i's are independent. And under these circumstances the modularity of L requires that $r = (q_1 \vee q_2) \wedge (p_1 \vee p_3)$ is an atom. (Proof?) The condition $r = p_1$ implies that $p_1 \leq q_1 \vee q_2$ and hence that

$$q_1 \vee q_2 = p_1 \vee q_1 \vee q_2 = p_1 \vee p_2 \vee q_2 = p_1 \vee p_2 \vee p_3,$$

an impossibility. Therefore $r \neq p_1$, and, similarly, $r \neq p_3$. We have now found an atom r, distinct from p_1 and p_3, with $r \leq p_1 \vee p_3$, and we conclude that $p_1 \sim p_3$.

Now suppose that L is subdirectly irreducible. Any two prime quotients of L are therefore projective, and hence if p_1 and p_2 are any two distinct atoms of L, for some integer $n \geq 2$, $p_1/0$ and $p_2/0$ are projective in n steps. We will prove that $p_1 \sim p_2$ by induction on n. When $n = 2$, there is a quotient x/y such that both p_1 and p_2 are complements of y in $x/0$, and it is easy to check that $y \wedge (p_1 \vee p_2)$ is an atom that is distinct from both p_1 and p_2. Suppose that the desired conclusion holds for each integer k less than n, and let $p_1/0 = x_0/y_0, x_1/y_1, \ldots, x_n/y_n = p_2/0$ be a sequence of $n + 1$ quotients such that each x_{i-1}/y_{i-1} is a transpose of x_i/y_i. Furthermore, we can assume that none of these quotients is superfluous (p. 76). In this situation x_2/y_2 is a lower transpose of both x_1/y_1 and x_3/y_3. Also, if q is a complement of y_2 in $x_2/0$, then q is an atom, and $q/0$ is a lower transpose of both x_1/y_1 and x_3/y_3. Therefore $p_1/0$ and $q/0$ are projective in two steps, so that $p_1 \sim q$, and $q/0$ and $p_2/0$ are projective in $n - 2$ steps, so by the induction, $q \sim p_2$. Consequently $p_1 \sim p_2$, completing the proof.

An important illustration of the preceding theorem comes from vector space lattices. If v is a vector space and L is the lattice of all subspaces of v, then L is compactly generated, complemented, and modular. The atoms of L are the one-dimensional subspaces of v, and if p_1 and p_2 are distinct atoms of L generated, say, by vectors x_1 and x_2, respectively, then the subspace generated by the vector $x_1 + x_2$ is an atom of L that is different from p_1 and p_2 and contained in $p_1 \vee p_2$. Thus L is subdirectly irreducible and hence a geomodular lattice.

Theorem 13.2 allows us to link lattice theory and geometry. Recall that a *projective space* is a system consisting of a set P of *points* and certain subsets of P called *lines* such that the following axioms are satisfied:

(1) Two distinct points lie on one and only one line.
(2) If a, b, c are three points not on a line, and if distinct points d and e are such that b, c, d are on a line and c, a, e are on a line, then there is a point f such that a, b, f are on a line and d, e, f are on a line. (In other words, a line intersecting two sides of a triangle, not at a vertex, also intersects the third side.)
(3) Each line contains at least three distinct points.

A subset S of P is a *subspace* if any line containing two distinct points of S is also included in S. It is clear that any subspace together with those lines it contains is itself a projective space.

Dimension is introduced in a projective space by defining a point to be of dimension 0, a line to be of dimension 1, and, inductively, a subspace S to be of dimension n if there is a point $a \in S$ and a subspace $T \subseteq S$ of dimension $n - 1$ that does not contain the point a such that each point in S lies on a line containing a and some point in T. Those projective spaces of dimension 2 are familiarly called projective planes.

The connection between projective spaces and lattices is established by the following theorem: *The set of all subspaces of a projective space, partially ordered by set-inclusion, is a geomodular lattice. Conversely, if L is a geomodular lattice, then the set P of all the atoms of L becomes a projective space when the line containing two distinct atoms $p_1, p_2 \in P$ is defined to be the set $\{q \in P \mid q \leq p_1 \vee p_2\}$, and L is isomorphic to the lattice of all subspaces of P.*[3] (The proof is a nontrivial exercise.)

A basic condition in projective geometry is Desargues' law. Letting pq designate the line through the points p and q in a projective space P, Desargues' law asserts: If $\langle a_0, a_1, a_2 \rangle$ and $\langle b_0, b_1, b_2 \rangle$ are two triples of distinct points such that the lines $a_0 b_0$, $a_1 b_1$, and $a_2 b_2$ intersect in a common point d, then the pairs of lines $a_0 a_1$ and $b_0 b_1$, $a_0 a_2$ and $b_0 b_2$, and $a_1 a_2$ and $b_1 b_2$ intersect in three points c_2, c_1, c_0, respectively, that lie on a line; in other words, two triangles that are centrally perspective are also axially perspective. (See Fig. 13-1.)

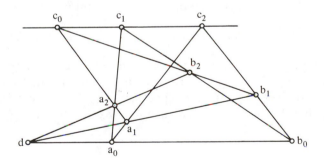

Fig. 13-1

Desargues' law holds in any projective space of dimension 3 or more, but, of course, there are projective planes in which Desargues' law fails. An example of such a plane is easy to construct. We start with the ordinary Euclidean plane endowed with the usual Cartesian coordinates. Let M be the set of all points in the Euclidean plane together with new points $\langle \infty, \infty \rangle$

[3] G. Birkhoff [12], O. Frink [39], M. L. Mousinho [69].

and $\langle \infty, r \rangle$, where r ranges over the real numbers. As a line in M we take (1) any line in the Euclidean plane parallel with the x-axis, with the point $\langle \infty, 0 \rangle$ adjoined; (2) any line in the Euclidean plane parallel with the y-axis, with the point $\langle \infty, \infty \rangle$ adjoined; (3) any line of the Euclidean plane of negative slope r with the point $\langle \infty, r \rangle$ adjoined, (4) any line in the Euclidean plane of positive slope r bent at the x-axis so that its part above the x-axis has slope $r/2$, with the point $\langle \infty, r \rangle$ adjoined; and (5) the line consisting of all the points $\langle \infty, \infty \rangle$ and $\langle \infty, r \rangle$. It is now routine to check that M is indeed a projective plane and that Desargues' law fails to hold in M.

Desargues' law can be formulated quite simply in lattice theoretic terms. Given a geomodular lattice L, two triples of atoms $\langle a_0, a_1, a_2 \rangle$ and $\langle b_0, b_1, b_2 \rangle$ are said to be *centrally perspective* if

$$(a_0 \vee b_0) \wedge (a_1 \vee b_1) \le a_2 \vee b_2,$$

and these two triples are said to be *axially perspective* if

$$(a_0 \vee a_1) \wedge (b_0 \vee b_1) \le [(a_0 \vee a_2) \wedge (b_0 \vee b_2)] \vee [(a_1 \vee a_2) \wedge (b_1 \vee b_2)].$$

We say that *Desargues' law* holds in the lattice L if any two triples of atoms that are centrally perspective are also axially perspective.

Certain special cases of Desargues' law hold in any modular lattice. In the presence of modularity, the axial perspectivity of $\langle a_0, a_1, a_2 \rangle$ and $\langle b_0, b_1, b_2 \rangle$ follows from their central perspectivity if any two of the a_i's are equal, or more generally if the a_i's are not independent, or if any $a_i = b_i$. (Proof?) Further, Desargues' law is trivial if the element $(a_0 \vee b_0) \wedge (a_1 \vee b_1)$ is either a two-dimensional element or the least element of the modular lattice.

13.3: *Desargues' law holds in every Arguesian geomodular lattice.*[4]

PROOF: Suppose L is an Arguesian geomodular lattice with least element 0 and $\langle a_0, a_1, a_2 \rangle$ and $\langle b_0, b_1, b_2 \rangle$ are two triples of atoms that are centrally perspective. In view of the preceding remarks, we can assume that the a_i's as well as the b_i's are distinct, that each $a_i \ne b_i$, and that the element $p = (a_0 \vee b_0) \wedge (a_1 \vee b_1)$ is an atom. Set

$$z_0 = (a_1 \vee a_2) \wedge (b_1 \vee b_2),$$
$$z_1 = (a_0 \vee a_2) \wedge (b_0 \vee b_2),$$
$$z_2 = (a_0 \vee a_1) \wedge (b_0 \vee b_1),$$
$$c = z_2 \wedge (z_1 \vee z_0).$$

Since $(a_0 \vee b_0) \wedge (a_1 \vee b_1)$ is an atom, $a_0 \vee b_0 \vee a_1 \vee b_1$ is necessarily a three-dimensional element, and therefore z_2 is also an atom. Furthermore, since $p \le (a_0 \vee b_0) \wedge (a_1 \vee b_1) \wedge (a_2 \vee b_2)$, the Arguesian condition yields

[4] B. Jónsson [54].

that

$$p \leq (a_0 \wedge (c \vee a_1)) \vee (b_0 \wedge (c \vee b_1)).$$

This shows that $c \neq 0$, for otherwise

$$0 < p \leq (a_0 \wedge a_1) \vee (b_0 \wedge b_1) = 0,$$

an impossibility. Hence $0 < c \leq z_2$, and as z_2 is an atom, we infer that $z_2 = c \leq z_1 \vee z_0$. Thus Desargues' law holds in L.

Theorem 13.3 makes it clear how to construct a modular lattice that is not Arguesian; we need only form the lattice of all subspaces of the non-Desarguean projective plane M constructed above.

The presence of Desargues' law in a projective space allows the space to be coordinatized from a suitable division ring. The principal result of this chapter is the following strong lattice-theoretic version of this coordinatization theorem.

13.4: *If Desargues' law holds in a geomodular lattice L of dimension 3 or more, then L is isomorphic to the lattice of all subspaces of a vector space over some division ring Δ. In particular, every Arguesian geomodular lattice of dimension 3 or more is isomorphic to the lattice of all subspaces of a vector space over some division ring.*[5]

Observe that inasmuch as the lattice of subspaces of a vector space has a representation of type 1 and hence is Arguesian, 13.3 and 13.4 combine to show that *Desargues' law holds in a geomodular lattice L if and only if L is Arguesian.*

PROOF OF 13.4: The proof of 13.4 is made in several steps. The main part is to construct the division ring Δ and an isomorphism of a quotient sublattice of L onto the lattice of subspaces of a vector space V over Δ.[6] The proof is then completed by extending this isomorphism to an isomorphism of L onto the lattice of all subspaces of an extension of V.

Let 0 and 1 denote the least and greatest elements of L, respectively. Choose an element $w \in L$, which will remain fixed throughout the proof, such that

$$w \prec 1,$$

and let W denote the set of atoms not less than w, $W = \{p \in L \mid 0 \prec p$ and $p \nleq w\}$.

The assumption that the lattice L is subdirectly irreducible and has

---

[5] G. Birkhoff [12], O. Frink [39]. The phrase "of dimension 3 or more" allows infinite dimensional lattices.

[6] The approach here is essentially due to Artin [2]; see also Jónsson and Monk [63].

dimension at least 3 implies the following two lemmas, which will be needed at several points in the proof.

A. If a and b are two-dimensional elements in L, then $a/0 \cong b/0$.

Assuming that $a \neq b$, pick an atom $p \leq a$ with $p \not\leq b$, and an atom $q \leq b$ with $q \not\leq a$, and set $x = p \vee q$. Clearly, both $a \wedge x$ and $b \wedge x$ are atoms. If $a \wedge b$ is an atom, choose an atom $r \leq p \vee q$ with $r \neq p$ and $r \neq q$ (here we use 13.2), and observe that $r \wedge a = r \wedge b = 0$, while $r \vee a = r \vee b = a \vee b$, whence $a/0 \cong b/0$. This shows that, under any circumstances, $a/0 \cong x/0 \cong b/0$, the desired result.

B. If p and q are distinct atoms in W, then there exists an atom $r \in W$ such that $r \not\leq p \vee q$.

For as L has dimension at least 3, the sublattice $w/0$ has dimension at least 2, and we infer that $w/0$ contains an atom u that is distinct from the atom $v = (p \vee q) \wedge w$. $p \neq u$ since $p \not\leq w$, and 13.2 yields the existence of an atom r, distinct from p and u, such that $r \leq p \vee u$. Now $p \leq r \vee u$, and as $p \not\leq w$, we see that $r \not\leq w$. The condition $r \leq p \vee q$ implies that $p \vee q = r \vee p \geq u$ and hence that $v = (p \vee q) \wedge w = u$, contrary to the choice of u. Thus $r \not\leq p \vee q$.

An automorphism f of L is defined to be a *dilation* if $f(x) = x$ for all $x \leq w$. A dilation f is called a *translation* if, for every $p, q \in W$,

$$(p \vee f(p)) \wedge w = (q \vee f(q)) \wedge w.$$

When f is a translation, we define the *trace* of f to be that element $tr\, f$ such that

$$tr\, f = (p \vee f(p)) \wedge w \qquad \text{all } p \in W.$$

The identity automorphism of L is certainly a translation. In addition, note that if $p \in W$, then $p \wedge w = 0$ and $f(p) \wedge f(w) = f(p) \wedge w = 0$, whence $f(p) \in W$ whenever $p \in W$. Further for any $p \in W$,

$$p \vee tr\, f = p \vee ((p \vee f(p)) \wedge w) = (p \vee f(p)) \wedge (p \vee w)$$
$$= p \vee f(p) = f(p) \vee tr\, f.$$

Consequently, if we further have that $f(p) \neq p$ for some $p \in W$, then $tr\, f \succ 0$. It follows that *if a translation f is different from the identity, then $tr\, f$ is an atom, and $f(p) \neq p$ for every $p \in W$.*

C. If f is a translation, $p, q \in W$ and $q \not\leq p \vee f(p)$, then

$$f(q) = (q \vee tr\, f) \wedge [f(p) \vee ((p \vee q) \wedge w)].$$

To prove this, recall that $q \vee tr\, f = q \vee f(q) \geq f(q)$. Also from the fact that $q \leq p \vee q = p \vee ((p \vee q) \wedge w)$ and f is a translation we get that $f(q)$

$\leq f(p) \vee ((p \vee q) \wedge w)$. Now the inequality $q \vee tr f \geq f(p)$ yields that $q \leq f(p) \vee tr f = p \vee f(p)$, contrary to assumption. Therefore $q \vee tr f \neq f(p) \vee ((p \vee q) \wedge w)$, and the formula of C follows.

D. If f and g are translations such that $f(p) = g(p)$ for some $p \in W$, then $f = g$.

To prove D, we first show that if $f(p) = g(p)$ and $f(q) = g(q)$ for two distinct atoms $p, q \in W$, then $f = g$. Under these assumptions, if r is an atom with $r \not\leq p \vee q$, then

$$r = (r \vee p) \wedge (r \vee q) = [p \vee ((p \vee r) \wedge w)] \wedge [q \vee ((q \vee r) \wedge w)],$$

and since f and g are automorphisms of L that agree on the elements p, q, $(p \vee r) \wedge w$, and $(q \vee r) \wedge w$, we infer that $f(r) = g(r)$. If $r \leq p \vee q$, then using B, we pick an atom $s \in W$ with $s \not\leq p \vee q$ and invoke the preceding sentence to obtain that $f(s) = g(s)$, and as $r \not\leq p \vee s$, the preceding sentence again yields that $f(r) = g(r)$. Thus f and g agree on all the atoms of L, and hence they must be equal.

Now suppose that $f(p) = g(p)$ for some $p \in W$. Choosing an atom $q \in W$ with $q \not\leq p \vee f(p)$ and invoking C, we obtain that

$$f(q) = (q \vee tr\, f) \wedge [f(p) \vee ((p \vee q) \wedge w)]$$
$$= (q \vee tr\, g) \wedge [g(p) \vee ((p \vee q) \wedge w)] = g(q).$$

Hence the preceding paragraph applies, yielding that $f = g$.

E. If $p, q \in W$, then there exists a unique translation f such that $f(p) = q$.

We may assume that $p \neq q$, since otherwise the identity translation meets the requirements of E, Set

$$u = (p \vee q) \wedge w.$$

As suggested by C, whenever $r \in W$ and $r \not\leq p \vee q$, define

$$f(r) = (r \vee u) \wedge [q \vee ((p \vee r) \wedge w)].$$

Then

$$r \vee f(r) = r \vee [(r \vee u) \wedge [q \vee ((p \vee r) \wedge w)]]$$
$$= (r \vee u) \wedge [r \vee q \vee ((p \vee r) \wedge w)]$$
$$= (r \vee u) \wedge (p \vee q \vee r) = r \vee u,$$

whence $f(r) \in W$ and $(r \vee f(r)) \wedge w = u$. In defining $f(r)$ when $r \leq p \vee q$, we need to be more elaborate. Suppose that $r \in W$ and $r \leq p \vee q$. For each $s \in W$ with $s \not\leq p \vee q$, define

$$f_s(r) = (p \vee q) \wedge [f(s) \vee ((r \vee s) \wedge w)].$$

Again $r \vee f_s(r) = p \vee q = r \vee u$, so $f_s(r) \in W$ and $(r \vee f_s(r)) \wedge w = u$. Next we show that $f_s(r)$ is independent of the choice of s.

Suppose s and t are distinct atoms in W with $s, t \not\leq p \vee q$. Set

$$s_1 = (p \vee s) \wedge w, \qquad t_1 = (p \vee t) \wedge w,$$
$$s_2 = (r \vee s) \wedge w, \qquad t_2 = (r \vee t) \wedge w,$$

and observe that

$$p \vee s_1 = p \vee s, \qquad f(s) \vee s_1 = q \vee s_1, \qquad s \vee s_2 = s \vee r,$$

with corresponding formulas for s replaced by t.

When $u \leq s \vee t$, we have $s \vee t = f(s) \vee f(t)$, and hence $(s \vee t) \wedge w = (f(s) \vee f(t)) \wedge w$. The last equality also holds when $u \not\leq s \vee t$. For in this case $(s \vee f(s)) \wedge (t \vee f(t)) = u \leq p \vee q$, so that the triples $\langle s, t, p \rangle$ and $\langle f(s), f(t), q \rangle$ are centrally perspective, whence they are axially perspective; i.e.,

$$(s \vee t) \wedge (f(s) \vee f(t)) \leq [(s \vee p) \wedge (f(s) \vee q)] \vee [(t \vee p) \wedge (f(t) \vee q)]$$
$$= [(p \vee s_1) \wedge (q \vee s_1)] \vee [(p \vee t_1) \wedge (q \vee t_1)] = s_1 \vee t_1 \leq w.$$

$f(s) \neq f(t)$ since $s \vee u \neq t \vee u$, and since $s \vee t \vee f(s) \vee f(t) = s \vee t \vee u$, we infer that $(s \vee t) \wedge (f(s) \vee f(t))$ is an atom equal to

$$(1) \qquad\qquad (s \vee t) \wedge w = (f(s) \vee f(t)) \wedge w.$$

Now under any circumstances

$$f_s(p) = (p \vee q) \wedge (f(s) \vee s_1) = (p \vee q) \wedge (q \vee s_1) = q.$$

Also, the calculations in the first paragraph show that $f_s(q) \not\leq w$ and that $f_s(q) \neq q$. Consequently, if $p \vee q/0$ contains precisely three atoms, then $f_s(q) = p$. In other words, if $p \vee q/0$ contains precisely three atoms, then $f_s(r) = f_t(r)$. We can assume, therefore, that $p \vee q/0$ contains at least four atoms.

If $r \leq s \vee t$, we have $s_2 = t_2 = (s \vee t) \wedge w \leq f(s) \vee f(t)$. This means that $f(s) \vee s_2 = f(t) \vee t_2$, and hence

$$f_s(r) = (p \vee q) \wedge (f(s) \vee s_2) = (p \vee q) \wedge (f(t) \vee t_2) = f_t(r).$$

Therefore we can further assume that $r \not\leq s \vee t$.

Suppose $u \not\leq t$. Set $v = (s \vee t) \wedge w$. A straightforward calculation yields $v \vee s_2 = v \vee t_2$, and because of (1) it follows that $f(s) \vee f(t) \vee s_2 \vee t_2 = f(s) \vee f(t) \vee s_2$ is a three-dimensional element. Therefore $(f(s) \vee f(t)) \wedge (s_2 \vee t_2) = v$, and we infer that $\langle f(s), s_2, s \rangle$ and $\langle f(t), t_2, t \rangle$ are centrally and hence axially perspective:

$$(f(s) \vee s_2) \wedge (f(t) \vee t_2) \leq [(f(s) \vee s) \wedge (f(t) \vee t)] \vee [(s_2 \vee s) \wedge (t_2 \vee t)]$$
$$= [(s \vee u) \wedge (t \vee u)] \vee [(s \vee r) \wedge (t \vee r)] = u \vee r = p \vee q.$$

And this inequality again gives us that $f_s(r) = f_t(r)$. If $u \leq s \vee t$, then inasmuch as $p \vee q/0$ and hence $p \vee s/0$ contains at least four atoms, there is an atom $z \leq p \vee s$ that is distinct from p, s, and s_1. Since necessarily $z \in W, z \nleq p \vee q$, and $z \nleq s \vee t$, the preceding calculations applied to s and z and then to z and t show that $f_s(r) = f_z(r) = f_t(r)$. Thus $f_s(r)$ does not depend on s.

Now define, for each $r \in W$ with $r \leq p \vee q$,

$$f(r) = f_s(r) \qquad \text{any } s \in W, s \nleq p \vee q.$$

At this point we need to derive the following property: If $s, t \in W, s \neq t$, $0 \prec v \leq w$, and $s \leq t \vee v$, then $f(s) \leq f(t) \vee v$. The first case to handle is when $t \vee v = p \vee q$. In this situation $v = u$, and inasmuch as $f(s), f(t) \leq p \vee q$, it follows that $f(t) \vee v = p \vee q \geq f(s)$. If $t \vee v \neq p \vee q$ but $s \leq p \vee q$, then $t \nleq p \vee q$ and $v \nleq p \vee q$, whence

$$f(s) = (p \vee q) \wedge (f(t) \vee ((s \vee t) \wedge w))$$
$$\leq f(t) \vee ((s \vee t) \wedge w) = f(t) \vee v.$$

Finally, if $t \vee v \neq p \vee q$, $t \nleq p \vee q$, and $s \nleq p \vee q$, then by (1),

$$v = (s \vee t) \wedge w = (f(s) \vee f(t)) \wedge w \leq f(s) \vee f(t),$$

yielding $f(s) \leq f(t) \vee v$.

We can now complete the definition of the map f. If $x \in L$ and $x \leq w$, we define $f(x) = x$. If $x \nleq w$, then $x \wedge w \prec x$ and there is an atom $s \in W$ such that $s \vee (x \wedge w) = x$, so we define

$$f(x) = f(s) \vee (x \wedge w).$$

This definition also does not depend on the atom s. For if $t \in W, t \neq s$, and $t \vee (x \wedge w) = x$, then $v = (s \vee t) \wedge x \wedge w \succ 0$ and $s \leq t \vee v$, and applying the property derived in the preceding paragraph, we see that $f(s) \leq f(t) \vee v \leq f(t) \vee (x \wedge w)$ and hence that $f(s) \vee (x \wedge w) = f(t) \vee (x \wedge w)$.

It is clear that the function f is order-preserving, and it is easy to check that its restriction to W is one-to-one. It also preserves joins of atoms: If $r, s \in W$, then $r \vee s = r \vee v = s \vee v$, where $v = (r \vee s) \wedge w$, whence $f(r \vee s) = f(r) \vee v = f(s) \vee v = f(r) \vee f(s)$.

Having defined f, we interchange the roles of p and q and define a function g in exactly the same way we defined f except with p and q replacing each other. All the properties obtained above for f also hold for g. Moreover, if $r \in W$ and $r \nleq p \vee q$,

$$gf(r) = (f(r) \vee u) \wedge [p \vee ((q \vee f(r)) \wedge w)]$$
$$= (r \vee u) \wedge (p \vee r) = r,$$

and interchanging p and q, we obtain that $fg(r) = r$. When $r \leq p \vee q$, we have to work a little harder. Pick any $s \in W, s \nleq p \vee q$. Then $gf(r) = (p \vee q) \wedge (g(s) \vee v_1)$, where $v_1 = (f(r) \vee s) \wedge w$. Also, $r \vee g(s) = r \vee v_2$, where $v_2 = (r \vee g(s)) \wedge w$, and therefore

$$f(r) \vee s = f(r) \vee fg(s) = f(r \vee g(s)) = f(r \vee v_2) = f(r) \vee v_2.$$

This shows that $v_1 = v_2$ and hence that $r \vee g(s) \geq v_1$. Thus $r \leq g(s) \vee v_1$, and we infer that $r = (p \vee q) \wedge (g(s) \vee v_1) = gf(r)$. Again, symmetry yields that $fg(r) = r$. It now follows that the functions f and g are inverses of each, and we conclude that f is an automorphism of L and hence a translation. This completes the proof of E.

An immediate corollary of E is:

F. If $0 \prec u \leq w$, then there is a translation f such that $tr\, f = u$.

Let G denote the collection of all translations together with the operation of composition of functions. We have already remarked that the identity automorphism of L belongs to G, and if f is any translation, then it is clear the inverse f^{-1} of f is also a translation.

G. G is an abelian group. In addition, if $f, g \in G$, then tr $fg \leq tr\, f \vee tr\, g$.

To show that G is an abelian group, we need to show that it is closed under the operation of composition of functions and that this operation is commutative. Let $f, g \in G$. In any case fg is a dilation.

Observe that if p and q are distinct atoms in W and $u = (p \vee q) \wedge w$, then $p \vee q = p \vee u = q \vee u$, and this implies that $g(p) \vee g(q) = g(p) \vee u = g(q) \vee u$ and that $fg(p) \vee fg(q) = fg(p) \vee u = fg(q) \vee u$.

Next, we need to prove that if $fg(p) = p$ for some $p \in W$, then fg is the identity automorphism. Suppose $p \in W$ and $fg(p) = p$. Note that under these circumstances we must have $tr\, f = tr\, g = v$. If $q \nleq p \vee v$, then $g(q) \nleq p \vee v$, and applying C with p and q replaced by $g(p)$ and $g(q)$ respectively, we get

$$fg(q) = (g(q) \vee v) \wedge [fg(p) \vee ((g(p) \vee g(q)) \wedge w)]$$
$$= (q \vee v) \wedge (p \vee ((p \vee q) \wedge w)) = (q \vee v) \wedge (p \vee q) = q.$$

If $q \leq p \vee v$, then picking an atom $r \in W$ with $r \nleq p \vee v$, we know that $fg(r) = r$, and the preceding calculation with r replacing p gives us $fg(q) = q$. Thus fg is the identity.

Now we prove that if p and q are distinct atoms of W, then

$$(2) \qquad\qquad (p \vee fg(p)) \wedge w = (q \vee fg(q)) \wedge w.$$

If $fg(p) \vee fg(q) = p \vee q$, then in view of the preceding paragraph it is clear that (2) holds, so we may assume that $fg(p) \vee fg(q) \neq p \vee q$. In this case the calculations in the second paragraph show that the triples $\langle p, fg(p), g(p) \rangle$ and $\langle q, fg(q), g(q) \rangle$ are centrally perspective and hence axially perspective:

$$(p \vee fg(p)) \wedge (q \vee fg(q)) \leq [(p \vee g(p)) \wedge (q \vee g(q))]$$
$$\vee [(g(p) \vee fg(p)) \wedge (g(q) \vee fg(q))].$$

And if $tr\,f$, $tr\,g \not\le p \vee q$, it follows that $p \vee fg(p)) \wedge (q \vee fg(q)) \le$ $tr\,g \vee tr\,f \le w$, which implies (2). Suppose either $tr\,f \le p \vee q$ or $tr\,g \le p \vee q$, say $tr\,g \le p \vee q$. If $p \vee q/0$ contains exactly three atoms and neither f nor g is the identity, then $g(p) = q$ and $g(q) = p$, and as $f(p) \vee f(q) = f(p) \vee tr\,g = f(q) \vee tr\,g$, we must also have $gf(p) = f(q) = fg(p)$ and $gf(q) = f(p) = fg(q)$. Therefore

$$g((p \vee fg(p)) \wedge (q \vee fg(q))) = (g(p) \vee gf(q)) \wedge (g(q) \vee gf(p))$$
$$= (q \vee fg(q)) \wedge (p \vee fg(p)),$$

and as g is not the identity, this ensures that $(p \vee fg(p)) \wedge (q \vee fg(q)) \le w$ and hence that (2) holds. On the other hand, if $p \vee q/0$ contains at least four distinct atoms, $v \le w$ is an atom distinct from $tr\,f$ and $tr\,g$, and $z \le p \vee v$ is an atom distinct from p, v, and $(p \vee v) \wedge (q \vee tr\,f)$, then $tr\,f$, $tr\,g \not\le p \vee z$, and $tr\,f$, $tr\,g \not\le q \vee z$, and the preceding results show that

$$(p \vee fg(p)) \wedge w = (z \vee fg(z) \wedge w = (q \vee fg(q)) \wedge w.$$

Hence fg is a translation.

At this point observe that

$$tr\,f \vee tr\,g = ((p \vee g(p)) \wedge w) \vee ((g(p) \vee fg(p)) \wedge w)$$
$$= [((p \vee g(p)) \wedge w) \vee g(p) \vee fg(p)] \wedge w$$
$$= [p \vee g(p) \vee fg(p)] \wedge w \ge tr\,fg.$$

If $tr\,f \ne tr\,g$ and $p \in W$, then $g(p) \not\le p \vee f(p)$, and applying C with $q = g(p)$, we get

$$fg(p) = (g(p) \vee tr\,f) \wedge (f(p) \vee tr\,g).$$

The righthand side of this equation is symmetric in f and g, so $fg(p) = gf(p)$ and hence $fg = gf$. If $tr\,f = tr\,g$, we use F to obtain a translation h, different from the identity, such that $tr\,h \ne tr\,f$. As just seen, $hf = fh$ and $hg = gh$. Also, hf and f have different traces, since otherwise the preceding paragraph shows that $h = (hf)f^{-1}$ and f have the same trace, contrary to the choice of h. Consequently $hgf = ghf = hfg$, and we conclude that $gf = fg$. The proof of G is therefore complete.

Let E denote the collection of all endomorphisms of G. For a translation $f \in G$ and an endomorphism $\sigma \in E$, we write the image of f under σ as

$$f^{\sigma}.$$

Given two endomorphisms $\sigma, \tau \in E$, we define the endomorphisms $\sigma + \tau$ and $\sigma\tau$ by

$$f^{\sigma+\tau} = f^{\sigma}f^{\tau} \quad \text{and} \quad f^{\sigma\tau} = (f^{\sigma})^{\tau}.$$

It is well known that E together with these two operations is a ring.

We define an endomorphism $\sigma \in E$ to be *trace-preserving* if

$$tr\,f^{\sigma} \le tr\,f \quad \text{all } f \in G.$$

If Δ denotes the collection of all trace-preserving endomorphisms, then it is clear from the second part of G that Δ is a subring of E.

H. If f and g are translations with different traces, neither of which is the identity translation, and $p, q \in W$ are such that $q \leq p \vee tr\, f$, then $(p \vee tr\, g) \wedge (q \vee tr\, gf^{-1}) \in W$.

     If $s = (p \vee tr\, g) \wedge (q \vee tr\, gf^{-1})$, then the reader can easily check that $s \vee tr\, gf^{-1} = q \vee tr\, gf^{-1}$ and $s \wedge w = 0$, from which the desired conclusion follows.

I. If f and g are translations with different traces and neither is the identity translation, then for any $p \in W$ and $\sigma \in \Delta$,

$$g^{\sigma}(p) = (p \vee tr\, g) \wedge (f^{\sigma}(p) \vee tr\, gf^{-1}).$$

     It is certainly true that $g^{\sigma}(p) \leq p \vee tr\, g^{\sigma} = p \vee tr\, g$ and

$$g^{\sigma}(p) = (gf^{-1})^{\sigma}(f^{\sigma}(p)) \leq f^{\sigma}(p) \vee tr\, (gf^{-1})^{\sigma} = f^{\sigma}(p) \vee tr\, gf^{-1}.$$

Therefore, if $s = (p \vee tr\, g) \wedge (f^{\sigma}(p) \vee tr\, gf^{-1})$, then $g^{\sigma}(p) \leq s$, and as s is an atom by H, we infer that $g^{\sigma}(p) = s$.

J. If $f \in G$ is different from the identity translation and $\sigma, \tau \in \Delta$ are such that $f^{\sigma} = f^{\tau}$, then $\sigma = \tau$.

     For let $h \in G$, and let $g \in G$ be different from the identity translation such that $tr\, g \neq tr\, f$ and $tr\, g \neq tr\, h$. Applying I to f and g, we see that $g^{\sigma} = g^{\tau}$, and again applying it to g and h, we see that $h^{\sigma} = h^{\tau}$. As h was an arbitrary element of G, we infer that $\sigma = \tau$.

K. If f and k are translations such that $tr\, f = tr\, k$, then there exists $\tau \in \Delta$ such that $f^{\tau} = k$.

     We can assume that $f \neq k$. Choose an atom $p \in W$. If $g \in G$ is such that $tr\, g \neq tr\, f$, then by H and E there is a translation g^{σ} such that

$$g^{\sigma}(p) = (p \vee tr\, g) \wedge (k(p) \vee tr\, gf^{-1}).$$

In this way we define a map $g \rightarrow g^{\sigma}$ of $\{g \in G \,|\, tr\, g \neq tr\, f\}$ to G.
     Suppose g and h are translations, neither of which is the identity translation, such that $tr\, g \neq tr\, f$ and $tr\, h \neq tr\, f$. Then

$$p \vee k(p) = p \vee tr\, k = p \vee tr\, f = f(p) \vee tr\, f,$$

$$g(p) \vee tr\, gf^{-1} = gf^{-1}(f(p)) \vee tr\, gf^{-1} = f(p) \vee tr\, gf^{-1},$$

and $tr\, f \neq tr\, gf^{-1}$, so

$$(p \vee k(p)) \wedge (g(p) \vee tr\, gf^{-1}) = (f(p) \vee tr\, f) \wedge (f(p) \vee tr\, gf^{-1})$$
$$= f(p) \leq h(p) \vee tr\, hf^{-1},$$

whence $\langle p, g(p), h(p) \rangle$ and $\langle k(p), tr\, gf^{-1}, tr\, hf^{-1} \rangle$ are centrally perspective. Hence they are axially perspective,

$$(p \vee g(p)) \wedge (k(p) \vee tr\, gf^{-1}) \leq [(p \vee h(p)) \wedge (k(p) \vee tr\, hf^{-1})]$$
$$\vee [(g(p) \vee h(p)) \wedge (tr\, gf^{-1} \vee tr\, hf^{-1})];$$

i.e., $g^\sigma(p) \leq h^\sigma(p) \vee v$, where $v = (g(p) \vee h(p)) \wedge (tr\, gf^{-1} \vee tr\, hf^{-1})$. But $v \leq g(p) \vee h(p) = g(p) \vee hg^{-1}(g(p)) = g(p) \vee tr\, hg^{-1}$, so that $v = (g(p) \vee h(p)) \wedge w = tr\, hg^{-1} = tr\, gh^{-1}$, whence

$$(3) \qquad\qquad g^\sigma(p) \leq h^\sigma(p) \vee tr\, hg^{-1}.$$

If, in addition, $tr\, g \neq tr\, h$, then it follows from the preceding formula that

$$(4) \qquad\qquad g^\sigma(p) = (p \vee g(p)) \wedge (h^\sigma(p) \vee tr\, hg^{-1}).$$

We can now extend the map σ to all of G. Set $f_0 = f$, and choose two translations f_1 and f_2 such that $tr\, f_0$, $tr\, f_1$ and $tr\, f_2$ are distinct atoms. Set $k = k_0$, $k_1 = f_1^\sigma$, and $k_2 = f_2^\sigma$, and set $\sigma_0 = \sigma$. For $i = 1$ and 2, define the map σ_i of $\{g \in G \,|\, tr\, g \neq tr\, f_i\}$ to G exactly as we defined σ above except with k replaced by k_i and f by f_i: g^{σ_i} is that translation such that

$$g^{\sigma_i}(p) = (p \vee tr\, g) \wedge (k_i(p) \vee tr\, gf_i^{-1}).$$

It is clear that the properties shown to hold for σ, in particular (3) and (4), also hold for the σ_i's. Note further that if $i \neq 0$, then $k_i(p) = f_i^\sigma(p) \leq k(p) \vee tr\, ff_i^{-1}$ and hence $k(p) \leq k_i(p) \vee tr\, ff_i^{-1}$, and $k(p) \leq p \vee tr\, k = p \vee tr\, f$, so

$$k(p) \leq (p \vee tr\, f) \wedge (k_i(p) \vee tr\, ff_i^{-1}) = f^{\sigma_i}(p),$$

whence $k = f^{\sigma_i}$ for $i = 1, 2$. When $i \neq 0$ and $j \neq i$, condition (4) yields directly that $f^{\sigma_j} = k_i$. Every translation belongs to the domain of at least two of the σ_i's. If g is a translation for which $tr\, g \neq tr\, f_i$, $tr\, g \neq tr\, f_j$, and $i \neq j$, using condition (4) for σ_j we see that

$$g^{\sigma_i}(p) = (p \vee tr\, g) \wedge (k_i(p) \vee tr\, gf_i^{-1})$$
$$= (p \vee tr\, g) \wedge (f_i^{\sigma_j}(p) \vee tr\, gf_i^{-1}) = g^{\sigma_j}(p).$$

Therefore any two of the σ_i's agree wherever they are both defined, and it follows that σ_0, σ_1, and σ_2 have a common extension τ to all of G.

Observe that in view of the definition of τ, if g is any translation, then $p \vee g^\tau(p) \leq p \vee tr\, g$. This yields that $tr\, g^\tau \leq tr\, g$, so that map τ is at least trace-preserving.

Observe next that if g and h are any two translations, neither the identity translation, then g and h both belong to the domain of at least one σ_i. Using (3) for σ_i, we obtain

$$(5) \qquad\qquad g^\tau(p) \leq h^\tau(p) \vee tr\, gh^{-1}.$$

Replacing g by gh in (5), we get $(gh)^\tau(p) \leq h^\tau(p) \vee tr\, g$, and because g and h commute, interchanging g and h, we get $(gh)^\tau(p) \leq g^\tau(p) \vee tr\, h$. If we further stipulate that $tr\ g \neq tr\ h$, then

$$(gh)^\tau(p) = (g^\tau(p) \vee tr\ h) \wedge (h^\tau(p) \vee tr\ g).$$

On the other hand,

$$g^\tau h^\tau(p) \leq g^\tau h^\tau(p) \vee tr\ g^\tau = h^\tau(p) \vee tr\ g^\tau,$$

and since g^τ and h^τ commute, $g^\tau h^\tau(p) \leq g^\tau(p) \vee tr\ h^\tau$. Thus

$$g^\tau h^\tau(p) = (g^\tau(p) \vee tr\ h^\tau) \wedge (h^\tau(p) \vee tr\ g^\tau) = (gh)^\tau(p),$$

and we infer that $(gh)^\tau = g^\tau h^\tau$ whenever $tr\ g \neq tr\ h$. In the case that $tr\ g = tr\ h$, pick f_i with $tr\ f_i \neq tr\ g$, and since $tr\ gh = tr\ g$ and $tr\ h \neq tr\ hf_i$, we can use the preceding case to obtain that

$$(gh)^\tau f_i^\tau = (ghf_i)^\tau = g^\tau(hf_i)^\tau = g^\tau h^\tau f^\tau$$

and hence that $(gh)^\tau = g^\tau h^\tau$. Thus $\tau \in \Delta$, and as we have already noted that $f^\tau = k$, the proof of K is complete.

L. Δ is a division ring.

Let σ and τ be any elements of Δ, σ nonzero. Pick a translation f that is not the identity translation. Then by K there exists $\rho \in \Delta$ such that $f^\tau = (f^\sigma)^\rho = f^{\sigma\rho}$, and J yields that $\sigma\rho = \tau$. This guarantees that Δ is a division ring.

Since Δ is a division ring, the abelian group G is a vector space over Δ. Here, of course, G is a multiplicative abelian group, and the scalars in Δ act as exponents on the vectors in G. Furthermore, K shows that the sets

$$\{f \in G \mid tr\ f \leq v\} \qquad 0 \prec v \leq w,$$

are precisely the one-dimensional subspaces of G.

For each $x \leq w$, define

$$\varphi(x) = \{f \in G \mid tr\ f \leq x\}.$$

This defines a map φ of the quotient sublattice $w/0$ to the lattice of all sub-spaces of the vector space G.

M. φ is an isomorphism of $w/0$ onto the lattice of all subspaces of G.

It is easy to check that φ is one-to-one and that it and its inverse are order-preserving, so we only need to verify that φ is onto. First we prove: If $u, v \leq w$, then $\varphi(u \vee v) = \varphi(u) \vee \varphi(v)$. To prove this, we need to show that if $f \in G$ is such that $tr\ f \leq u \vee v$, then f belongs to the subspace of G spanned by $\varphi(u)$ and $\varphi(v)$. Set $z = tr\ f$. We can certainly assume that $0 \prec z \nleq u, v$ and that $u \wedge v = 0$ (if the latter condition does not hold, we replace v by a complement of $u \wedge v$ in $v/0$). In addition, we can assume that u and v are atoms; again if this is not the case, we replace u and v by the atoms $u \wedge (v \vee z)$ and

$v \wedge (u \vee z)$, respectively. Under these conditions, choose an atom $p \in W$ and observe that

$$q = (p \vee u) \wedge (f(p) \vee v) \in W.$$

Let g and h be translations such that $g(p) = q$ and $h(q) = f(p)$. Then $tr\, g = = u$, $tr\, h = v$, and because of D, we must have $f = hg$. Thus $f \in \varphi(u) \vee \varphi(v)$, as desired. Now suppose that S is a subspace of G. Set $x = \bigvee \{tr\, f \,|\, f \in S\}$. Since φ is order-preserving and S is the join of its one-dimensional subspaces, we at least have $\varphi(x) \supseteq S$. On the other hand, if $f \in \varphi(x)$, then there are finitely many translations $f_1, \ldots, f_n \in S$ such that $tr\, f \leq tr\, f_1 \vee \cdots \vee tr\, f_n$. And as we have just proved, this implies that

$$f \in \varphi(tr\, f_1 \vee \cdots \vee tr\, f_n) = \varphi(tr\, f_1) \vee \cdots \vee \varphi(tr\, f_n) \subseteq S.$$

Consequently $\varphi(x) = S$, and the map φ is onto.

Having the vector space G, let H be a vector space over Δ that contains G as a subspace in such a way that H/G is a one-dimensional vector space. Again we write H as a multiplicative abelian group with the scalars in Δ acting on the elements of H as exponents. Since H/G is a one-dimensional, there is a vector $e \in H$ such that each vector in H is uniquely of the form

$$e^\sigma f, \qquad f \in G \text{ and } \sigma \in \Delta.$$

We will complete the proof of 13.4 by extending φ to an isomorphism of L onto the lattice of all subspaces of H.

Choose an atom $p \in W$ which will remain fixed for the rest of the proof. For each atom $q \in W$, let f_q be that translation such that $f_q(p) = q$. Note that, for any atom $v \leq w$, the image of the map $q \to f_q$ ($q \leq p \vee v$, $q \in W$) is the entire one-dimensional subspace $\varphi(v)$. Now extend the map φ to W by defining $\varphi(q)$ to be that subspace of H spanned by

$$e f_q.$$

N. If $q, r \in W$ and $0 \prec x \leq w$, then $r \leq q \vee x$ if and only if $\varphi(r) \leq \varphi(q) \vee \varphi(x)$.

Under any circumstance $\varphi(q)$ is spanned by $e f_q$ and $\varphi(r)$ is spanned by $e f_r$. If $r \leq q \vee x$ and h is that translation such that $h(q) = r$, then $tr\, h \leq x$. Moreover, $hf_q = f_r$, and this implies that $ef_r = (ef_q)h$. Consequently $\varphi(r)$ is a subspace of the span of ef_q and h; i.e., $\varphi(r) \subseteq \varphi(q) \vee \varphi(x)$.

Conversely, suppose that $\varphi(r) \subseteq \varphi(q) \vee \varphi(x)$. This says that for some $\sigma \in \Delta$ and some translation $g \in \varphi(x)$,

$$ef_r = (ef_q)^\sigma g = e^\sigma(f_q^\sigma g).$$

Because of our choice of e, we must have $\sigma = 1$, so that $g = f_r f_q^{-1}$. Thus $g(q) = f_r(f_q^{-1}(q)) = r$, and inasmuch as $tr\, g \leq x$, we infer that $r \leq q \vee x$.

The definition of φ is completed using the same technique as in the proof of E. If $x \in L$ and $x \nleq w$, then $x \wedge w \prec x$, and there is an atom $q \in W$ such that $q \vee (x \wedge w) = x$; under these circumstances we define

$$\varphi(x) = \varphi(q) \vee \varphi(x \wedge w).$$

This definition of $\varphi(x)$ is independent of the atom q, and hence defines a function φ on L to the lattice of all subspaces of H. Using N, it is easy to verify that φ is one-to-one, onto, and it and its inverse are order-preserving. Thus L is isomorphic to the lattice of all subspaces of H, and the proof of 13.4 is complete.

The following theorem clarifies the scope of 13.4.

13.5:   *Every subdirectly irreducible, complemented modular lattice of dimension 4 or more is Arguesian.*[7]

PROOF: First we prove that if L is a geomodular lattice of dimension 4 or more, then L is Arguesian. In view of the remark following the statement of 13.4, it is enough to show that Desargues' law holds in L. Let 0 be the least element of L, and let $\langle a_0, a_1, a_2 \rangle$ and $\langle b_0, b_1, b_2 \rangle$ be two triples of atoms in L that are centrally perspective. Again we can assume that the a_i's as well as the b_i's are independent, that each $a_i \neq b_i$, and the element $p = (a_0 \vee b_0) \wedge (a_1 \vee b_1)$ is an atom. Under these assumptions, the element

$$u = a_0 \vee a_1 \vee a_2 \vee b_0 \vee b_1 \vee b_2$$

has dimension at least 3, and the central perspectivity of $\langle a_0, a_1, a_2 \rangle$ and $\langle b_0, b_1, b_2 \rangle$ requires that the dimension of u not exceed 4. As in the classical proof of Desargues' theorem in a projective space of dimension 3 or more, we now consider two cases.

Suppose the dimension of u is 4. In this case

$$v = (a_0 \vee a_1 \vee a_2) \wedge (b_0 \vee b_1 \vee b_2)$$

must have dimension exactly 2. Set

$$z_0 = (a_1 \vee a_2) \wedge (b_1 \vee b_2),$$
$$z_1 = (a_0 \vee a_2) \wedge (b_0 \vee b_2),$$
$$z_2 = (a_0 \vee a_1) \wedge (b_0 \vee b_1).$$

Since $(a_2 \vee b_2) \wedge (a_1 \vee b_1) \geq p > 0$, the element $a_2 \vee b_2 \vee a_1 \vee b_1$ has dimension at most 3, and hence $z_0 > 0$. Similarly, $z_1 > 0$. Furthermore, if $z_0 = z_1$, then inasmuch as $a_1 \vee a_2 \geq z_0$ and $a_0 \vee a_2 \geq z_1$, we would necessarily have

$$a_2 = (a_1 \vee a_2) \wedge (a_0 \vee a_2) = z_0 = z_1,$$

and symmetrically $b_2 = z_0 = z_1 = a_2$, contrary to assumption. Therefore z_0 and z_1 are distinct nonzero elements. But observe that $z_i \leq v$ for each

[7] B. Jónsson [58].

$i = 0, 1, 2$, and as v has dimension 2, we infer that $z_0 \vee z_1 = v \geq z_2$, as desired.

Suppose that u has dimension 3. Using the fact that the dimension of L is 4 or more, pick an atom $q \not\leq u$, and pick an atom $r \leq p \vee q$ that is distinct from p and q. Note that

$$a_i \vee q \vee b_i \vee r = a_i \vee b_i \vee p \vee q = a_i \vee b_i \vee q,$$

whence $c_i = (a_i \vee q) \wedge (b_i \vee r)$ is an atom for each $i = 0, 1, 2$. And since $q, r \not\leq u$ and $a_i \neq b_i$, it follows that each $c_i \neq a_i$. Moreover, the c_i's are necessarily distinct. Now the triples $\langle a_0, a_1, a_2 \rangle$ and $\langle c_0, c_1, c_2 \rangle$ are centrally perspective since

$$(a_0 \vee c_0) \wedge (a_1 \vee c_1) = q \leq a_2 \vee c_2.$$

Also, $a_0 \vee a_1 \vee a_2 \vee c_0 \vee c_1 \vee c_2 = u \vee q$ is a four-dimensional element. Therefore by the preceding paragraph, $\langle a_0, a_1, a_2 \rangle$ and $\langle c_0, c_1, c_2 \rangle$ are axially perspective:

(1) $\quad (a_0 \vee a_1) \wedge (c_0 \vee c_1) \leq [(a_0 \vee a_2) \wedge (c_0 \vee c_2)]$
$$\vee [(a_1 \vee a_2) \wedge (c_1 \vee c_2)].$$

If $i \neq j$, then $u \vee c_i \vee c_j = u \vee q \succ u$, so that $u \wedge (c_i \vee c_j)$ is an atom. A similar argument shows that $(a_i \vee a_j) \wedge (c_i \vee c_j)$, $(b_i \vee b_j) \wedge (c_i \vee c_j)$ and $(a_i \vee a_j) \wedge (b_i \vee b_j)$ are also atoms, and as $(a_i \vee a_j) \wedge (c_i \vee c_j)$ and $(b_i \vee b_j) \wedge (c_i \vee c_j)$ are equal to or less than $u \wedge (c_i \vee c_j)$, it follows that all four atoms coincide:

$$(a_i \vee a_j) \wedge (c_i \vee c_j) = (b_i \vee b_j) \wedge (c_i \vee c_j)$$
$$= u \wedge (c_i \vee c_j) = (a_i \vee a_j) \wedge (b_i \vee b_j).$$

And substituting into (1), we obtain the axial perspectivity of $\langle a_0, a_1, a_2 \rangle$ and $\langle b_0, b_1, b_2 \rangle$. Thus Desargues' law holds in L, and L is Arguesian.

If L is an arbitrary subdirectly irreducible, complemented modular lattice of dimension 4 or more, than by 13.1 there is a compactly generated, complemented modular lattice K containing L as a sublattice. Now K is a direct product of geomodular lattices K_i ($i \in I$), and therefore L is embedded in $X_{i \in I} K_i$. Consequently, since L is subdirectly irreducible, there is some index $h \in I$ such that L is embedded in K_h. The dimension of K_h is necessarily 4 or more, so K_h is Arguesian. Thus L is Arguesian, completing the proof.

Theorems 13.4 and 13.5 give us a clear picture of the geomodular lattices, except for dimension 3. A two-element chain is a geomodular lattice, and it is obviously isomorphic to the lattice of all subspaces of any one-dimensional vector space. A two-dimensional modular lattice with three or more atoms is a geomodular lattice. In this connection, if Δ is a division ring, then the two-dimensional vector space over Δ has exactly $|\Delta| + 1$ one-dimensional subspaces. There is a field of every infinite cardinality, and a finite division ring is a finite field with a prime-power number of elements. Consequently a two-dimensional geomodular lattice L is isomorphic to the lattice of all subspaces of some vector space if and only if the number of atoms in L is either infinite or one more than a prime power. Under any circumstances every two-dimensional geomodular lattice can be embedded in the lattice of all subspaces of some two-dimensional vector space. The non-Arguesian geomodular lattices of dimension 3, of course, are a mystery, while every geomodular lattice of dimension greater than 3 is isomorphic to the lattice of all subspaces of some vector space.

The foregoing remarks combine with 13.1 to give the following general embedding theorem: *Each complemented modular lattice L can be embedded in the direct product of a family of lattices, each of which is either a non-Arguesian geomodular lattice of dimension 3 or the lattice of all subspaces of some vector space; if L is further Arguesian, then L can be embedded in the direct product of a family of lattices, each the lattice of all subspaces of some vector space.*

Observe that if K is the lattice of all subspaces of a vector space V, then concentrating on the group structure of V, it is apparent that K is a sublattice of the lattice of all subgroups of the abelian group V. Further, if each $K_i (i \in I)$ is a sublattice of the lattice of all subgroups of an abelian group V_i, and V is the direct product of the V_i's [i.e., V consists of all functions x with domain I such that $x(i) \in V_i$ and $x(i)$ is the identity for all but finitely many i, with the group operations defined componentwise], then V is an abelian group, and $\mathsf{X}_{i \in I} K_i$ is embedded in the lattice of all subgroups of V. (Proof?) This observation together with the embedding theorem in the preceding paragraph shows that every Arguesian complemented lattice can be embedded in the lattice of all subgroups of some abelian group, and as the lattice of all subgroups of an abelian group has a representation of type 1, we obtain the following theorem alluded to in the opening paragraph of this chapter.

13.6: *If L is a complemented lattice, then the following conditions are equivalent:*

(1) *L has a representation of type* 1.
(2) *L is Arguesian.*
(3) *L can be embedded in the lattice of all subgroups of some abelian group.*[8]

This theorem is false without the assumption of complementation. Jónsson [59] has constructed a simple lattice of dimension 5 that has a representation of type 1 but cannot be embedded in the lattice of all subgroups of an abelian group.

[8] B. Jónsson [59].

14

COMBINATORIAL THEORY

Two of the most challenging open problems encountered in the preceding two chapters—that of embedding any finite lattice in a finite partition lattice and that of describing the non-Arguesian geomodular lattices—arise under the most stringent finiteness conditions. Both of these problems lie in the realm of combinatorial lattice theory, and before passing to a discussion of continuous complemented modular lattices, we will discuss a few of these combinatorial results and problems.

Many combinatorial questions can be expressed as questions involving finite dimensional, semimodular, relatively complemented lattices. This class of lattices is central to combinatorial lattice theory, and customarily its members are referred to as *geometric lattices*. The class of geometric lattices obviously includes all finite dimensional, complemented, modular lattices as well as all finite partition lattices. And although, at the moment, we do not know if each finite lattice can be embedded in a finite partition lattice, we do know that the larger class of geometric lattices does provide such embeddings.

14.1: *Each finite lattice can be embedded in a finite geometric lattice.*[1]

PROOF: It should be pointed out that the proof of 14.1 involves a basic technique for constructing lattices, described in lemmas C, D and E to follow.

To start the proof of 14.1, let L be any finite lattice with least element 0 and greatest element 1. (No problem arises in distinguishing these elements from the integers 0 and 1.) We first observe that something resembling a dimension function can be defined in L.

[1] R. P. Dilworth (unpublished).

125

A. There exists an integer-valued function σ defined in L such that

(1) $\sigma(0) = 0$.
(2) $\sigma(a) > \sigma(b)$ whenever $a > b$.
(3) $\sigma(a \vee b) + \sigma(a \wedge b) \leq \sigma(a) + \sigma(b)$ for all $a, b \in L$.

To show this, define an integer-valued function τ in L by induction as follows:

$$\tau(1) = 0,$$
$$\tau(a) = \tau(a_1) + 1$$

if a is irreducible and $a \prec a_1$, and

$$\tau(a) = max\{\tau(x) + \tau(y) - \tau(x \vee y) \mid a = x \wedge y, a < x \text{ and } a < y\}$$

if a is not irreducible. With this definition we clearly have

$$\tau(a \vee b) + \tau(a \wedge b) \geq \tau(a) + \tau(b)$$

for all $a, b \in L$. Suppose that $a < b$, and suppose that $\tau(x) > \tau(y)$ whenever $a < x < y$. If a is irreducible, then $a \prec a_1 \leq b$, and we have

$$\tau(a) = \tau(a_1) + 1 \geq \tau(b) + 1 > \tau(b).$$

If a is not irreducible, then $a = x \wedge y$, where $a < x \leq b$ and $a < y$, and as $\tau(y) > \tau(x \vee y)$, we obtain

$$\tau(a) \geq \tau(x) + \tau(y) - \tau(x \vee y) > \tau(x) \geq \tau(b).$$

Thus $\tau(a) > \tau(b)$ whenever $a < b$. Now if, for all $a \in L$, we define $\sigma(a) = \tau(0) - \tau(a)$, then it is clear that σ satisfies (1)–(3).

At this point in the proof, we need two new concepts. Given a finite set X, we define a collection $\mathcal{L}$ of subsets of X to be a *lattice of subsets* of X if the null set $\varnothing$ and the set X are in $\mathcal{L}$ and $\mathcal{L}$ is closed under set-intersection; i.e., $A \cap B \in \mathcal{L}$ whenever $A, B \in \mathcal{L}$. Obviously a lattice of subsets of X is a lattice; its partial order is set-inclusion, and the meet of two of its members is their set-intersection.

Let $\mathcal{L}$ be a lattice of subsets of a finite set X. An integer-valued function ρ defined in $\mathcal{L}$ is called a *rank function* if

(1) $\rho(\varnothing) = 0$.
(2) $\rho(A) \geq \rho(B)$ whenever $A \supseteq B$.
(3) $\rho(A \vee B) + \rho(A \cap B) \leq \rho(A) + \rho(B)$ all $A, B \in \mathcal{L}$.
(4) $\rho(A) - \rho(B) \leq |A - B|$ whenever $A \supseteq B$.

We say that the rank function ρ is *strictly increasing* if

(5) $\rho(A) > \rho(B)$ whenever $A \supset B$.

Observe that (2) and (4) combine to show that (4) holds without the restriction $A \supseteq B$, for if A and B are any two sets in $\mathcal{L}$,

$$p(A) - p(B) \leq p(A) - p(A \cap B) \leq |A - A \cap B| = |A - B|.$$

B. There exists a lattice $\mathcal{L}$ of subsets of a finite set, in which a strictly increasing rank function is defined, such that $L \cong \mathcal{L}$. ·

Let σ be the function defined in L given by A, and let I be the collection of all nonzero join-irreducible elements of L. For each $r \in I$ choose a set X_r such that

$$|X_r| = \sigma(r) - \sigma(r_1), \qquad \text{where } r \succ r_1,$$

and such that

$$X_r \cap X_s = \varnothing \qquad \text{when } r \neq s.$$

Set $X = \bigcup_{r \in I} X_r$. And for each $a \in L$, define

$$S_a = \bigcup_{r \in I, r \leq a} X_r.$$

Then $S_0 = \varnothing$, $S_1 = X$, and $S_{a \wedge b} = S_a \cap S_b$ for every $a, b \in L$. Consequently the collection $\mathcal{L} = \{S_a \mid a \in L\}$ is a lattice of subsets of X, and the map $a \rightarrow S_a$ is an isomorphism of L onto $\mathcal{L}$. For each $a \in L$ define

$$p(S_a) = \sigma(a).$$

Certainly p satisfies (1)–(3) and (5). We will show that it also satisfies (4) by induction on $\sigma(a)$. The proof of this requires the following combinatorial formula: For any three sets $S \supseteq T \supseteq U$,

(1) $$|S - U| = |S - T| + |T - U|.$$

[This formula is immediate since $S - U = (S - T) \cup (T - U)$ and $S - T$ and $T - U$ are disjoint.] Now if $a = b$ (and hence if $a = 0$), condition (4) is trivial. Suppose $a \succ b$. Pick a join-irreducible element r such that $r \leq a$ and $r \nleq b$. Then $a = b \vee r$, and we have

$$\sigma(a) - \sigma(b) = \sigma(b \vee r) - \sigma(b) \leq \sigma(r) - \sigma(b \wedge r).$$

Also, as r is join-irreducible, $r \succ r_1 \geq b \wedge r$, and this together with the assumption of the induction yields

$$\sigma(a) - \sigma(b) \leq \sigma(r) - \sigma(r_1) + \sigma(r_1) - \sigma(b \wedge r)$$
$$\leq \sigma(r) - \sigma(r_1) + |S_{r_1} - S_{b \wedge r}|.$$

By the choice of X_r we have $\sigma(r) - \sigma(r_1) = |X_r|$. In addition, there is no join-irreducible element s with $s < r$ and $s \nleq r_1$, and if s is a join-irreducible element with $s \leq r_1$ and $s \nleq b \wedge r$, then $s \leq a$ and $s \nleq b$. Consequently

$$\sigma(a) - \sigma(b) \leq |X_r| + |S_{r_1} - S_{b \wedge r}| \leq |S_a - S_b|.$$

Finally, suppose that $a > b$. Choosing a_1 such that $a \succ a_1 \geq b$, the preceding formula together with (1) and the assumption of the induction yields that

$$\sigma(a) - \sigma(b) = \sigma(a) - \sigma(a_1) + \sigma(a_1) - \sigma(b) \leq |S_a - S_{a_1}|$$
$$+ |S_{a_1} - S_b| = |S_a - S_b|,$$

completing the proof of B.

For the remainder of the proof of 14.1, *let X be any finite set and $\mathfrak{L}$ be any lattice of subsets of X in which a strictly increasing rank function ρ is defined.*

C. For each subset $S \subseteq X$, define

$$\pi(S) = \min \{\rho(A) + |S - A| \,|\, A \in \mathfrak{L}\}.$$

Then the function π so defined is a rank function defined in the lattice of all subsets of X, and the restriction of π to $\mathfrak{L}$ coincides with ρ.

To show that π is a rank function, we need two additional combinatorial formulas: For any sets S, T, U and W,

(2) $$|S - U| \leq |S - T| + |T - U|,$$

(3) $$|S \cup T - U \cup W| + |S \cap T - U \cap W| \leq |S - U| + |T - W|.$$

[Formula (2) is immediate since $S - U \subseteq (S - T) \cup (T - U)$ and $S - T$ and $T - U$ are disjoint. Formula (3) holds inasmuch as any element which is in exactly one of the two sets on the left-hand side of (3) is also in exactly one of the two sets on the right, and an element in both sets on the left is also in both sets on the right.] Now $\rho(\varnothing) + |\varnothing - \varnothing| = 0$, so we certainly have $\pi(\varnothing) = 0$. If $S \supseteq T$, then $\rho(A) + |S - A| \geq \rho(A) + |T - A|$ for all $A \in \mathfrak{L}$, whence $\pi(S) \geq \pi(T)$. If S and T are any subsets of X, there are subsets A, $B \in \mathfrak{L}$ such that $\pi(S) = \rho(A) + |S - A|$ and $\pi(T) = \rho(B) + |T - B|$. And using formula (3) and the fact that $A \vee B \supseteq A \cup B$, we get

$$\pi(S \cup T) + \pi(S \cap T) \leq \rho(A \vee B) + |S \cup T - A \vee B| + \rho(A \cap B)$$
$$+ |S \cap T - A \cap B|$$
$$\leq \rho(A \vee B) + \rho(A \cap B) + |S \cup T - A \cup B|$$
$$+ |S \cap T - A \cap B|$$
$$\leq \rho(A) + \rho(B) + |S - A| + |T - B|$$
$$= \pi(S) + \pi(T).$$

Again, if $S \subseteq T$, choosing $A \in \mathfrak{L}$ so that $\pi(S) = \rho(A) + |S - A|$, and using (1), we obtain

$$\pi(T) \leq \rho(A) + |T - A| \leq \rho(A) + |T - S| + |S - A| = \pi(S) + |T - S|.$$

Thus π is a rank function. Finally, if $A \in \mathfrak{L}$, then for any choice of $B \in \mathfrak{L}$ we have

$$\pi(A) \leq \rho(A) + |A - A| = \rho(A) \leq \rho(B) + |A - B|,$$

and it follows that $\pi(A) = \rho(A)$. completing the proof of C.

Before stating the next lemma, recall our observation in Chap. 3 that if a map $S \to S^c$ of the set of all subsets of X to itself is a closure operator and satisfies the exchange axiom, then the lattice of all closed subsets of X is a semimodular lattice in which each element is a join of atoms. In addition, 4.1 guarantees that this lattice of closed subsets is a finite geometric lattice.

D. For each subset $S \subseteq X$, define

$$S^\pi = \{x \in X \mid \pi(S \cup \{x\}) = \pi(S)\}.$$

Then the map $S \to S^\pi$ of the set of all subsets of X to itself is a closure operator which satisfies the exchange axiom. If K_π denotes the geometric lattice of all closed subsets of X, then the dimension of any closed subset S in K_π is precisely $\pi(S)$.

First note the following: If $T \subseteq S \subseteq X$ and $\pi(S) = \pi(T)$, then $\pi(S \cup U) = \pi(T \cup U)$ for any subset $U \subseteq X$. For we have

$$\pi(S \cup U) = \pi(T \cup U \cup S) \leq \pi(T \cup U) + \pi(S) - \pi((T \cup U) \cap S)$$
$$\leq \pi(T \cup U) + \pi(S) - \pi(T)$$
$$= \pi(T \cup U) \leq \pi(S \cup U).$$

It is clear that each $S^\pi \supseteq S$. If $S \subseteq T$ and $x \in S^\pi$, then $\pi(S \cup \{x\}) = \pi(S)$, and using the result of the preceding paragraph, we get

$$\pi(T \cup \{x\}) = \pi(S \cup \{x\} \cup T) = \pi(S \cup T) = \pi(T),$$

so that $x \in T^\pi$, whence $S^\pi \subseteq T^\pi$. Repeated application of the result of the preceding paragraph yields $\pi(S^\pi) = \pi(S)$. Consequently, if $x \in (S^\pi)^\pi$, then

$$\pi(S) = \pi(S^\pi) = \pi(S^\pi \cup \{x\}) = \pi(S \cup \{x\}),$$

and we infer that $x \in S^\pi$ and hence that $(S^\pi)^\pi = S^\pi$. Thus the map $S \to S^\pi$ is a closure operator.

At this point notice that if $x \notin S^\pi$, then $\pi(S \cup \{x\}) = \pi(S) + 1$. This is true because

$$\pi(S \cup \{x\}) \leq \pi(S) + |S \cup \{x\} - S| = \pi(S) + 1,$$

while necessarily $\pi(S \cup \{x\}) > \pi(S)$.

Now to show that the closure operator $S \to S^\pi$ satisfies the exchange axiom, suppose $x \in (S \cup \{y\})^\pi$ but $x \notin S^\pi$. Then $y \notin S^\pi$, and by the preceding argument,

$$\pi(S \cup \{x, y\}) = \pi(S \cup \{y\}) = \pi(S) + 1 = \pi(S \cup \{x\}),$$

whence $y \in (S \cup \{x\})^\pi$, as desired. Finally, suppose $S \in K_\pi$ and

$$\varnothing = S_0 \prec S_1 \prec \cdots \prec S_k = S$$

is a maximal chain in $S/\varnothing$. If $x_i \in S_i$ but $x_i \notin S_{i-1}$, then $S_i = (S_{i-1} \cup \{x_i\})^\pi$, and as seen in the preceding paragraph, this implies that $\pi(S_i) = \pi(S_{i-1}) + 1$. Consequently $k = \pi(S)$, and the proof of D is completed.

E. $\mathcal{L}$ is a sublattice of K_π.

The proof of E is based on a description of the closure of a subset of X. To start, observe that if $S, T \subseteq X$ and $A, B \in \mathcal{L}$ are such that $\pi(S \cup T) + \pi(S \cap T) = \pi(S) + \pi(T)$, $\pi(S) = \pi(A) + |S - A|$, and $\pi(T) = \pi(B) + |T - B|$, then

$$(4) \qquad \pi(S \cup T) = \pi(A \vee B) + |S \cup T - A \vee B|.$$

(Here, and below, joins refer to the lattice $\mathcal{L}$.) This holds because

$$\begin{aligned}
\pi(S \cup T) &\leq \pi(A \vee B) + |S \cup T - A \vee B| \\
&\leq \pi(A) + \pi(B) - \pi(A \cap B) + |S - A| + |S - B| \\
&\quad - |S \cap T - A \cap B| \\
&= \pi(S) + \pi(T) - (\pi(A \cap B) + |S \cap T - A \cap B|) \\
&\leq \pi(S) + \pi(T) - \pi(S \cap T) = \pi(S \cup T).
\end{aligned}$$

It follows from (4) that, given any subset $S \subseteq X$, if J_S denotes the join in $\mathcal{L}$ of all those $A \in \mathcal{L}$ with $\pi(S) = \pi(A) + |S - A|$, then

$$(5) \qquad \pi(S) = \pi(J_S) + |S - J_S|.$$

When $S \supseteq T$, formulas (4) and (5) combine to give

$$\pi(S) = \pi(J_S \vee J_T) + |S - J_S \vee J_T|,$$

and this shows that $J_S \supseteq J_S \vee J_T \supseteq J_T$. In particular, for any two subsets $S, T \subseteq X$, we have $J_{S \cup T} \supseteq J_S, J_T$, and hence in $\mathcal{L}$

$$(6) \qquad J_{S \cup T} \supseteq J_S \vee J_T.$$

If $A \in \mathcal{L}$, then $\pi(A) = \pi(A) + |A - A|$, so $A \subseteq J_A$. On the other hand,

$$\pi(A) = \pi(J_A) + |A - J_A| \geq \pi(J_A) \geq \pi(A),$$

and since the restriction of π to $\mathcal{L}$ is strictly increasing, we must have $J_A = A$.

The description of the closure we are seeking is now the following: $S^\pi = J_S \cup S$ for any $S \subseteq X$. For if $x \in S^\pi$, $x \notin S$, and $T = S \cup \{x\}$, then

$$\pi(S) = \pi(T) = \pi(J_T) + |T - J_T| \geq \pi(J_T) + |S - J_T| \geq \pi(S),$$

and we infer that

$$|S \cup \{x\} - J_T| = |T - J_T| = |S - J_T|,$$
$$\pi(S) = \pi(J_T) + |S - J_T|.$$

These two formulas give us in turn that $x \in J_T$ and that $J_T \subseteq J_S$, and hence $x \in J_S$. Thus $S^\pi \subseteq J_S \cup S$. Conversely, if $x \in J_S$,

$$\pi(S) \leq \pi(S \cup \{x\}) \leq \pi(J_S) + |S \cup \{x\} - J_S| = \pi(J_S) + |S - J_S| = \pi(S).$$

Therefore $\pi(S) = \pi(S \cup \{x\})$, so that $x \in S^\pi$. Hence $S^\pi = J_S \cup S$.

The conclusion of E now follows easily. If $A \in \mathcal{L}$, then $A^\pi = J_A \cup A = A$, whence $A \in K_\pi$. If $A, B \in \mathcal{L}$, then their meet in both $\mathcal{L}$ and K_π is $A \cap B$. On the other hand, $A \vee B$ (the join of A and B in $\mathcal{L}$) certainly includes $A \cup B$, so that $A \vee B \supseteq (A \cup B)^\pi$, while in view of (6) we have $(A \cup B)^\pi \supseteq J_{A \cup B} \supseteq J_A \vee J_B = A \vee B$. Thus the join of A and B in K_π coincides with their join in $\mathcal{L}$, and we conclude that $\mathcal{L}$ is a sublattice of K_π.

The proof of 14.1 is also finished; B and E combine to give the desired conclusion.

We have already remarked that every (finite) distributive lattice can be embedded in a (finite) complemented distributive lattice, and this would suggest that 14.1 might be strengthened in the case of modular lattices to assert that each finite modular lattice can be embedded in a finite complemented modular lattice. This, however, is not the case, for *there exist modular lattices that cannot be embedded in any complemented modular lattice.*[2] To prove this, choose any non-Arguesian geomodular lattice K, e.g., the lattice of all subspaces of the non-Desarguean projective plane constructed in the preceding chapter. (There exist finite non-Desarguean projective planes, and a finite example can be obtained by starting with the lattice of subspaces of one of these.) Designate an atom $a \in K$. Let M be a five-element modular nondistributive lattice, and designate an atom $b \in M$. Identify a and the greatest element of M, and identify b and the least element of K. With these identifications, let L be the set-union of K and M, together with the binary relation $\leq$ defined in L as follows: $x \leq y$ if (1) $x, y \in K$ and $x \leq y$ in K; (2) $x, y \in M$ and $x \leq y$ in M; (3) $x \in M, y \in K$, and $a \leq y$; or (4) $x \in M, y \in K$, and $x \leq b$. It is easy to verify that L is a modular lattice whose diagram is shown in Fig. 14-1. Also it is apparent that the dimension of L is 4, and that L is simple (any two prime quotients are projective). Furthermore, since K is a sublattice of L, the lattice L is non-Arguesian. Now if L were embedded in a complemented modular lattice, then in view of the results of the preceding chapter, L would be embedded in a direct product of geomodular lattices, and as L is subdirectly irreducible,

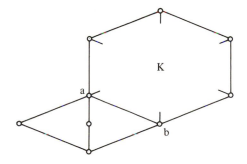

Fig. 14-1

[2] M. Hall and R. P. Dilworth [47].

it follows that L would be embedded in some geomodular lattice. This geomodular lattice would necessarily have dimension at least 4 and hence be Arguesian, a contradiction since L is not Arguesian. Thus L cannot be embedded in any complemented modular lattice.

Finite complemented modular lattices display some interesting combinatorial properties. For example, if K is a finite, Arguesian geomodular lattice of dimension at least 3, by 13.4, K is isomorphic to the lattice of all subspaces of a finite vector space v over some finite field Δ. And if $\bar{v}$ is the dual space of v, i.e., $\bar{v}$ is the set of all linear transformations of v to Δ with addition and scalar multiplication defined in the obvious way, then it is a familiar fact that $\bar{v}$ and v are isomorphic vector spaces. Moreover, if for each subspace s of v we define s^a to be the set of all those linear transformations in $\bar{v}$ that map each member of s to the zero vector,

$$s^a = \{f \in \bar{v} \mid f(s) = 0\},$$

then each s^a is a subspace of $\bar{v}$, and for any two subspaces s and t, $s \subset t$ if and only if $s^a \supset t^a$. Consequently the map $s \longrightarrow s^a$ is an isomorphism of the lattice of all subspaces of v onto the dual lattice of the lattice of all subspaces $\bar{v}$, and we infer that K and its dual lattice are isomorphic.

Now the dual lattice of a direct product is the direct product of the dual lattices,

$$(\mathsf{X}_{i \in I} K_i)^{\wedge} = \mathsf{X}_{i \in I} \hat{K}_i.$$

(Prove!) And as any finite complemented modular lattice is a direct product of finite geomodular lattices, the preceding remarks show that *a finite, Arguesian complemented lattice and its dual lattice are isomorphic.*

It is not true that every finite, complemented modular lattice is isomorphic with its dual lattice. An example of a projective plane whose lattice of subspaces is not isomorphic to its dual is given by T. G. Room and P. B. Kirkpatrick, *Miniquaternion geometry* (Cambridge, 1971), p. 128. We can, however, prove a weaker statement in this special case. For each finite geometric lattice L, let

$$w_k(L)$$

denote the number of elements in L of dimension precisely k. Because of the duality result in the preceding paragraph, it is clear that if L is a finite Arguesian complemented lattice of dimension n, then $w_k(L) = w_{n-k}(L)$ for each integer k. On the other hand, suppose that L is any geomodular lattice of dimension 3. If p and q are two distinct atoms of L, r is a third atom with $r \leq p \vee q$ and t is a complement of $p \vee q$ in the sublattice $1/r$, then t is a complement of both p and q, and it follows that $1/p \cong 1/q \cong t/0$. Dually, if s and t are any two-dimensional elements, then $s/0 \cong t/0$. Consequently there is an integer m such that each two-dimensional element is greater than exactly m atoms, and each atom is less than exactly m two-dimensional elements. Counting the number e of order pairs $\langle p, t \rangle$, where p is an atom of L and $p \prec t$, first summing over the p's and then summing over the t's, we get

$$e = w_1(L)m = w_2(L)m,$$

whence $w_1(L) = w_2(L)$.

The numbers $w_k(L)$, when L is a finite geomodular lattice, behave nicely in another way. Let L be a geomodular lattice of dimension $n \geq 4$, and think of L as the lattice of all subspaces of some vector space v. Let k be an integer with $0 < k \leq n/2$. Then there are integer l and m such that each k-dimensional element of L is equal to or greater than exactly l atoms, and each $(k - 1)$-dimensional element is covered by exactly k-dimensional elements; furthermore, $l < m$. (Why?) Counting the number e of ordered pairs $\langle s, t \rangle$, where s is a $(k - 1)$-dimensional element and $s \prec t$, we get

$$e = w_{k-1}(L)m = w_k(L)l,$$

so that $w_{k-1}(L) < w_k(L)$. As L and its dual are isomorphic, we also get $w_{k-1}(L) > w_k(L)$ whenever $n/2 < k \leq n$.

The foregoing property of geomodular lattices suggests the following *unimodality conjecture*: For each finite geometric lattice L there is an integer h such that $w_{k-1}(L) \leq w_k(L)$ for $k \leq h$ and $w_{k-1}(L) \geq w_k(L)$ for $k > h$. So far, all attempts to settle this conjecture have been unsuccessful. The only general result in this direction, at the present, is the following theorem.

14.2: *If L is a finite geometric lattice of dimension $n > 1$, then $w_1(L) \leq w_k(L)$ for each $k = 1, \ldots, n - 1$.*[3]

PROOF: If the elements of dimension exceeding k in any geometric lattice are identified, the result is again a geometric lattice in which the k-dimensional elements are covered by the greatest element of the lattice. (Proof?) Thus it is enough to prove 14.2 in the case that $k = n - 1$. The theorem is trivial when $n = 2$, so proceeding by induction we assume that it is true for each geometric lattice of dimension less than n.

Let 0 denote the least element of L, P the set of all atoms of L, and Q the set of all $(n - 1)$-dimensional elements of L. For simplicity, during the proof we will write w_k for $w_k(L)$. For each $p \in P$, let

$$\varphi(p) = |Q \cap 1/p|,$$

and for each $q \in Q$, let

$$\pi(q) = |P \cap q/0|.$$

Observe that if $p \in P$ and $q \in Q$ are such that $p \wedge q = 0$, then $\varphi(p) \geq \pi(q)$. For q has dimension $n - 1$, so by the induction the number of elements covered by q is at least $\pi(q)$. Also, if x and y are distinct elements covered

(3) J. G. Basterfield and L. M. Kelly [6], C. Greene [46].

by q, then $p \vee x$ and $p \vee y$ are distinct $(n-1)$-dimensional elements in $1/p$, whence $\varphi(p) \geq \pi(q)$.

Now suppose that $w_{n-1} < w_1$. Then for each $q \in Q$,

$$\frac{w_1 - \pi(q)}{w_{n-1} - \pi(q)} > \frac{w_1}{w_{n-1}},$$

and we get

$$w_1 = \sum_{p \in P} \frac{w_{n-1} - \varphi(p)}{w_{n-1} - \varphi(p)} = \sum_{p \in P, q \in Q \, p \wedge q = 0} \frac{1}{w_{n-1} - \varphi(p)}$$

$$\geq \sum_{p \in P, q \in Q, \, p \wedge q = 0} \frac{1}{w_{n-1} - \pi(q)} = \sum_{q \in Q} \frac{w_1 - \pi(q)}{w_{n-1} - \pi(q)}$$

$$> \sum_{q \in Q} \frac{w_1}{w_{n-1}} = w_1,$$

a contradiction. Thus 14.2 is true.

The preceding theorem shows that if L is a finite modular geometric lattice of dimension $n > 1$, then $w_1(L) = w_{n-1}(L)$. Interestingly enough, this equality occurs in no other instance.

14.3: *If L is a finite geometric lattice of dimension $n > 1$ and $w_1(L) = w_k(L)$ for some k with $1 < k < n$, then L is modular and $k = n - 1$.*[4]

PROOF: Again let 0 and 1 denote the least and greatest elements of L, P the set of atoms of L, and Q the set of $(n-1)$-dimensional elements. Define the maps φ and π as in the proof of 14.2. We first show that under the assumption that $w_1(L) = w_{n-1}(L) = w$, the lattice L is modular. The proof is by induction on n, so we assume that the preceding assertion is true for all lattices of dimension less than n.

We know from the proof of 14.2 that if $p \in P$ and $q \in Q$ are a pair of elements with $p \wedge q = 0$, then $\varphi(p) \geq \pi(q)$. Suppose for at least one such pair that we have the strict inequality $\varphi(p) > \pi(q)$. Then as in the proof of 14.2 we obtain

$$w = \sum_{p \in P} \frac{w - \varphi(p)}{w - \varphi(p)} = \sum_{p \in P, q \in Q, \, p \wedge q = 0} \frac{1}{w - \varphi(p)}$$

$$> \sum_{p \in P, q \in Q, \, p \wedge q = 0} \frac{1}{w - \pi(q)} = \sum_{q \in Q} \frac{w - \pi(q)}{w - \pi(q)} = w,$$

a contradiction. Thus $\varphi(p) = \pi(q)$ whenever $p \in P, q \in Q$, and $p \wedge q = 0$.

Next let q be any element of Q. If the number of elements covered by q exceeds $\pi(q)$, then picking any atom p with $p \wedge q = 0$, the map $x \to x \vee p$ is a one-to-one map of the elements covered by q to $Q \cap 1/p$, whence $\varphi(p) > \pi(q)$, an impossibility. Consequently the number of elements covered by q equals the number of atoms of $q/0$, and we infer that $q/0$ is modular.

[4] C. Greene [46].

Let q_1 and q_2 be any two distinct elements of Q. Pick any atom p such that $p \leq q_1$ and $p \not\leq q_2$. Then inasmuch as the number of elements covered by q_2 is equal to $\varphi(p)$, the map $x \longrightarrow x \vee p$ takes the set $\{x \mid x \prec q_2\}$ onto the set $Q \cap 1/p$. As $q_1 \geq p$, it follows that there is some element x covered by q_2 such that $x \vee p = q_1$. Therefore $q_1 \wedge q_2 = x$, and we have shown that q_1, $q_2 \succ q_1 \wedge q_2$.

Now suppose that $x, y \in L$ are such that $x \vee y \succ x$. If $x \vee y \neq 1$, then there is some $q \in Q$ such that $q \geq x \vee y$, and as $q/0$ is modular, it follows that $y \succ x \wedge y$. Assume that $x \vee y = 1$ and that $y \neq 1$. Pick $q \in Q$ such that $q \geq y$. Since $1 \succ x$, the preceding paragraph shows that $x, q \succ x \wedge q$. Moreover, it is clear that

$$y \vee (x \wedge q) = q \succ x \wedge q,$$

and consequently the modularity of $q/0$ yields that $y \succ x \wedge q \wedge y = x \wedge y$. Thus L is lower semimodular and hence modular.

Finally, assume that $w_1(L) = w_k(L)$, where $1 < k < n - 1$. Choose an element $a \in L$ of dimension $k - 2$. Since $1/a$ has dimension at least 4, there are four independent elements $p_1, p_2, p_3, p_4 \in 1/a$, each covering a. The sublattice generated by the p_i's is a 16-element Boolean algebra, and the two-dimensional elements in this sublattice have dimension k in L. Now let L' be that lattice obtained from L by identifying all the elements of L of dimension greater than k. The lattice L' is a geometric lattice of dimension $k + 1$ for which $w_1(L') = w_k(L')$, and therefore L' is modular. On the other hand, the sublattice of L' generated by the p_i's is isomorphic to the nonmodular lattice of Fig. 3-2. This contradiction shows that $k < n - 1$ is impossible, completing the proof.

Again the properties of geomodular lattices together with 14.2 suggest another unanswered question: Is it true that for each geometric lattice of dimension $n > 1$, $w_k(L) \leq w_{n-k}(L)$ whenever $0 \leq k \leq n/2$?

We have already remarked that in a finite modular geometric lattice L of dimension $n > 1$, $w_1(L) = w_{n-1}(L)$. Even without complementation, finite modular lattices possess a much stronger combinatorial property. Given a finite lattice L, let $B_k(L)$ and $C_k(L)$ denote, respectively, the set of all those elements in L that are covered by exactly k elements and the set of all those elements in L that cover exactly k elements. Observe that if L is a geometric lattice, then $|C_1(L)| = w_1(L)$ and $|B_1(L)| = w_{n-1}(L)$.

14.4: *If L is a finite modular lattice, then $|B_k(L)| = |C_k(L)|$ for each integer k.*[5]

PROOF: The proof of this theorem is made in two stages. It is first proved in the special case when L is complemented, and then the general case is reduced

[5] R. P. Dilworth [34].

to the complemented case. The principal tool in this reduction process is the Möbius function, a basic concept in combinatorial lattice theory, and preliminary to the second part of the proof, this function is introduced and a few of its properties developed.

It is clear from the duality results above that if K is a finite geomodular lattice, then $|B_k(K)| = |C_k(K)|$ for each k. Suppose that L is any finite complemented modular lattice. Then $L \cong \mathsf{X}_{i \in I} K_i$, where $I = \{1, 2, \ldots, r\}$ and each K_i is a finite geomodular lattice, and for notational convenience we can suppose that L and $\mathsf{X}_{i \in I} K_i$ are actually equal. If $x, y \in L$, then $x \prec y$ if and only if there is some integer $h \in I$ such that $y(h) \succ x(h)$ while $y(i) = x(i)$ for all $i \neq h$. It follows that x is covered by precisely k elements in L if and only if

$$k = N(x(1)) + \cdots + N(x(r)),$$

where $N(x(i))$ is the number of elements in K_i covering $x(i)$. If $k = \sum_{i \in I} k_i$, we infer that there are exactly $\prod_{i \in I} |B_{k_i}(K_i)|$ elements $x \in L$ which are covered by precisely k elements in L and are such that $x(i)$ is covered by precisely k_i elements of K_i. Therefore

$$|B_k(L)| = \sum_{k = k_1 + \cdots + k_r} \prod_{i \in I} |B_{k_i}(K_i)|,$$

and dually

$$|C_k(L)| = \sum_{k = k_1 + \cdots + k_r} \prod_{i \in I} |C_{k_i}(K_i)|.$$

Since we know that $|B_k(K_i)| = |C_k(K_i)|$ for each k and i, we conclude that $|B_k(L)| = |(C_k L)|$ for each positive integer k. Thus the conclusion of 14.4 holds for every finite complemented modular lattice, and the first stage of the proof is complete.

Now let P be any finite partially ordered set. We define an integer-valued function μ on P^2 inductively as follows: $\mu(x, x) = 1$; $\mu(x, y) = 0$ whenever $x \not\leq y$; and if $x < y$ and $\mu(x, z)$ has been defined for all z such that $x \leq z < y$, then

$$\mu(x, y) = - \sum_{x \leq z < y} \mu(x, z).$$

Note that the function μ so defined necessarily satisfies the dual relation:

$$\mu(x, y) = - \sum_{x < z \leq y} \mu(z, y) \qquad \text{when } x < y.$$

For if this relation holds for every pair of elements $x, w \in P$ with $x < w < y$, then

$$\mu(x, y) = -\mu(x, x) - \sum_{x < w < y} \mu(x, w)$$

$$= -1 + \sum_{x < w < y} \sum_{x < z \leq w} \mu(z, w)$$

$$= -\mu(y, y) + \sum_{x < z < y} \sum_{z \leq w < y} \mu(z, w) = - \sum_{x < z \leq y} \mu(z, y).$$

This function μ is called the *Möbius function* of P.[6] It is defined so that the

---

[6] See G.-C. Rota [78] for a definitive discussion of the Möbius function.

following inversion property holds: *If f is any real-valued function on P and the function g is defined by the formula* $g(x) = \sum_{y \leq x} f(y)$, *then*

$$f(x) = \sum_{y \leq x} g(y)\mu(y, x).$$

Substituting for $g(y)$ and using the dual relation, we get

$$\sum_{y \leq x} g(y)\mu(y, x) = \sum_{y \leq x} \sum_{z \leq y} f(z)\mu(y, x) = \sum_{z \leq x} f(z) \sum_{z \leq y \leq x} \mu(y, x)$$

$$= f(x)\mu(x, x) + \sum_{z < x} f(z) \sum_{z \leq y \leq x} \mu(y, x) = f(x).$$

When the partially ordered set is a lattice, the Mobius function has a useful alternative description. For each element x in a finite lattice L let P_x denote the set of those elements in L that cover x, and for any $y \in L$ let $N_k(x, y)$ denote the number of k-element subsets of P_x whose join (in the sublattice $1/x$) is y. Then *if μ is the Möbius function of L,*

$$\mu(x, y) = \sum_{k \geq 0} (-1)^k N_k(x, y).$$

To prove this, set $\mu'(x, y) = \sum_{k \geq 0}(-1)^k N_k(x, y)$. Since the empty set is the only subset of P_x whose join (in $1/x$) is x, we have $\mu'(x, x) = 1$, and when $y \not\geq x$, no subset of P_x has its join equal to y, so that $\mu'(x, y) = 0$. Furthermore, if $y > x$, then

$$\sum_{x \leq z \leq y} \mu'(x, z) = \sum_{x \leq z \leq y} \sum_{k \geq 0} (-1)^k N_k(x, z)$$

$$= \sum_{k \geq 0} (-1)^k \sum_{x \leq z \leq y} N_k(x, z) = \sum_{k \geq 0} (-1)^k \binom{N}{k} = (1 - 1)^N = 0,$$

where N is the number of elements in $P_x \cap y/0$. Therefore μ' satisfies those relations that define μ, so we must have $\mu' = \mu$.

Another necessary property is: *If μ is the Möbius function of a finite lattice L and $x, y, z \in L$ with $x \leq z \leq y$, then*

$$\sum_{z \vee t = y} \mu(x, t) = \begin{cases} \mu(x, y), & \text{if } z = x, \\ 0, & \text{if } z \neq x. \end{cases}$$

Certainly $\mu(x, t) = 0$ unless $x \leq t$. Therefore if $z = x$ and $x \leq t$, then $t = x \vee t = y$, so that the formula holds in this case. Suppose $z \neq x$, and suppose that $\sum_{z \vee t = s} \mu(x, t) = 0$ whenever $z \leq s < y$. Then

$$\sum_{z \vee t = y} \mu(x, t) = \sum_{z \leq s < y} \sum_{z \vee t = s} \mu(x, t) + \sum_{z \vee t = y} \mu(x, t)$$

$$= \sum_{z \leq s \leq y} \sum_{z \vee t = s} \mu(x, t)$$

$$= \sum_{t \leq y} \mu(x, t) = \sum_{x \leq t \leq y} \mu(x, t) = 0,$$

and hence the formula is true by induction.

If μ is the Möbius function of a finite lattice L with least element 0, we can define the *restricted Möbius function* λ of L by

$$\lambda(x) = \mu(0, x).$$

Actually one does not lose anything in passing to the restricted Möbius function, for it is apparent that $\mu(x, y)$ is just the value at y of the restricted Möbius function of $1/x$.

We can now complete the proof of 14.4. Throughout the rest of this section, L denotes a finite modular lattice with least element 0 and greatest element 1. (Again there is no problem in distinguishing these elements from the integers 0 and 1.) For each element $a \in L$ we set

$$u_a = \bigvee\{p \in L \,|\, p \succ a\}, \qquad v_a = \bigwedge\{q \in L \,|\, q \prec a\}.$$

In particular u_0 is the join of all the atoms of L, and the sublattice

$$K = u_0/0$$

is complemented. Observe that if λ is the restricted Möbius function of L, then the restriction of λ to K coincides with the restricted Möbius function of K. The number of atoms in L will be denoted by w.

The proof proceeds in a number of steps, beginning with

A.
$$\sum_{a \in K} \lambda(a) |B_k(1/a)| = \begin{cases} 1, & \text{if } w = k, \\ 0, & \text{if } w \neq k. \end{cases}$$

$B_k(1/a) = B_k(L) \cap 1/a$, and therefore if $b \in K$ and

$$T_k(b) = \{x \in B_k(L) \,|\, x \wedge u_0 = b\},$$

then $T_k(b) \subseteq B_k(1/a)$ whenever $b \geq a$. Furthermore, if b_1 and b_2 are distinct elements of K, both in $1/a$, then the sets $T_k(b_1)$ and $T_k(b_2)$ are disjoint. In addition, if $x \in B_k(1/a)$, then $x \wedge u_0 \in K$ and $x \wedge u_0 \geq a$. Consequently

$$B_k(1/a) = \bigcup_{b \in K \cap 1/a} T_k(b),$$

and hence

$$|B_k(1/a)| = \sum_{b \in K \cap 1/a} |T_k(b)|.$$

It follows that

$$\sum_{a \in K} \lambda(a) |B_k(1/a)| = \sum_{a \in K} \sum_{b \in K \cap 1/a} \lambda(a) |T_k(b)|$$
$$= \sum_{b \in K} |T_k(b)| \sum_{a \leq b} \lambda(a) = |T_k(0)|.$$

But $x \in T_k(0)$ means that $x \wedge u_0 = 0$ and hence that $x = 0$. Consequently $T_k(0)$ is nonempty only if $w = k$, in which case $T_k(0)$ contains the single element 0; that is, $|T_k(0)| = 1$ if $w = k$, and $|T_k(0)| = 0$ if $w \neq k$.

Set $S_k(x) = \{a \in K \,|\, x \in C_k(1/a)\}$.

B. If $x \notin K$, then $\sum_{a \in S_k(x)} \lambda(a) = 0$.

Define an equivalence relation $\sim$ in K by the rule

$$a \sim b \text{ if } a \vee (v_x \wedge u_0) = b \vee (v_x \wedge u_0).$$

Let E be any equivalence class. If b is a fixed element of E, then E is precisely the set of all those elements $a \in K$ such that $a \vee (v_x \wedge u_0) = b \vee (v_x \wedge u_0)$. Furthermore, $v_x \wedge u_0 \neq 0$, for otherwise $v_x = 0$, and this requires that $x/0$ is a complemented sublattice and hence that x is a join of atoms, contrary to $x \notin K$. Therefore by the property of the Möbius function derived above,

$$\sum_{a \in E} \lambda(a) = 0.$$

Next assume that $S_k(x)$ and E have an element a in common. Let b be any other element of E. If $y \in L$ is such that $x \succ y \geq a$, then $y \geq v_x$, and therefore

$$y \geq a \vee (v_x \wedge u_0) = b \vee (v_x \wedge u_0) \geq b.$$

Similarly, if $x \succ y \geq b$, then $y \geq a$. We infer that x covers exactly the same set of elements in $1/a$ as in $1/b$, and hence $a \in S_k(x)$ implies that $b \in S_k(x)$. Summarizing, if the equivalence class E and $S_k(x)$ have an element in common, then $E \subseteq S_k(x)$. It follows that $S_k(x)$ is the set-union of those equivalence classes it contains, and thus

$$\sum_{a \in S_k(x)} \lambda(a) = \sum_{E \subseteq S_k(x)} \sum_{a \in E} \lambda(a) = 0.$$

C.
$$\sum_{a \in K} \lambda(a) |C_k(1/a)| = \begin{cases} 1, & \text{if } w = k, \\ 0, & \text{if } w \neq k. \end{cases}$$

Certainly

$$\sum_{a \in K} \lambda(a) |C_k(1/a)| = \sum_{a \in K} \lambda(a) \sum_{x \in L} \varphi_k(a, x),$$

where $\varphi_k(a, x) = 1$ if x covers exactly k elements in $1/a$ and is zero otherwise. Thus, with B in mind, we get

$$\sum_{a \in K} \lambda(a) |C_k(1/a)| = \sum_{x \in L} \sum_{a \in K} \lambda(a) \varphi_k(a, x)$$
$$= \sum_{x \in L} \sum_{a \in S_k(x)} \lambda(a) = \sum_{x \in K} \sum_{a \in S_k(x)} \lambda(a)$$
$$= \sum_{x \in K} \sum_{a \in K} \lambda(a) \varphi_k(a, x) = \sum_{a \in K} \lambda(a) \sum_{x \in K} \varphi_k(a, x)$$
$$= \sum_{a \in K} \lambda(a) |C_k(u_0/a)|.$$

We know that 14.4 holds in the complemented case, so $|C_k(u_0/a)| = |B_k(u_0/a)|$, and in view of A and the fact that K and L both have w atoms, we have

$$\sum_{a \in K} \lambda(a) |C_k(1/a)| = \sum_{a \in K} \lambda(a) |B_k(u_0/a)| = \begin{cases} 1, & \text{if } w = k, \\ 0, & \text{if } w \neq k. \end{cases}$$

The proof of 14.4 is now easily finished. The theorem is trivial for those lattices of dimension 1, and proceeding by induction, we assume that it holds for all the sublattices $1/a$ of L with $a \neq 0$. Combining A and C, we see that

$$\sum_{a \in K} \lambda(a)[|B_k(1/a)| - |C_k(1/a)|] = 0.$$

By the induction hypothesis, $|B_k(1/a)| - |C_k(1/a)| = 0$ for all $a \neq 0$. Therefore

$$\lambda(0)[|B_k(1/0)| - |C_k(1/0)|] = 0,$$

and inasmuch as $\lambda(0) = 1$ and $1/0 = L$, the conclusion of 14.4 follows.

In this chapter we have discussed only those combinatorial properties of geometric lattices which relate directly to lattice structure theory. There are many other combinatorial aspects of geometric lattices which arise from geometric and graph-theoretic considerations. A detailed account of this approach to combinatorial theory may be found in H. H. Crapo and G.-C. Rota [16].

15

DIMENSION THEORY

If δ is the dimension function of a finite dimensional modular lattice with least element 0 and greatest element 1 and if the function d is defined in the lattice by the rule $d(x) = \delta(x)/\delta(1)$, then this function d has the properties

(1) $d(0) = 0$ and $d(1) = 1$.
(2) $d(x) > d(y)$ whenever $x > y$.
(3) $d(x \vee y) + d(x \wedge y) = d(x) + d(y)$.

Any real-valued function d defined in a lattice L (with least element 0 and greatest element 1) that satisfies (1)–(3) is called a *normalized dimension function* in L. Observe that *any lattice having a normalized dimension function is necessarily modular*. (Proof?)

Normalized dimension functions are not necessarily unique: *There is a unique normalized dimension function in a finite dimensional modular lattice L if and only if L is simple.* (The reader should devise a proof of this nontrivial result. *Hint:* Use the structure theory of Chap. 11.)

The complexity of the situation when the assumption of finite dimensionality is dropped is suggested by the fact that there are no known nontrivial sufficient conditions for the existence of a normalized dimension function that encompass all finite dimensional modular lattices as well as some that are not finite dimensional. Certain necessary conditions do exist; for example, in a lattice having a normalized dimension function no quotient is projective to one of its proper subquotients.

In the presence of complements more can be said; one of lattice theory's most profound results is the following theorem of von Neumann, the proof of which will occupy us for most of this chapter.

15.1: *Every indecomposable, continuous, complemented modular lattice has a unique normalized dimension function. Moreover, any such lattice is simple.*[1]

---

[1] This was announced by von Neumann in [71].

A couple of examples may help illuminate von Neumann's theorem. Note that any complete Boolean algebra is a continuous complemented modular lattice, and the complete Boolean algebra of all subsets of an uncountable set contains uncountable well-ordered chains. On the other hand, any lattice having a normalized dimension function contains only countable well-ordered chains, so it is clear that the assumption of indecomposability cannot be dropped from the hypothesis of 15.1. The continuity assumption cannot be dropped either. To see this, let v be a vector space of countably infinite dimension, and let K be the lattice of all subspaces of v. K is then a complete, atomic, complemented, modular lattice, and as we observed in Chap. 13, $\Theta(K)$ is an atomic lattice having a unique atom σ, the congruence relation generated by identifying any finite dimensional subspace with 0. Suppose that x is an infinite dimensional subspace of v such that v/x is also infinite dimensional and x' is a complement of x. If $\{e_0, e_1, e_2, \ldots\}$ is a basis of x, $\{e'_0, e'_1, e'_2, \ldots\}$ is a basis of x', and y is that subspace spanned by $e_0 + e'_0$, $e_1 + e'_1$, $e_2 + e'_2$, $\ldots$, then x, x', y, v, and 0 form a five-element sublattice of K. But this means that the least congruence relation collapsing $x/0$ collapses every quotient of K, i.e., that $\Theta(K)$ consists of the three congruence relations 1, σ, 0. In particular, K/σ is a simple, complemented, modular lattice, with the additional property that any two nonzero complementary elements have a common complement. Now observe that if a complemented modular lattice L has a normalized dimension function d and a and a' are complements in L, then

$$d(a) + d(a') = d(a \lor a') + d(a \land a') = 1 + 0 = 1,$$

so that two elements in L having a common complement must have the same value under d. Applying this to K/σ, it follows that if K/σ did have a normalized dimension function, each element different from the least and greatest elements would have to have the value 1/2 under this function, an impossibility. The same considerations, by the way, show also that no normalized dimension function is possessed by K, a lattice satisfying all the conditions of 15.1 except lower continuity.

While we are talking about examples, we should point out that 15.1 does have content; there do exist indecomposable continuous complemented modular lattices that are not finite dimensional. At the end of this chapter we will describe a construction of von Neumann's of a family of such lattices derived from the family of division rings.

Before launching into the proof of 15.1, it is perhaps instructive to give a brief outline and a little motivation for the plan of attack. The first step in the construction of a normalized dimension function is to gather together those lattice elements that must be assigned the same value under the function. The key to this is suggested by the observation above that the same value must be assigned to two lattice elements having a common complement. Thus we are led to the following two definitions. We define two elements a and b in a complemented modular lattice L to be *perspective* (in symbols, $a \sim b$) if a and b have a common complement in L. The elements a and b are *projective* (in symbols, $a \approx b$) if there is a finite sequence $a = a_0$, $a_1, \ldots, a_n = b$ such that $a_{i-1} \sim a_i$ for each $i = 1, \ldots, n$. The idea, of course, is to ultimately assign each member in a projectivity class the same value under the normalized dimension function.

Because the lattice is modular, two distinct perspective elements cannot be comparable—an important property inasmuch as the normalized dimension function we hope to construct must satisfy property (2). On the other hand, it is not at all clear that the same holds for projective elements; in fact, the lattice K above contains distinct comparable projective elements. Consequently an important step in the proof is to show that with the added assumption of continuity, perspectivity is transitive, i.e., that the notions of perspectivity and projectivity coincide.

Once the transitivity of perspectivity is established, the next step is to show that the perspectivity classes have a natural ordering. Here the key property is the following: If a and b are elements of our lattice, then there is an element x such that either $a \sim x \leq b$ or $b \sim x \leq a$. In the first case we order the perspectivity class containing a below that containing b, reversing this order if the second case holds. Also, as perspectivity is transitive, it follows that under the foregoing order the perspectivity classes form a chain.

Real numbers still have to be attached to the perspectivity classes. When L is finite dimensional, this can be done with the dimension function. When L is not finite dimensional, the main step is to show that there are complementary elements c_0 and c_0' in L which are also perspective. The value $1/2$ is then assigned to the perspectivity class containing c_0. Similarly, perspective elements c_1 and c_1' are found that are complements in $c_0/0$, and the perspectivity class containing these elements is given the value $1/4$. Continuing in this way, a subset C is obtained in which a function d is defined taking on rational values of the form $k/2^n$, and this function d is extended to the whole lattice by defining $d(x) = \sup\{d(c) \mid c \in C(x)\}$, where $C(x)$ denotes those elements of C whose perspectivity classes lie below the perspectivity class containing x.

Now to supply the details. *For the remainder of this chapter, L will denote a complemented modular lattice with least element 0 and greatest element 1.* At this point no other conditions on L are assumed; *further assumptions will be explicitly imposed as they are required.*

We begin the proof with two lemmas giving alternative characterizations of perspectivity.

15.2:   *Two elements $a, b \in L$ are perspective if and only if they are perspective in any quotient sublattice to which they both belong.*

PROOF: If a and b belong to the quotient sublattice c/d and x is a common complement of a and b in L, then $c \wedge (d \vee x)$ is a common complement of a and b in c/d. Conversely, if y is a common complement of a and b in c/d and if c' and d' are complements of c and d in L, then $c' \vee (d' \wedge y)$ is a common complement of a and b in L.

Applying the preceding lemma to the quotient $a \vee b/0$, we get

15.3: *Two elements $a, b \in L$ are perspective if and only if there is an element $x \in L$ such that $a \vee x = b \vee x = a \vee b$ and $a \wedge x = b \wedge x = 0$.*

The element x provided by 15.3 for two perspective elements a and b is called an *axis of perspectivity* for $a \sim b$. Note that if x is an axis of perspectivity for $a \sim b$, then the map $z \longrightarrow (z \vee x) \wedge b$, henceforth called a *perspectivity map* from $a/0$ to $b/0$, is an isomorphism of $a/0$ onto $b/0$. More generally, if $a = a_0 \sim a_1 \sim \cdots \sim a_n = b$ and if ψ_i is a perspectivity map from $a_{i-1}/0$ to $a_i/0$, then $\psi = \psi_n \cdots \psi_1$ is an isomorphism of $a/0$ onto $b/0$, and we will refer to ψ as a *projectivity map* from $a/0$ to $b/0$. Perspectivity maps have a very useful property:

15.4: *If $a \sim b$ in L with axis of perspectivity x and ψ is the corresponding perspectivity map from $a/0$ to $b/0$, then $z \sim \psi(z)$ with axis of perspectivity $x \wedge (z \vee \psi(z))$ for each $z \in a/0$.*

(The proof of 15.4 is left as an exercise.)

As pointed out above, we cannot get the transitivity of perspectivity in the present general setting; we can, however, get it in an important special case.

15.5: *If $a, b, c \in L$, $a \sim b \sim c$, and $(a \vee b) \wedge c = 0$, then $a \sim c$.*

PROOF: Let x and y be axes of perspectivity for $a \sim b$ and $b \sim c$, respectively. Then

$$a \vee (x \vee y) = a \vee x \vee y = a \vee b \vee y = a \vee b \vee c,$$

and, similarly, $c \vee (x \vee y) = a \vee b \vee c$. Further,

$$(a \vee b) \wedge y = (a \vee b) \wedge (b \vee c) \wedge y$$
$$= (b \vee ((a \vee b) \wedge c)) \wedge y = b \wedge y = 0,$$

so that

$$a \wedge (x \vee y) = a \wedge (a \vee b) \wedge (x \vee y) = a \wedge (x \vee ((a \vee b) \wedge y))$$
$$= a \wedge x = 0.$$

Similarly, $c \wedge (x \vee y) = 0$, and a and c are perspective in $a \vee b \vee c/0$.

The next lemma provides conditions for the preservation of perspectivity under join.

15.6: *If* $a, b, c, d \in L$, $a \sim b$ *with axis of perspectivity* x, $c \sim d$ *with axis of perspectivity* y, *and* $(a \vee b) \wedge (c \vee d) = 0$, *then* $a \vee c \sim b \vee d$ *with axis of perspectivity* $x \vee y$.

PROOF: Clearly $(a \vee c) \vee (x \vee y) = a \vee b \vee c \vee d = (b \vee d) \vee (x \vee y)$. Moreover,

$$(a \vee b \vee c) \wedge y = (a \vee b \vee c) \wedge (c \vee d) \wedge y$$
$$= ([(a \vee b) \wedge (c \vee d)] \vee c) \wedge y = c \wedge y = 0,$$

whence

$$(a \vee c) \wedge (x \vee y) = (a \vee c) \wedge (a \vee b \vee c) \wedge (x \vee y)$$
$$= (a \vee c) \wedge (x \vee ((a \vee b \vee c) \wedge y)) = (a \vee c) \wedge x$$
$$= (a \vee c) \wedge (a \vee b) \wedge x = [a \vee (c \wedge (a \vee b))] \wedge x$$
$$= a \wedge x = 0.$$

A similar calculation yields that $(b \vee d) \wedge (x \vee y) = 0$, and therefore $a \vee c \sim b \vee d$ with axis of perspectivity $x \vee y$.

The existence of perspectivities and the failure of the distributive law are closely related; certainly when two distinct elements have a common complement, distributivity fails somewhere in the lattice. To help bring this relationship into sharper focus, let us define two elements $a, b \in L$ to be a *distributive pair*, in symbols $a \, D \, b$, if

$$x \wedge (a \vee b) = (x \wedge a) \vee (x \wedge b) \qquad \text{all } x \in L.$$

Further, define the elements a and b to be *orthogonal*, in symbols $a \perp b$, if $a \, D \, b$ and $a \wedge b = 0$. Both D and $\perp$ are clearly symmetric relations. Additional properties are listed in the four following lemmas, the proofs of which are straightforward and left as exercises, with this hint: Prove them in sequence.

15.7: *If* $a, b \in L$, *then* $a \, D \, b$ *if and only if, for all* $x \in L$,

$$a \wedge (x \vee b) = (a \wedge x) \vee (a \wedge b).$$

15.8: *If* $a, b \in L$, *then* $a \perp b$ *if and only if* $a \wedge (x \vee b) \leq a \wedge x$ *for all* $x \in L$.

15.9: *If* $a, b, c \in L$, $a \perp b$, *and* $a \perp c$, *then* $a \perp (b \vee c)$.

15.10: *If* $a, b, c, d \in L$, $a \perp b$, $c \leq a$, *and* $d \leq b$, *then* $c \perp d$.

Our next theorem embodies the basic relationship between the existence of a perspectivity and the failure of distributivity.

15.11: *For any two elements* $a, b \in L$, *the relation* $a \perp b$ *is equivalent to the condition*

(∗)   *For all* $c, d \in L$, $c \leq a$, $d \leq b$, *and* $c \sim d$ *imply that* $c = d = 0$.

PROOF: Assume that $a \perp b$ and that $c, d \in L$ are such that $c \leq a, d \leq b$, and $c \sim d$. Then $c \perp d$ by 15.10, and if x is an axis of perspectivity for $c \sim d$,
$$c = c \wedge (x \vee c) = c \wedge (x \vee d) = (c \wedge x) \vee (c \wedge d) = 0, \quad \text{with} \quad d = 0$$
following similarly.

Conversely, assume that a and b satisfy condition (∗). Then immediately we get $a \wedge b = 0$, inasmuch as $a \wedge b \leq a, b$, and $a \wedge b \sim a \wedge b$. Now let x be any element L, and let y be a complement of $(x \wedge a) \vee (x \wedge b)$ in $x \wedge (a \vee b)/0$. We then have
$$y \wedge a = y \wedge x \wedge a = y \wedge ((x \wedge a) \vee (x \wedge b)) \wedge (x \wedge a) = 0,$$
and likewise $y \wedge b = 0$. Therefore $y \wedge (a \wedge (y \vee b)) = y \wedge (b \wedge (y \vee a))$ $= 0$, and as $y \vee (a \wedge (y \vee b)) = (y \vee a) \wedge (y \vee b) = y \vee (b \wedge (y \vee a))$, it follows that $a \wedge (y \vee b) \sim b \wedge (y \vee a)$. This together with condition (∗) implies that
$$a \wedge (y \vee b) = b \wedge (y \vee a) = 0.$$
Consequently $b = b \vee (a \wedge (y \vee b)) = (b \vee a) \wedge (y \vee b) \geq y$, and by symmetry $a \geq y$, so that $0 = a \wedge b \geq y$. Thus $(x \wedge a) \vee (x \wedge b) = x \wedge (a \vee b)$, completing the argument.

Restating 15.11, if $a \wedge b = 0$ and a and b do not form a distributive pair, then there exist elements $c, d \in L$, both of which are nonzero, such that $c \leq a, d \leq b$ and $c \sim d$. Stated slightly differently, if $a \wedge b = 0$ and $a D b$ does not hold, then there is a nondistributive five-element sublattice of the form $\{c, d, x, c \vee d, 0\}$, where $c \leq a$ and $d \leq b$.

As a corollary of 15.11 we get

15.12:   *If* $a, b, c \in L$, $a \perp b$, *and* $b \sim c$, *then* $a \perp c$.

PROOF: If d is the image of $a \wedge c$ under a perspectivity map from $c/0$ to $b/0$, then 15.4 assures us that $d \sim a \wedge c$. But $d \leq b$ and $a \wedge c \leq a$, and so by (∗) we infer that $a \wedge c = 0$. Now pick any $u \leq a$ and $v \leq c$ with $u \sim v$. Again, if $w \leq b$ is the image of v under the perspectivity map from $c/0$ to $b/0$, then $w \sim v$, and as $a \perp b$, we have
$$u \wedge (v \vee w) \leq a \wedge (c \vee b) = (a \wedge c) \vee (a \wedge b) = 0,$$
and 15.5 yields that $u \sim w$. Another application of (∗) gives $u = w = 0$, and therefore $u = v = 0$. Invoking (∗) again, we conclude that $a \perp c$.

At this point let us define an element $a \in L$ to be *distributive* if $a D x$ for all $x \in L$. With 15.7 in mind, it is clear that *the following statements are equivalent*: (1) *the element* a *is distributive*, (2) $a \wedge (x \vee y) = (a \wedge x) \vee (a \wedge y)$ *for all* $x, y \in L$, and (3) $x \wedge (a \vee y) = (x \wedge a) \vee (x \wedge y)$ *for all* $x, y \in L$.

The collection of all distributive elements in L is called the *center* of L and is denoted by $C(L)$. Under any circumstances $1, 0 \in C(L)$.

15.13: *An element $a \in L$ belongs to $C(L)$ if and only if a has a unique complement.*

PROOF: Suppose that $a \in C(L)$ and that a' and a'' are complements of a. Making the familiar calculation,

$$a' = a' \wedge (a \vee a'') = (a' \wedge a) \vee (a' \wedge a'') = a' \wedge a'',$$

with $a'' = a' \wedge a''$ following by symmetry. Thus $a' = a''$.

Conversely, suppose a has a unique complement a' in L. Pick any $x \in L$, and let z be a complement of $(x \wedge a) \vee (x \wedge a')$ in $x/0$. Observe that

$$z \wedge a = z \wedge x \wedge a \leq z \wedge ((x \wedge a) \vee (x \wedge a')) = 0,$$

and, similarly, $z \wedge a' = 0$. Choosing a complement w of $a \vee z$ in $1/z$, we see that $a \vee w = a \vee z \vee w = 1$, and $a \wedge w = a \wedge (a \vee z) \wedge w = a \wedge z = 0$. Thus w is a complement of a, which means that $a' = w$. Therefore $a' \geq z$, and this implies that $z = z \wedge a' = 0$. Consequently $(x \wedge a) \vee (x \wedge a') = x$. Now if y is any other element in L,

$$
\begin{aligned}
x \vee y &= [(x \wedge a) \vee (x \wedge a')] \vee [(y \wedge a) \vee (y \wedge a')] \\
&= [(x \wedge a) \vee (y \wedge a)] \vee [(x \wedge a') \vee (y \wedge a')],
\end{aligned}
$$

and as $a \geq (x \wedge a) \vee (y \wedge a)$ and $a \wedge [(x \wedge a') \vee (y \wedge a')] = 0$, with the help of modularity we conclude that $a \wedge (x \vee y) = (x \wedge a) \vee (y \wedge a)$. Hence $a \in C(L)$.

Notice that the foregoing argument also shows that if $a \in C(L)$ and a' is the complement of a, then a' is a distributive element; i.e., $a' \in C(L)$. Moreover, the statement that a has a unique complement is self-dual, and consequently an element a belongs to $C(L)$ if and only if either of the duals of (2) or (3) above holds. Now if $a, b \in C(L)$, using (3) it is easy to check that $a \wedge b \in C(L)$, and likewise using the dual of (2) that $a \vee b \in C(L)$. Thus

15.14: *$C(L)$ is a sublattice of L, and as a sublattice $C(L)$ is a Boolean algebra.*

Note further that if $a \in C(L)$, then the map $x \longrightarrow \langle x \wedge a, x \wedge a' \rangle$ is a one-to-one map of L onto the direct product of $a/0$ and $a'/0$. Conversely, if there is an isomorphism of L onto the direct product of two lattices L_1 and L_2 and a is that element of L whose image under this isomorphism is the largest element of L_1, then a must belong to $C(L)$. Therefore we have

15.15: *L is indecomposable if and only if $C(L) = \{0, 1\}$.*

We will need two additional lemmas, the first characterizing the elements of $C(L)$ in terms of perspectivity and the second showing that perspectivity is preserved under meets and joins with elements of $C(L)$.

15.16: *An element $a \in C(L)$ if and only if, for all $x, y \in L$, $x \sim y \leq a$ implies that $x \leq a$.*

PROOF: If $a \in C(L)$, then a', the complement of a, also belongs to $C(L)$, and this in conjunction with the fact that $a' \wedge y = 0$ implies that $a' \perp y$. By 15.12 we get $x \perp a'$, and as a is a distributive element, $x = x \wedge (a \vee a') = (x \wedge a) \vee (x \wedge a') = x \wedge a \leq a$.

Conversely, suppose that a satisfies the condition of 15.16. Let a' be a complement of a. If $a \perp a'$ does not hold, then by 15.11 there are nonzero elements $x \leq a'$ and $y \leq a$ with $x \sim y$. But then $x \leq a$, forcing $x \leq a \wedge a' = 0$, a contradiction. Therefore a and a' are a distributive pair, and this is enough to ensure that a' is the unique complement of a.

15.17: *If $a, b \in L$, $c \in C(L)$, and $a \sim b$, then $a \vee c \sim b \vee c$ and $a \wedge c \sim b \wedge c$.*

PROOF: To prove this, let x be an axis of perspectivity for $a \sim b$. Then $(a \vee c) \vee x = (b \vee c) \vee x$, and

$$(a \vee c) \wedge x = (a \wedge x) \vee (c \wedge x) = (b \wedge x) \vee (c \wedge x) = (b \vee c) \wedge x,$$

so that $a \vee c \sim b \vee c$ follows by 15.2. A dual calculation shows that $a \wedge c \sim b \wedge c$.

Up to this point the only assumptions imposed on the lattice L are that it is complemented and modular, and each of the results 15.2–15.17 holds in this general setting. Further progress, however, requires additional assumptions. Therefore *from this point on we assume that the lattice L is upper continuous as well as complemented and modular*. One form of upper continuity that we will use is the following: For each $a \in L$ and each upper-directed set $S \subseteq L$, $a \wedge \bigvee S = \bigvee_{s \in S} a \wedge s$. Here a subset S is *upper-directed* if every finite subset of S has an upper bound in S. That the foregoing condition is actually equivalent to upper continuity is clear from 2.4.

Our first use of upper continuity is to construct elements of $C(L)$. For each $a \in L$, define

$$a^\perp = \bigvee \{x \in L \,|\, a \perp x\}.$$

Notice that the set $\{x \in L \,|\, a \perp x\}$ is upper-directed by 15.9, and therefore an application of upper continuity shows that $a \wedge a^\perp = 0$. Moreover, if y is any element of L, then

$$a \wedge (y \vee a^\perp) = a \wedge \bigvee_{x \perp a}(y \vee x) = \bigvee_{x \perp a}(a \wedge (y \vee x)) = \bigvee_{x \perp a}(a \wedge y) = a \wedge y.$$

Thus $a \, D \, a^\perp$, and we obtain

15.18: *For each $a \in L$, $a \perp a^\perp$, and consequently $a^{\perp\perp} \geq a$.*

15.19: *For each $a \in L$, $a^\perp \in C(L)$.*

PROOF: We prove 15.19 with 15.16: If $x \sim y \leq a^\perp$, then $y \perp a$ by 15.18 and 15.10, and 15.12 yields that $x \perp a$ and hence that $x \leq a^\perp$.

Additional properties are given by the following three lemmas.

15.20: *If $a, b \in L$ and $a \geq b$, then $a^\perp \leq b^\perp$.*

15.21: *For each $a \in L$, $a^{\perp\perp} = a$ if and only if $a \in C(L)$.*

15.22: *If $a, b \in L$, then $a \perp b$ if and only if $a^{\perp\perp} \wedge b^{\perp\perp} = 0$.*

If $a \geq b$ in the lattice L, then from the relation $a \perp a^\perp$ and 15.10 we obtain that $b \perp a^\perp$, and this gives $b^\perp \geq a^\perp$, the conclusion of 15.20.

The equation $a^{\perp\perp} = a$ certainly implies that $a \in C(L)$ in view of 15.19. On the other hand, if $a \in C(L)$ and a' is the complement of a, then $a \perp a'$ and therefore $a^\perp \geq a'$. This implies that $a \vee a^\perp = 1$, and as $a \wedge a^\perp = 0$, we infer that $a^\perp = a'$. It follows that $a^{\perp\perp} = (a')' = a$, as required in 15.21.

The relation $a \perp b$ implies that $a^\perp \geq b$, so that $a^{\perp\perp} \leq b^\perp$, and as $b \perp b^\perp$, we get $a^{\perp\perp} \perp b$. Now, repeating the argument with b yields $a^{\perp\perp} \perp b^{\perp\perp}$, and therefore that $a^{\perp\perp} \wedge b^{\perp\perp} = 0$. Conversely, if $a^{\perp\perp} \wedge b^{\perp\perp} = 0$, then $a^{\perp\perp} \perp b^{\perp\perp}$, and applying 15.18 and 15.10, we see that $a \perp b$, completing the proof of 15.22.

The next lemma provides the principal tool for constructing truly useful perspectivities out of existing ones.

15.23: *Let φ be a one-to-one map of an independent subset $S \subseteq L$ onto an independent subset $\varphi(S) \subseteq L$ such that $s \sim \varphi(s)$ for each $s \in S$. Then if $(\bigvee S) \wedge (\bigvee \varphi(S)) = 0$, we have $\bigvee S \sim \bigvee \varphi(S)$.*

PROOF: For each $s \in S$ let x_s be an axis of perspectivity for $s \sim \varphi(s)$. The first step is to prove that if F is a finite subset of S, then $\bigvee F \sim \bigvee \varphi(F)$ with axis of perspectivity $x_F = \bigvee_{s \in F} x_s$. This we do by induction on $|F|$. If $s \in F$ and we set $G = F - \{s\}$, then by induction $\bigvee G \sim \bigvee \varphi(G)$ with axis of perspectivity x_G. Now $S \cup \varphi(S)$ is independent by 8.1, and hence $F \cup \varphi(F)$ is also, and this implies that $(s \vee \bigvee G) \wedge (\varphi(s) \vee \bigvee \varphi(G)) = 0$. The conditions of 15.6 are therefore satisfied, and we infer that $\bigvee F = s \vee \bigvee G \sim \varphi(s) \vee \bigvee \varphi(G) = \bigvee \varphi(F)$ with axis of perspectivity $x_s \vee x_G = x_F$. Set $x = \bigvee_{s \in S} x_s$. Clearly $x \vee \bigvee S = \bigvee_{s \in S} x_s \vee s = \bigvee_{s \in S} x_s \vee \varphi(s) = x \vee \bigvee \varphi(S)$. Moreover, if $\mathcal{S}$ denotes the collection of all finite subsets of S,

$$x \wedge \bigvee S = \bigvee_{F \in \mathcal{S}} (x \wedge \bigvee F) = \bigvee_{F \in \mathcal{S}} (\bigvee F) \wedge \bigvee_{G \in \mathcal{S}} x_G = \bigvee_{F, G \in \mathcal{S}} (x_G \wedge \bigvee F)$$
$$\leq \bigvee_{F, G \in \mathcal{S}} (x_{G \cup F} \wedge \bigvee(F \cup G)) = 0.$$

Similarly $x \wedge \bigvee \varphi(S) = 0$, and we conclude that $\bigvee S \sim \bigvee \varphi(S)$.

We are now in the position to prove the basic theorem that will give the comparability of perspectivity classes when L is indecomposable.

15.24: *If $a, b \in L$, then there exist $a_1, a_2, b_1, b_2 \in L$ such that $a = a_1 \vee a_2$, $b = b_1 \vee b_2$, $a_1 \sim b_1$, and $a_2^{\perp\perp} \wedge b_2^{\perp\perp} = 0$.*

PROOF: First we take up the case when $a \wedge b = 0$. Consider the collection of all ordered pairs $\langle \varphi, S \rangle$, where φ is a one-to-one map of the independent subset $S \subseteq a/0$ onto an independent subset $\varphi(S) \subseteq b/0$ such that $s \sim \varphi(s)$ for each $s \in S$. Partially order these pairs by defining $\langle \varphi, S \rangle \le \langle \psi, T \rangle$ if $S \subseteq T$ and ψ restricted to S coincides with φ. By Zorn's lemma there exists a maximal pair $\langle \varphi, S \rangle$. (It is permissible for S to be empty.) Let $a_1 = \bigvee S$, $b_1 = \bigvee \varphi(S)$. And let a_2 be a complement of a_1 in $a/0$ and b_2 be a complement of b_1 in $b/0$. Then $a_1 \wedge b_1 \le a \wedge b = 0$, and the preceding lemma implies that $a_1 \sim b_1$. Also, $a = a_1 \vee a_2$ and $b = b_1 \vee b_2$. Therefore to complete the proof in this case, we need to show that $a_2^{\perp\perp} \wedge b_2^{\perp\perp} = 0$, or, what is equivalent in view of 15.22, that $a_2 \perp b_2$. If this last relation does not hold, then by 15.11 there are nonzero elements $s \le a_2$ and $t \le b_2$ such that $s \sim t$. But then $\{s\} \cup S$ and $\{t\} \cup \varphi(S)$ are independent sets, and 15.6 guarantees that $s \vee \bigvee S \sim t \vee \bigvee \varphi(S)$, contrary to the maximality of $\langle \varphi, S \rangle$.

In the case that $a \wedge b \ne 0$, let c and d be complements of $a \wedge b$ in $a/0$ and $b/0$, respectively. Since $c \wedge d = 0$, we can apply the first part of the proof to these elements, obtaining $c_1, c_2, d_1, d_2 \in L$ such that $c = c_1 \vee c_2$, $d = d_1 \vee d_2$, $c_1 \sim d_1$, and $c_2^{\perp\perp} \wedge d_2^{\perp\perp} = 0$. Set

$$a_1 = c_1 \vee (a \wedge b), \qquad b_1 = d_1 \vee (a \wedge b), \qquad a_2 = c_2, \qquad b_2 = d_2.$$

Then $a = c \vee (a \wedge b) = a_1 \vee a_2$ and $b = d \vee (a \wedge b) = b_1 \vee b_2$. In addition,

$$c \wedge (a \wedge b) = 0, \qquad [c \vee (a \wedge b)] \wedge d = a \wedge d = a \wedge b \wedge d = 0,$$

so that the set $\{c, a \wedge b, d\}$ is independent. Hence $\{c_1, a \wedge b, d_1\}$ is independent, and 15.6 shows that $a_1 = c_1 \vee (a \wedge b) \sim d_1 \vee (a \wedge b) = b_1$. And as $a_2^{\perp\perp} \wedge b_2^{\perp\perp} = c_2^{\perp\perp} \wedge d_2^{\perp\perp} = 0$, the proof is complete.

As suggested above, a primary application of 15.24 comes when L is indecomposable. Under these circumstances $C(L) = \{0, 1\}$, and as $a_2^{\perp\perp}$, $b_2^{\perp\perp} \in C(L)$ by 15.19, $a_2^{\perp\perp} \wedge b_2^{\perp\perp} = 0$ implies $a_2^{\perp\perp} = 0$ or $b_2^{\perp\perp} = 0$ and hence that $a_2 = 0$ or $b_2 = 0$. Consequently, *if the lattice L is indecomposable, then for any two elements $a, b \in L$ there is an element $x \in L$ such that either $a \sim x \le b$ or $b \sim x \le a$.*

We can also prove the theorem which enables us to construct elements of specified dimension.

15.25: *There exists elements a, $b \in L$ such that $a \wedge b = 0$, $a \sim b$, and $1/a \vee b$ is distributive.*

PROOF: Again consider the collection of all pairs $\langle \varphi, S \rangle$, where φ is a one-to-one map of an independent set S onto an independent set $\varphi(S)$ such that $s \sim \varphi(s)$ for each $s \in S$ and $(\bigvee S) \wedge (\bigvee \varphi(S)) = 0$. As in the proof of the preceding theorem, there is a maximal such pair $\langle \varphi, S \rangle$. Setting $a = \bigvee S$ and $b = \bigvee \varphi(S)$, we have $a \wedge b = 0$ and $a \sim b$. Suppose that $1/a \vee b$ is not distributive. If c is a complement of $a \vee b$, then $c/0 \cong 1/a \vee b$, and therefore $c/0$ is not distributive; i.e., $c/0$ contains a five-element nondistributive sublattice $\{x, y, z, x \vee y, x \wedge y\}$. We can assume that $x \wedge y = 0$, for if this is not the case, we choose a complement c' of $x \wedge y$ in $c/0$ and replace x and y by their images under the isomorphism from $c/x \wedge y$ to $c'/0$. Under these circumstances we have $x \sim y$. Moreover, as $(\bigvee S) \wedge (\bigvee \varphi(S)) = 0$, the set $S \cup \varphi(S)$ is independent by 8.1, and as

$$[\bigvee(S \cup \varphi(S))] \wedge (x \vee y) \leq (a \vee b) \wedge c = 0,$$

the set $S \cup \varphi(S) \cup \{x, y\}$ is independent. Therefore $(x \vee \bigvee S) \wedge (y \vee \bigvee \varphi(s)) = 0$, and 15.6 shows that $x \vee \bigvee S \sim y \vee \bigvee \varphi(S)$, contrary to the maximality of $\langle \varphi, S \rangle$.

Below we will see that when L is indecomposable, continuous, and not finite dimensional, the distributivity of $1/a \vee b$ implies that $a \vee b = 1$. Therefore the elements a and b of 15.25 are perspective complements and must be assigned the dimension $1/2$. Repeating this for appropriate quotients, we obtain elements of dimension $k/2^n$, where k and n are any positive integers with $k \leq 2^n$.

Even though upper continuity is insufficient to give generally the transitivity of perspectivity, it is enough to give it under considerably weaker conditions than we have considered so far.

15.26: *If $a, b \in L$, then $a \approx b$ and $a \wedge b = 0$ imply $a \sim b$.*

PROOF: It is helpful to first prove a lemma: *If $a, b \in L$, $a \neq 0$, $a \approx b$, and φ is a projectivity map from $a/0$ to $b/0$, then there exists $e \in a/0$ such that $e \neq 0$ and $e \sim \varphi(e)$.* To prove the lemma, it is enough to handle the case when $a \sim c \sim b$, since repeated use of the result in this case in conjunction with 15.4 gives the result in general. Let x be an axis of perspectivity for $a \sim c$, and let ψ_1 be the associated perspectivity map from $a/0$ to $c/0$. Let y be an axis of perspectivity for $c \sim b$, and ψ_2 be the perspectivity map of $c/0$ to $b/0$. Set $\varphi = \psi_2 \psi_1$. If $a \wedge c \neq 0$, then

$$\psi_1(a \wedge c) = ((a \wedge c) \vee x) \wedge c = (x \wedge c) \vee (a \wedge c) = a \wedge c,$$

and therefore by 15.4 we have $\varphi(a \wedge c) = \psi_2 \psi_1(a \wedge c) = \psi_2(a \wedge c) \sim$

$a \wedge c$. A corresponding argument handles the case when $b \wedge c \neq 0$, and so we may assume that $a \wedge c = b \wedge c = 0$. With this asumption observe further that if $a \vee c = b \vee c$, then $a \sim b = \varphi(a)$. Consequently we may also assume that $a \vee c \neq b \vee c$ and hence that either $a > a \wedge (b \vee c)$ or $b > b \wedge (a \vee c)$. In the case that $a > a \wedge (b \vee c)$, let e be a complement of $a \wedge (b \vee c)$ in $a/0$. Then, inasmuch as $e \wedge (b \vee c) = 0$, we get

$$e \wedge (\psi_1(e) \vee \psi_2\psi_1(e)) \leq e \wedge (c \vee b) = 0,$$

and as 15.4 guarantees that $e \sim \psi_1(e) \sim \psi_2\psi_1(e) = \varphi(e)$, we infer that $e \sim \varphi(e)$ by 15.5. A similar argument holds when $b > b \wedge (a \vee c)$.

Taking up the proof of 15.26, let φ be a projectivity map from $a/0$ to $b/0$, and let S be a maximal independent subset of $a/0$ such that $s \sim \varphi(s)$ all $s \in S$. Since φ is an isomorphism, $\varphi(S)$ is also independent, and as $(\bigvee S) \wedge (\bigvee\varphi(S)) \leq a \wedge b = 0$, 15.23 assures us that $\bigvee S \sim \bigvee\varphi(S)$. Suppose that $\bigvee S < a$. Then if c is a complement of $\bigvee S$ in $a/0$, it follows that $\varphi(c)$ is a complement of $\varphi(\bigvee S) = \bigvee\varphi(S)$ in $b/0$. Furthermore, we infer from 15.4 that $c \approx \varphi(c)$ and that the restriction of φ to $c/0$ is a projectivity map from $c/0$ to $\varphi(c)/0$. Consequently our lemma above asserts the existence of an element e such that $0 < e \leq c$ and $e \sim \varphi(e)$. But $e \wedge \bigvee S = 0$, so that $S \cup \{e\}$ is independent by 8.1, contrary to the maximality of S. Hence $a = \bigvee S \sim \bigvee\varphi(S) = b$.

Further progress in the proof of the transitivity of perspectivity requires the assumption of lower as well as upper continuity. In consequence *from now on we assume that L is a continuous complemented modular lattice.* Actually in the entire proof of 15.1, lower continuity is used only once, in the proof of the following lemma, which establishes a property that necessarily holds in any lattice having a normalized dimension function.

15.27:   *If $a_0, a_1, a_2, \ldots$ is an infinite sequence of independent elements in L such that $a_0 \sim a_1 \sim a_2 \sim \cdots$, then $a_0 = 0$.*

PROOF: Noting that $a_0 \sim a_n$ for each integer n by 15.26, pick an axis of perspectivity for $a_0 \sim a_n$, say x_n, for each $n > 0$. Then

$$a_0 \leq a_0 \vee x_n = a_n \vee x_n \leq \bigvee_{k \geq n} a_k \vee \bigvee_{k \geq 1} x_k,$$

and therefore by lower continuity,

$$a_0 \leq \bigwedge_{n>0} (\bigvee_{k \geq n} a_k \vee \bigvee_{k \geq 1} x_k) = \bigvee_{k \geq 1} x_k \vee \bigwedge_{n>0} \bigvee_{k \geq n} a_k = \bigvee_{k \geq 1} x_k$$

since 8.2 ensures that $\bigwedge_{n>0}\bigvee_{k \geq n}a_k = 0$. Also, for each $n > 0$,

$$x_{n+1} \wedge (a_0 \vee x_1 \vee \cdots \vee x_n) = x_{n+1} \wedge (a_0 \vee a_{n+1}) \wedge (a_0 \vee a_1 \vee \cdots \vee a_n)$$
$$= x_{n+1} \wedge a_0 = 0,$$

and using 8.1 and induction, we see that $\{a_0, x_1, x_2, \ldots\}$ is an independent set. Therefore $a_0 = a_0 \wedge \bigvee_{k \geq 1}x_k = 0$, as asserted.

One additional lemma, actually a special case of the transitivity of perspectivity, is needed before we tackle the proof of the transitivity: *If a and b are elements of L and $a \approx b \leq a$, then $a = b$.* To see this, let φ be a projectivity map from $a/0$ to $b/0$. Let a_0 be a complement of b in $a/0$, and for each $n > 0$ define a_n by the rule $a_n = \varphi(a_{n-1}) = \varphi^n(a_0)$. Set $b_0 = b$, and define b_n for each $n > 0$ by $b_n = \varphi(b_{n-1}) = \varphi^n(b) = \varphi^{n+1}(a)$. Since φ is an isomorphism, we have

$$b_{n-1} = \varphi^n(a) = \varphi^n(a_0 \vee b) = \varphi^n(a_0) \vee \varphi^n(b) = a_n \vee b_n,$$

$$a_n \wedge b_n = \varphi^n(a_0 \wedge b) = \varphi^n(0) = 0.$$

Therefore for each k and n with $k < n$,

$$a_k \wedge (a_{k+1} \vee \cdots \vee a_n) \leq a_k \wedge (b_k \vee \cdots \vee b_{n-1}) = a_k \wedge b_k = 0,$$

and we infer that the sequence $a_0, a_1, a_2, \ldots$ is independent. Moreover, $a_0 \approx a_1 \approx a_2 \approx \cdots$ since φ is a projectivity map, and 15.26 implies that $a_0 \sim a_1 \sim a_2 \sim \cdots$. Consequently 15.27 applies, yielding that $a_0 = 0$ and hence that $a = b$.

And now the transitivity of perspectivity.

15.28: *If $a \approx b$ in L, then $a \sim b$.*

PROOF: By 15.24 there exist elements $a_1, a_2, b_1, b_2 \in L$ such that $a = a_1 \vee a_2$, $b = b_1 \vee b_2$, $a_1 \sim b_1$, and $a_2^{\perp\perp} \wedge b_2^{\perp\perp} = 0$. Observe that we can assume that $a_1 \wedge a_2 = 0$, for if this is not the case, we replace a_2 by a complement of $a_1 \wedge a_2$ in $a_2/0$, preserving the conditions on a_2 in view of 15.20. Similarly, we can assume that $b_1 \wedge b_2 = 0$. Now from 15.19 and 15.17 we infer that $a_1 \wedge a_2^{\perp\perp} \sim b_1 \wedge a_2^{\perp\perp}$ and that $a \wedge a_2^{\perp\perp} \approx b \wedge a_2^{\perp\perp}$, and as $b_2 \wedge a_2^{\perp\perp} \leq b_2^{\perp\perp} \wedge a_2^{\perp\perp} = 0$, we have

$$a \wedge a_2^{\perp\perp} \approx b \wedge a_2^{\perp\perp} = (b_1 \vee b_2) \wedge a_2^{\perp\perp} = (b_1 \wedge a_2^{\perp\perp}) \vee (b_2 \wedge a_2^{\perp\perp})$$
$$= b_1 \wedge a_2^{\perp\perp} \sim a_1 \wedge a_2^{\perp\perp} \leq a \wedge a_2^{\perp\perp}.$$

Consequently $a \wedge a_2^{\perp\perp} = a_1 \wedge a_2^{\perp\perp}$ by the lemma proved in the preceding paragraph, and therefore

$$a_1 \geq a_1 \wedge a_2^{\perp\perp} = a \wedge a_2^{\perp\perp} = (a_1 \vee a_2) \wedge a_2^{\perp\perp} = (a_1 \wedge a_2^{\perp\perp}) \vee (a_2 \wedge a_2^{\perp\perp})$$
$$= (a_1 \wedge a_2^{\perp\perp}) \vee a_2 \geq a_2.$$

We conclude that $a_2 = a_1 \wedge a_2 = 0$, and, similarly, that $b_2 = 0$, whence $a = a_1 \sim b_1 = b$, completing the proof.

Having 15.28, we are able to obtain results concerning the preservation of perspectivity under join that are sharper than those available to us before now.

15.29: *If a, b, c, d are elements of L, then*

(1) $a \vee b \sim c \vee d$, $a \wedge b = c \wedge d = 0$, *and* $a \sim c$ *imply* $b \sim d$.
(2) $a \wedge b = c \wedge d = 0$, $a \sim c$, *and* $b \sim d$ *imply* $a \vee b \sim c \vee d$.

PROOF: Consider first the special case of (1) when $a \vee b = c \vee d$. Let x be a common complement of a and c, and set $y = (a \vee b) \wedge x$. Then $a \wedge y = 0 = a \wedge b$ and $a \vee y = (a \vee b) \wedge (a \vee x) = a \vee b$, so $y \sim b$. Similarly, $y = (c \vee d) \wedge x \sim d$, and 15.28 implies that $b \sim d$.

When the assumptions of (1) hold, let a_1 and b_1 be the images of a and b, respectively, under a perspectivity map from $a \vee b/0$ to $c \vee d/0$. Since this map is an isomorphism, we certainly have $a_1 \vee b_1 = c \vee d$. Moreover, $a_1 \sim a \sim c$, and 15.28 combined with the preceding paragraph yields the conclusion of (1).

To prove (2), let x and y be complements of $a \vee b$ and $c \vee d$, respectively. Then

$$a \wedge (b \vee x) = a \wedge (a \vee b) \wedge (b \vee x) = a \wedge [b \vee ((a \vee b) \wedge x)]$$
$$= a \wedge b = 0,$$

and, similarly, $c \wedge (d \vee y) = 0$. As $a \vee (b \vee x) = c \vee (d \vee y) = 1$ and $a \sim c$, we conclude from (1) that $b \vee x \sim d \vee y$. But $b \wedge x = d \wedge y = 0$ and $b \sim d$, so that $x \sim y$. Remembering that x and y are complements of $a \vee b$ and $c \vee d$ and applying (1) a third time, we infer that $a \vee b \sim c \vee d$, as desired.

Once again we must impose additional assumptions on our lattice L; *for the remainder of the proof of* 15.1, L *will be an indecomposable, continuous, complemented modular lattice.* We have already noted, as a corollary to 15.24, that under these assumptions, for any two elements a, $b \in L$, there exists $x \in L$ such that either $a \sim x \leq b$ or $b \sim x \leq a$. For convenience let us write

$$a \lesssim b$$

to designate that there exists an element x such that $a \sim x \leq b$. With this notation, the corollary to 15.25 becomes

15.30:   *For any two elements* a, $b \in L$, *either* $a \lesssim b$ *or* $b \lesssim a$.

From the transitivity of perspectivity it follows directly that the relation $\lesssim$ is transitive. Note further that if $a \leq y \sim b$, then $a \sim \varphi(b) \leq b$, where φ is a perspectivity map from $y/0$ to $b/0$, and hence $a \lesssim b$. Conversely, if $a \lesssim b$, i.e., $a \sim x \leq b$ for some x, then applying the argument in the preceding sentence to the dual of L, we see that $a \leq y \sim b$ for some $y \in L$. Consequently the conditions $a \lesssim b$ and $a \leq y \sim b$ for some element y are equivalent.

15.31:   *L is simple.*

PROOF: Suppose L has a nontrivial congruence relation θ. Pick $a > 0$ such that $a \, \theta \, 0$, and let a' be a complement of a. If $a' \lesssim a$, then inasmuch as θ identifies perspective elements, we have $a' \, \theta \, 0$, which implies that $1 = a \vee a'$ $\theta \, 0$, contrary to the assumption that θ is nontrivial. Therefore $a \lesssim a'$ by 15.30. Set $a = a_0$, and pick a_1 such that $a = a_0 \sim a_1 \leq a'$. Observing that $a_0 \wedge a_1 = 0$ and that $a_0 \vee a_1 \, \theta \, 0$, choose a complement $(a_0 \vee a_1)'$ of $a_0 \vee a_1$. Again $(a_0 \vee a_1)' \lesssim a_0 \vee a_1$ implies that $1 \, \theta \, 0$, so we must have $a_0 \vee a_1 \lesssim (a_0 \vee a_1)'$. Pick a_2 such that $a_1 \sim a_2 \leq (a_0 \vee a_1)'$. Then $a_2 \wedge (a_0 \vee a_1) = 0$, and $a_0 \sim a_1 \sim a_2$. Continuing in this way, we get an independent sequence $a_0, a_1, a_2, \ldots$ of pairwise perspective elements, and 15.27 yields that $a = a_0 = 0$, a contradiction. Thus L has no nontrivial congruence relations.

Now suppose that L contains a prime quotient p/q. If $\theta_{p,q}$ is the least congruence relation collapsing p/q, then the preceding theorem shows that $1 \, \theta_{p,q} \, 0$, and therefore there is a finite sequence of elements $0 = e_0 < e_1 < \cdots < e_n = 1$ such that each e_i/e_{i-1} is projective to p/q. Each e_i/e_{i-1} is in consequence a prime quotient, and we conclude that *if L contains a prime quotient, then L is finite dimensional.*

When L is finite dimensional, a normalized dimension function in L can be constructed from its dimension function, as we described in the opening paragraphs of this chapter. We are left, therefore, with the case when L is not finite dimensional, and consequently we impose our final set of assumptions: *Henceforth L is an indecomposable, continuous, complemented modular lattice that is not finite dimensional.* Such a lattice is customarily referred to as a *continuous geometry.*

It is useful to observe that the property of being a continuous geometry is inherited by quotient sublattices: *If a and b are any two elements of L with $a > b$, then the sublattice a/b is a continuous geometry.* Since transposed quotient sublattices are isomorphic and L is relatively complemented, to prove this statement it is enough to show that $a/0$ is a continuous geometry whenever $a > 0$. Certainly $a/0$ contains no prime quotient and is continuous, complemented, and modular, so we have left to prove that $a/0$ is also indecomposable. Suppose x, y are orthogonal elements of $a/0$. If x and y are not orthogonal in L, then by 15.11 there are nonzero elements $u, v \in L$ such that $u \leq x$, $v \leq y$, and $u \sim v$ in L. But because of 15.2, it follows that $u \sim v$ in $a/0$, contrary to the assumption that x and y are orthogonal in $a/0$. Consequently $x \perp y$ in L, and 15.15, 15.18, 15.19, and 15.22 combine to show that either $x = 0$ or $y = 0$. Applying 15.15 again, we see that $a/0$ is indecomposable.

We are now about ready to construct a normalized dimension function in L. Here the basic tool is the following lemma: *For each element $a \in L$ there exist two elements $b, c \in L$ such that $a = b \vee c, b \wedge c = 0$, and $b \sim c$.*

This we prove by applying 15.25 to the sublattice $a/0$, obtaining elements b and c such that $b \wedge c = 0$, $b \sim c$, and the sublattice $a/b \vee c$ is distributive. The last condition yields that $a = b \vee c$, for otherwise the observation made in the preceding paragraph would require $a/b \vee c$ to be a simple Boolean algebra that is not finite dimensional, an impossibility, as each simple Boolean algebra is a two-element chain.

The first step in the construction of a normalized dimension function in L is to obtain a family of elements $a(n, k)$, n and k integers with $n \geq 0$ and $1 \leq k \leq 2^n$, such that the following properties hold:

(1) $a(0, 1) = 1$.
(2) $a(n, 1) \sim a(n, 2) \sim \cdots \sim a(n, 2^n)$ for each $n \geq 1$.
(3) The set $\{a(n, 1), a(n, 2), \ldots, a(n, 2^n)\}$ is independent for each $n \geq 1$.
(4) $a(n, 2k - 1) \vee a(n, 2k) = a(n - 1, k)$ for each $n \geq 1$ and $1 \leq k \leq 2^{n-1}$.

The element $a(0, 1)$ is given to us by (1). Suppose the elements $a(n - 1, 1)$, $\ldots, a(n - 1, 2^{n-1})$ have been constructed. Apply the lemma in the preceding paragraph to the element $a(n - 1, 1)$ to obtain two perspective elements $a(n, 1)$ and $a(n, 2)$ which are complements in $a(n - 1, 1)/0$. For each positive integer $k \leq 2^{n-1}$, let $a(n, 2k - 1)$ and $a(n, 2k)$ be the images of $a(n, 1)$ and $a(n, 2)$, respectively, under a perspectivity map from $a(n - 1, 1)/0$ to $a(n - 1, k)/0$. Under these circumstances it is clear that (2)–(4) are satisfied by $a(n, 1), \ldots, a(n, 2^n)$.

Let T be the set of all rational numbers of the form $k/2^n$, where k and n are nonnegative integers with $k \leq 2^n$. For each $r \in T$, define

$$c_r = a(n, 1) \vee \cdots \vee a(n, k) \qquad \text{if } r = k/2^n.$$

Note that this definition of c_r is independent of the particular representation of r, for if $r = k/2^n = 2k/2^{n+1}$, then the preceding formula for c_r coupled with property (4) above yields that

$$c_r = a(n + 1, 1) \vee a(n + 1, 2) \vee \cdots \vee a(n + 1, 2k - 1) \vee a(n + 1, 2k),$$

and an induction shows that the same value is obtained for c_r when r is written $r = 2^m k/2^{m+n}$.

It is certainly true that *for any two r, $s \in T$, $r < s$ implies $c_r < c_s$*; this becomes apparent by writing r and s with the same denominators and looking at the corresponding definitions of c_r and c_s. Moreover, as distinct comparable elements of L cannot have a common complement, *whenever $c_r \lesssim c_s$, then $r \leq s$*.

We need two additional lemmas.

15.32: *If r, $s \in T$ are such that $r + s \leq 1$, then there exists $e \in L$ such that $c_s \sim e$, $c_r \wedge e = 0$, and $c_r \vee e = c_{r+s}$.*

PROOF: Write $r = k/2^n$ and $s = l/2^n$. Then $k + l \leq 2^n$, and we can define

$$e = a(n, k + 1) \vee \cdots \vee a(n, k + l).$$

From property (3) and the definitions of c_r and c_{r+s} we obtain directly that $c_r \wedge e = 0$ and $c_r \vee e = c_{r+s}$. Further, since the map $a(n, i) \rightarrow a(n, k + i)$ ($i = 1, \ldots, l$) is one-to-one, properties (2) and (3) combine with 15.29 to guarantee that $c_s \sim e$.

15.33:   *If $a, b \in L$, $a \sim c_r$, $b \sim c_s$, and $a \wedge b = 0$, then $r + s \leq 1$.*

PROOF: Assume that $r + s > 1$, and set $t = 1 - r$. Then $t < s$, and therefore $c_t < c_s$. Also, if b_1 is the image of c_t under a perspectivity map from $c_s/0$ to $b/0$, then $b_1 \sim c_t$. By the preceding lemma there exists an element e such that $e \sim c_t$, $e \wedge c_r = 0$, and $e \vee c_r = c_{t+r} = c_1 = 1$. This means that $a \sim c_r$ and $b_1 \sim c_t \sim e$, so that in view of 15.29 we have

$$a \vee b_1 \sim c_r \vee e = 1;$$

i.e., $a \vee b_1 = 1$. But as $b \geq b_1$, the modularity of L yields that $b = b_1$, whence $c_s \sim b = b_1 \sim c_t$, contrary to $t < s$.

Now for each $x \in L$, define

$$d(x) = \sup \{r \in T \,|\, c_r \lesssim x\}.$$

Three properties of d are immediate: $d(0) = 0$, $d(1) = 1$, and $d(x) \leq d(y)$ whenever $x \leq y$.

Suppose x and y are elements of L with $x \wedge y = 0$. For a given $\epsilon > 0$, pick $r, s \in T$ such that $d(x) - \epsilon < r < d(x)$ and $d(y) - \epsilon < s < d(y)$. Then there exist $x_1 \leq x$ and $y_1 \leq y$ such that $c_r \sim x_1$ and $c_s \sim y_1$. Lemma 15.33 ensures that $r + s \leq 1$, and therefore by 15.32 there is an element e such that $c_s \sim e$, $c_r \wedge e = 0$, and $c_r \vee e = c_{r+s}$. Thus $e \sim c_s \sim y_1$, and applying 15.29, we get that $c_{r+s} = c_r \vee e \sim x_1 \vee y_1 \leq x \vee y$. Consequently

$$d(x \vee y) \geq r + s > d(x) + d(y) - 2\epsilon,$$

and as ϵ was an arbitrary positive number, we conclude that $d(x \vee y) \geq d(x) + d(y)$.

On the other hand, given $\epsilon > 0$, there exist $r, s \in T$ such that $d(x) < r < d(x) + \epsilon$ and $d(y) < s < d(y) + \epsilon$. These conditions imply that $x \lesssim c_r$ and $y \lesssim c_s$. If $r + s \leq 1$, then 15.32 provides an element e such that $c_s \sim e$, $c_r \wedge e = 0$, and $c_r \vee e = c_{r+s}$, and using 15.29, we see that $x \vee y \lesssim c_r \vee e = c_{r+s}$ and hence that $d(x \vee y) \leq r + s < d(x) + d(y) + 2\epsilon$. If $r + s > 1$, then $d(x \vee y) \leq 1 < r + s = d(x) + d(y) + 2\epsilon$. In either case we have $d(x \vee y) \leq d(x) + d(y) + 2\epsilon$,   so   that $d(x \vee y) \leq d(x) + d(y)$. Thus $d(x \vee y) = d(x) + d(y)$ whenever $x \wedge y = 0$.

Suppose now that x and y are arbitrary elements of L. Let w be a complement of $x \wedge y$ in $x/0$. Then, as just observed, $d(x) = d(x \wedge y) + d(w)$.

Also, $w \vee y = w \vee (x \wedge y) \vee y = x \vee y$ and $w \wedge y = w \wedge x \wedge y = 0$, whence

$$d(x \vee y) = d(w) + d(y) = d(x) + d(y) - d(x \wedge y).$$

Therefore, for any x, $y \in L$, $d(x \vee y) + d(x \wedge y) = d(x) + d(y)$.

Finally, suppose that $x > y$. Since L is simple, there is a finite sequence $0 = x_0 < x_1 < \cdots < x_n = 1$ such that each x_i/x_{i-1} is projective to a sub-quotient of x/y. Note that if a_1/b_1 and a_2/b_2 are projective quotients, then $d(a_1) - d(b_1) = d(a_2) - d(b_2)$. Consequently, if $d(x) = d(y)$, then $0 = d(0) = d(x_0) = d(x_1) = \cdots = d(x_n) = d(1) = 1$, a contradiction. Hence $d(x) > d(y)$, and we conclude that d is a normalized dimension function in L.

One small detail remains; we need to show that d is unique. To this end assume that d' is another normalized dimension function in L. Since $a(n, 1)$, $a(n, 2), \ldots, a(n, 2^n)$ are 2^n pairwise perspective independent elements whose join is 1, it follows that $d'(a(n, i)) = 1/2^n$ for each $i = 1, \ldots, 2^n$. In consequence, for each $r \in T$, say $r = k/2^n$, $d'(c_r) = k/2_n = r = d(c_r)$. From this we infer that $d(x) = \sup\{r \mid c_r \lesssim x\} = \sup\{d'(c_r) \mid c_r \lesssim x\} \leq d'(x)$ for any element $x \in L$. On the other hand, the inequality $d(x) < d'(x)$ cannot hold, for if it did, and if $r \in T$ were such that $d(x) < r < d'(x)$, then $x \lesssim c_r$ so that $d'(x) \leq d'(c_r) = r$, a contradiction. Thus $d(x) = d'(x)$ for each $x \in L$. This completes the proof of 15.1.

Passing now to the question of the existence of continuous geometries, we describe a technique, also due to von Neumann,[2] for constructing a continuous geometry $CG(\Delta)$ for each division ring Δ. Basic to this technique is the *metric completion* of a lattice which we first need to develop.

Let M be a modular lattice (with least element 0 and greatest element 1) having a normalized dimension function d. For each pair of elements a, $b \in M$, define

$$\partial(a, b) = d(a \vee b) - d(a \wedge b).$$

Certainly $\partial(a, b) = \partial(b, a)$, $\partial(a, b) \geq 0$, and $\partial(a, b) = 0$ if and only if $a = b$. It is also clear that if $a \geq b \geq c$, then $\partial(a, b) + \partial(b, c) = \partial(a, c)$, and if a/b is a transpose of c/d, then $\partial(a, b) = \partial(c, d)$. Moreover, for all $a, b, c \in M$, we have

$$\partial(a, c) \leq \partial(a, b) + \partial(b, c).$$

To see this, note that $a \vee c \geq (a \wedge b) \vee c \geq (a \vee b) \wedge c \geq a \wedge c$, whence

$$\partial(a, c) = \partial(a \vee c, a \wedge c) = \partial(a \vee c, (a \wedge b) \vee c)$$
$$+ \partial((a \wedge b) \vee c, (a \vee b) \wedge c) + \partial((a \vee b) \wedge c, a \wedge c).$$

Also, $a \vee c/(a \wedge b) \vee c$ is a transpose of $a/(a \wedge b) \vee (a \wedge c)$, so that

$$\partial(a \vee c, (a \wedge b) \vee c) = \partial(a, (a \wedge b) \vee (a \vee c)),$$

[2] J. von Neumann [72].

and likewise $\partial((a \vee b) \wedge c, a \wedge c) = \partial((a \vee b) \wedge (a \vee c), a)$. Therefore

$$\partial(a \vee c, (a \wedge b) \vee c) + \partial((a \vee b) \wedge c, a \wedge c)$$
$$= \partial((a \vee b) \wedge (a \vee c), (a \wedge b) \vee (a \wedge c)) \leq \partial(a, b),$$

and this combined with the fact that $\partial((a \wedge b) \vee c, (a \vee b) \wedge c) \leq \partial(b \vee c, b \wedge c) = \partial(b, c)$ gives the desired result. In particular, M together with ∂ is a metric space. Note further that as $a \vee b \vee c/(a \vee c) \wedge (b \vee c)$ is a transpose of $a \vee b/(a \vee c) \wedge (b \vee c) \wedge (a \vee b)$,

$$\partial(a \vee c, b \vee c) = \partial(a \vee b \vee c, (a \vee c) \wedge (b \vee c))$$
$$= \partial(a \vee b, (a \vee c) \wedge (b \vee c) \wedge (a \vee b))$$
$$\leq \partial(a \vee b, a \wedge b) = \partial(a, b),$$

with $\partial(a \wedge c, b \wedge c) \leq \partial(a, b)$ following similarly. These inequalities combine with the triangle inequality above to give

$$\partial(a \vee b, c \vee d) \leq \partial(a, c) + \partial(b, d),$$
$$\partial(a \wedge b, c \wedge d) \leq \partial(a, c) + \partial(b, d).$$

Now let P be the direct product of $\aleph_0$ copies of M; i.e., P consists of all functions x defined in the set of nonnegative integers such that $x(n) \in M$ for each $n \geq 0$. Let Q be that subset of P consisting of all those $x \in P$ with the property: There is a real number $r > 0$ such that $\partial(x(n-1), x(n)) \leq r/2^n$ for each $n \geq 1$. It is apparent from the inequalities above that Q is a sublattice of P, and in particular that Q is modular.

Define the relation ρ in the lattice Q by the rule

$$x \,\rho\, y \text{ if } \partial\big(x(n), y(n)\big) \longrightarrow 0 \text{ as } n \longrightarrow \infty.$$

The inequalities above show that ρ is a congruence relation in Q, so Q/ρ is also a modular lattice. If $a \in M$ and $x_a \in P$ is defined by $x_a(n) = a$ for each $n \geq 0$, then certainly $x_a \in Q$. And it is easy to verify that the map $a \longrightarrow x_a \rho$ is an isomorphism of M to Q/ρ. We will refer to this lattice Q/ρ as the *metric completion* of M. (In fact, Q/ρ is simply the familiar completion of M as a metric space.) One additional observation: If $x \in Q$, $n_0 < n_1 < n_2 < \cdots$ is an infinite sequence of nonnegative integers and $y(k) = x(n_k)$ for each $k \geq 0$, then $y \in Q$ and $y \,\rho\, x$.

Notice that if $x \in Q$, then $|d(x(n))) - d(x(n+1))| \leq \partial(x(n), x(n+1))$, and this guarantees that the sequence of real numbers $d(x(0))$, $d(x(1))$, $d(x(2))$, $\cdots$ converges. Furthermore, if $x \,\rho\, y$, then it is clear that $\lim_{n \to \infty} d(y(n)) = \lim_{n \to \infty} d(x(n))$. Consequently without ambiguity we can define $d(x\rho) = \lim_{n \to \infty} d(x(n))$. With this definition it is readily checked that d is a normalized dimension function in Q/ρ.

Suppose C is a chain of Q/ρ. Set $s = \sup\{d(x\rho) \mid x\rho \in C\}$, and pick a sequence $x_0\rho, x_1\rho, x_2\rho, \cdots \in C$ such that $d(x_n\rho) \longrightarrow s$ as $n \longrightarrow \infty$. Moreover, choose these x_n's in such a way that $x_0 \leq x_1 \leq x_2 < \cdots$ and $d(x_n\rho) -$

$d(x_{n-1}\rho) < 1/2^n$ for each $n \geq 1$. For each $n \geq 0$, pick an integer $k_n > 0$ such that $k_n > k_{n-1}$ and such that $\partial(x_n(l), x_n(m)) < 1/2^n$ whenever l, $m \geq k_n$. Observe that this last condition implies that $|d(x_n(l)) - d(x_n\rho)| \leq 1/2^n$ whenever $l \geq k_n$. Now define $w \in P$ by

$$w(n) = x_n(k_n), \qquad n = 0, 1, 2, \ldots .$$

$w \in Q$, since for each $n > 0$,

$$\partial\big(w(n-1), w(n)\big) \leq \partial\big(x_{n-1}(k_{n-1}), x_{n-1}(k_n)\big) + \partial\big(x_{n-1}(k_n), x_n(k_n)\big)$$
$$< 1/2^{n-1} + d\big(x_n(k_n)\big) - d\big(x_{n-1}(k_{n-1})\big)$$
$$\leq 1/2^{n-1} + |d\big(x_n(k_n)\big) - d(x_n\rho)| + |d(x_n\rho) - d(x_{n-1}\rho)|$$
$$+ |d\big(x_{n-1}(k_n)\big) - d(x_{n-1}\rho)|$$
$$\leq 6/2^n.$$

Also, $d\big(w(n)\big) \longrightarrow s$ as $n \longrightarrow \infty$, so $d(w\rho) = s$. In addition, $w(m) \geq x_n(m)$ if $m \geq k_n$, and this implies that $w\rho \geq x_n\rho$ for each $n \geq 0$. On the other hand, if $y \in Q$ and $y\rho \geq x_n\rho$ for each $n \geq 0$, then $w\rho \wedge y\rho \geq x_n\rho$ $(n = 0, 1, 2, \ldots)$, whence $d(w\rho \vee y\rho) \geq s = d(w\rho)$, and we infer that $y\rho \geq w\rho$. Thus $w\rho = \bigvee_{n \geq 0} x_n\rho$, and having this, it is apparent that $w\rho = \bigvee C$. Hence Q/ρ is a complete lattice.

If z is any element of Q and C is a chain of Q/ρ, then under any circumstances we have $z\rho \wedge \bigvee C \geq \bigvee_{x\rho \in C} z\rho \wedge x\rho$. Also,

$$d(z\rho \wedge \bigvee C) = d(z\rho) + d(\bigvee C) - d(z\rho \vee \bigvee C).$$

The argument in the preceding paragraph shows that $d(\bigvee C) = \sup\{d(z\rho)\,|\,z\rho \in C\}$, and consequently if ϵ is any positive real number there is some $y\rho \in C$ such that $d(\bigvee C) \leq d(y\rho) + \epsilon$. Therefore

$$d(\bigvee_{x\rho \in C} z\rho \wedge x\rho) \leq d(z\rho \wedge \bigvee C) \leq d(z\rho) + d(y\rho) - d(z\rho \vee y\rho) + \epsilon$$
$$= d(z\rho \wedge y\rho) + \epsilon \leq d(\bigvee_{x\rho \in C} z\rho \wedge x\rho) + \epsilon,$$

and as this is true for each $\epsilon > 0$, we conclude that $z\rho \wedge \bigvee C$ and $\bigvee_{x\rho \in C} z\rho \wedge x\rho$ have the same dimension and hence are equal. Thus Q/ρ is upper continuous, and a dual argument shows that it is also lower continuous.

Next we show that if M is complemented, then so is Q/ρ. Assuming that M is complemented, let $a, b \in M$ with $a \geq b$, and let a' be a complement of a. If e is any complement of $b \vee a'$ and $b' = a' \vee e$, then a straightforward calculation shows that b' is a complement of b and that $a/b \approx 1/b \vee a' \approx e/0 \approx a' \vee e/a' = b'/a'$, so that $\partial(a, b) = \partial(a', b')$. It now follows that if a and b are arbitrary elements of M and a' is a complement of a, then there is a complement b' of b such that

$$\partial(a', b') \leq \partial(a, b).$$

For by the preceding calculation there is a complement c of $a \wedge b$ such that $\partial(a', c) = \partial(a, a \wedge b)$, and dually there is a complement b' of b such that

$\partial(b, a \wedge b) = \partial(b', c)$, whence

$$\partial(a', b') \le \partial(a', c) + \partial(c, b') = \partial(a, a \wedge b) + \partial(b, a \wedge b)$$
$$= \partial(a \vee b, b) + \partial(b, a \wedge b) = \partial(a \vee b, a \wedge b) = \partial(a, b).$$

Having the last inequality, the complementation of Q/ρ is easy to demonstrate. If $x \in Q$, then picking any complement $x'(0)$ of $x(0)$ in M and applying the preceding result repeatedly, we obtain a complement $x'(n)$ of $x(n)$ such that $\partial(x'(n-1), x'(n)) \le \partial(x(n-1), x(n))$. The function x' so defined certainly belongs to Q and is a complement of x, so $x'\rho$ is a complement of $x\rho$ in Q/ρ.

Finally, we prove: If M has the property that each element $a \in M$ with $0 < d(a) \le 2/3$ has two complements $a', a'' \in M$ with $\partial(a', a'') \ge d(a)$, then Q/ρ is indecomposable. In view of 15.13–15.15, to prove this it suffices to show that if $x \in Q$ and $0 < d(x\rho) = s \le 1/2$, then $x\rho$ has two distinct complements in Q/ρ. By replacing x with a suitable member of the class $x\rho$, if necessary, we can assume that $s/2 < d(x(0)) < 2/3$ and that $\partial(x(n-1), x(n)) < s/2^{n+3}$ for each $n \ge 1$. Pick two complements a and b of $x(0)$ in M such that $\partial(a, b) \ge d(x(0)) > s/2$. Using the method of the preceding paragraph, construct two complements $x'\rho$ and $x''\rho$ of $x\rho$ such that $x'(0) = a$, $x''(0) = b$, and such that $\partial(x'(n-1), x'(n)) \le \partial(x(n-1), x(n))$ and $\partial(x''(n-1), x''(n)) \le \partial(x(n-1), x(n))$ for each $n \le 1$. It then follows that neither $\partial(a, x'(n))$ nor $\partial(b, x''(n))$ exceeds $s/16 + \cdots + s/2^{n+3} < s/8$, and therefore for each $n \ge 0$,

$$\partial(x'(n), x''(n)) \ge \partial(a, b) - \partial(a, x'(n)) - \partial(b, x''(n)) > \frac{s}{4}.$$

This establishes that $x'\rho \ne x''\rho$, completing the argument.

Now let Δ be an arbitrary division ring. For each $n \ge 0$, let v_n be a vector space over Δ of dimension 2^n such that $v_{n+1} = v_n \oplus v_n$, where $\oplus$ denotes vector space direct sum, and let M_n be the lattice of all subspaces of v_n. Note that there is a normalized dimension function d_n in M_n defined by

$$d_n(a) = \frac{1}{2^n} \dim a,$$

where $\dim a$ denotes the dimension of the subspace $a \in M_n$. Also, the map $a \longrightarrow a \oplus a (a \in M_n)$ is an embedding of M_n in M_{n+1}, and inasmuch as

$$d_{n+1}(a \oplus a) = \frac{1}{2^{n+1}} \dim a \oplus a = \frac{1}{2^n} \dim a = d_n(a),$$

this embedding preserves the dimension function. If we identify each element of M_n with its image in M_{n+1} under this embedding, then M_n and M_{n+1} have the same least and greatest elements, and we get an ascending chain of lattices

$$M_0 \subseteq M_1 \subseteq M_2 \subseteq \cdots.$$

Let M be the set-union of this chain of lattices. It is clear that M is a complemented modular lattice, and if we set $d(a) = d_n(a)$ when $a \in M_n$, then this defines a normalized dimension function d in M. Moreover, each element $a \in M_n$ with $0 < d(a) \leq 2/3$ has two complements a', $a'' \in M_n$ with $\partial(a', a'') \geq d(a)$ (proof?), and therefore M also has this property. Further, M is not finite dimensional since it contains arbitrarily large finite chains. Consequently if $CG(\Delta)$ denotes the metric completion of M, then $CG(\Delta)$ is a continuous geometry.

In connection with the foregoing construction, the reader should convince himself of two things: first, that it is possible that $CG(\Delta_1) \cong CG(\Delta_2)$ even though Δ_1 and Δ_2 are nonisomorphic division rings (*hint:* consider the field of real numbers and the division ring of real quaternions), and, second, that there do exist pairs of division rings giving rise to nonisomorphic continuous geometries.

In spite of our efforts in this chapter, we have, in fact, only scratched the surface of the theory of continuous geometries. Standing out among those results we have not discussed is von Neumann's truly remarkable *coordinatization theorem*, which asserts that any continuous geometry is isomorphic with the lattice of all principal left ideals of some regular ring. The proof of this can be found in von Neumann's published notes [73] edited by I. Halperin, or in F. Maeda's book [65]. An extension of the coordinatization theorem to arbitrary simple complemented modular lattices of dimension greater than 3 has been discovered by Jónsson [58]. And a revealing delineation of the roles of upper and lower continuity and the "finiteness" property stated in 15.27 has been developed by Amemiya and Halperin [1]. Thorough guides to the vast literature on continuous geometries and associated topics are found in Halperin's article [48] and in his editorial notes to [73].

16

FREE LATTICES

We say that a lattice F is *freely generated* by a subset X if F is generated by X and any map of the subset X to a lattice L extends to a homomorphism of F to L. When a lattice F is freely generated by one of its subsets, we refer to F as a *free lattice*.

It is a familiar fact from universal algebra that if a lattice L is generated by a subset X and two maps with domain L agree on X, then these two maps are equal. With this fact in hand, it is easy to derive the following uniqueness theorem for free lattices: *If F_1 and F_2 are freely generated by subsets X_1 and X_2, respectively, then any one-to-one map of X_1 onto X_2 extends to an isomorphism of F_1 onto F_2.* (Proofs are left as an exercise.)

Our purpose in this chapter is to give an explicit description of the lattice freely generated by a set of given cardinality and to use this description in the solution of some general lattice-theoretic problems.

To start, let X be an arbitrary nonempty set. Form the word algebra $W(X)$ over X. Define a binary relation $\leq$ in $W(X)$ by the rules:

(1) $p \leq q$ if $p, q \in X$ and $p = q$.
(2) $p \leq q$ if $p = (p_1 \wedge p_2)$ and either $p_1 \leq q$ or $p_2 \leq q$.
(3) $p \leq q$ if $p = (p_1 \vee p_2)$ and both $p_1 \leq q$ and $p_2 \leq q$.
(4) $p \leq q$ if $q = (q_1 \wedge q_2)$ and both $p \leq q_1$ and $p \leq q_2$.
(5) $p \leq q$ if $q = (q_1 \vee q_2)$ and either $p \leq q_1$ or $p \leq q_2$.

16.1: *The relation $\leq$ in $W(X)$ is reflexive and transitive.*

PROOF: Observe that $p \leq p$ certainly holds whenever $p \in X$. Suppose that $q \leq q$ whenever rank $q <$ rank p. If $p = (p_1 \vee p_2)$, then $p_1 \leq p_1$ and $p_2 \leq p_2$, so that $p \leq p$ follows from two applications of the definition of the relation $\leq$. The case $p = (p_1 \wedge p_2)$ follows by duality.

It is helpful to preface the proof of the transitivity with a lemma: *If $p, q \in W(X)$, $p = (p_1 \vee p_2)$, and $p \leq q$, then $p_1 \leq q$ and $p_2 \leq q$. The dual also* *holds.* The proof is by induction on the rank of q. When $q \in X$, the implication is clear from the definition of the relation $\leq$. If $q = (q_1 \vee q_2)$, then either the desired conclusion holds, or $p \leq q_i$ for $i = 1$ or 2, but then $p_1 \leq q_i$ and $p_2 \leq q_i$, whence $p_1 \leq q$ and $p_2 \leq q$. A similar argument handles the case $q = (q_1 \wedge q_2)$.

Now suppose that $p \leq q$ and $q \leq r$. We will show that $p \leq r$ by induction on rank p + rank q + rank r. Notice that the desired inequality follows trivially if either both p and q or both q and r belong to X. All the remaining possibilities for the forms of p, q, and r fall into at least one of the following seven cases: (1) $p = (p_1 \vee p_2)$, (2) $p \in X$ and $q = (q_1 \vee q_2)$, (3) $p = (p_1 \wedge p_2)$ and $q = (q_1 \vee q_2)$, (4) $q \in X$ and $r = (r_1 \vee r_2)$, (5) $r = (r_1 \wedge r_2)$, (6) $q = (q_1 \wedge q_2)$ and $r \in X$, and (7) $q = (q_1 \wedge q_2)$ and $r = (r_1 \vee r_2)$.

Case (1) follows easily, for the lemma yields that $p_1 \leq q$ and $p_2 < q$, so that $p_1 \leq r$ and $p_2 \leq r$, whence $p \leq r$. In the second case, $p \leq q$ implies that $p \leq q_i$ for $i = 1$ or 2, while $q \leq r$ implies that $q_i \leq r$, and so $p \leq r$. If case (3) holds, then from $p \leq q$ it follows that either $p_i \leq q$ or $p \leq q_i$ for $i = 1$ or 2. The first alternative yields that $p_i \leq r$ and hence that $p \leq r$, and the second alternative yields directly that $p \leq r$. In the fourth case, $q \leq r$ implies that $q \leq r_i$ for $i = 1$ or 2, and therefore $p \leq r_i$, which gives us $p \leq r$. Finally, cases (5), (6), and (7) are the duals of (1), (2), and (3), respectively, and consequently duality completes the proof.

Now define a second binary relation $\wedge$ in $W(X)$ by the rule

$$p \wedge q \text{ if } p \leq q \text{ and } q \leq p.$$

It is clear that $\wedge$ is an equivalence relation in $W(X)$. Moreover, the definition of the relation $\leq$ yields that $(p \vee r) \wedge (q \vee r)$ and $(p \wedge r) \wedge (q \wedge r)$ whenever $p, q, r \in W(X)$ and $p \wedge q$. Thus $\wedge$ is a congruence relation in $W(X)$. Let $FL(X)$ denote the factor system $W(X)/\wedge$; i.e., $FL(X)$ consists of the congruence classes $p\wedge$ ($p \in W(X)$) together with the binary operations $\vee$ and $\wedge$ defined by

$$p\wedge \vee q\wedge = (p \vee q)\wedge, \qquad p\wedge \wedge q\wedge = (p \wedge q)\wedge.$$

16.2: *$FL(X)$ is a lattice freely generated by $\{x\wedge \mid x \in X\}$. Moreover, the map $x \longrightarrow x\wedge$ ($x \in X$) is one-to-one.*[1]

PROOF: To show that $FL(X)$ is a lattice, observe that if we define

$$p\wedge \leq q\wedge \text{ if } p \leq q \text{ in } W(X),$$

then this relation $\leq$ in $FL(X)$ is a partial order, and for any two elements $p\wedge$, $q\wedge \in FL(X)$, $(p \vee q)\wedge$ and $(p \wedge q)\wedge$ are the least upper and greatest lower bounds of $p\wedge$ and $q\wedge$, respectively, relative to this partial order.

[1] P. Whitman [88].

Now suppose that φ is any map of $\{x\wedge \,|\, x \in X\}$ to a lattice L. By composing φ with the map $x \longrightarrow x\wedge$ $(x \in X)$, we get a map ψ of X to L. And as we pointed out in Chap. 2, this map ψ extends to a homomorphism f of $W(X)$ to L. The proof of 16.2 will be completed if we show that f preserves the relation $\wedge$, or, what is equivalent, that $p \leq q$ implies $f(p) \leq f(q)$. This we do by induction on rank $p +$ rank q. If $p, q \in X$, then the foregoing implication is clear. If $p = (p_1 \vee p_2)$, then $p \leq q$ implies that $p_1, p_2 \leq q$ and hence that $f(p_1), f(p_2) \leq f(q)$, so that $f(p) = f(p_1) \vee f(p_2) \leq f(q)$. A dual argument handles the case $q = (q_1 \wedge q_2)$. If $p = (p_1 \wedge p_2)$ and $q \in X$, then $p \leq q$ implies $p_i \leq q$ for $i = 1$ or 2, whence $f(p) \leq f(p_i) \leq f(q)$. The case $p \in X$ and $q = (q_1 \vee q_2)$ follows by duality. Finally, if $p = (p_1 \wedge p_2)$ and $q = (q_1 \vee q_2)$, then $p \leq q$ implies that either $p_i \leq q$ or $p \leq q_i$, for some $i = 1$ or 2. But then either $f(p) \leq f(p_i) \leq f(q)$ or $f(p) \leq f(q_i) \leq f(q)$. This completes the proof.

As a consequence of the preceding theorem we get a general characterization of those lattices freely generated by a set X.

16.3:   *A lattice F is freely generated by a set X if and only if F is generated by X and the following conditions hold:*

(W1)   *For all $x, y \in X$, if $x \leq y$, then $x = y$.*
(W2)   *For all $x \in X$ and $u, v \in F$, if $x \leq u \vee v$, then $x \leq u$ or $x \leq v$.*
(W3)   *For all $x \in X$ and $u, v \in F$, if $u \wedge v \leq x$, then $u \leq x$ or $v \leq x$.*
(W4)   *For all $s, t, u, v \in F$, if $s \wedge t \leq u \vee v$, then either $s \wedge t \leq u$,*
         $s \wedge t \leq v$, $s \leq u \vee v$, or $t \leq u \vee v$.

Actually conditions (W1), (W2), and (W3) can be replaced by two seemingly weaker conditions (the proof is left to the reader):

16.4:   *A lattice F is freely generated by a set X if and only if F is generated by X and satisfies (W4) together with the following two conditions:*

(W2')   *If $x, x_1, \ldots, x_n \in X$ are finitely many distinct elements, then $x \not\leq x_1 \vee \cdots \vee x_n$.*
(W3')   *If $x, x_1, \ldots, x_n \in X$ are finitely many distinct elements, then $x_1 \wedge \cdots \wedge x_n \not\leq x$.*

The reader might also prove that there is always at most one set of free generators in a lattice: *If F is freely generated by a set X and also freely generated by a set Y, then $X = Y$.*

Condition (W4) is clearly inherited by sublattices of a free lattice. Consequently the following is an immediate corollary of 16.4.

16.5: *A nonempty subset X of a free lattice F freely generates a sublattice of F if and only if X satisfies $(W2')$ and $(W3')$.*[2]

With 16.5 in hand, we are in a position to prove the following remarkable theorem of Whitman.

16.6: *A lattice freely generated by three elements contains a sublattice freely generated by infinitely many elements.*[2]

PROOF: Let F be freely generated by the three-element set $\{a, b, c\}$. With $y_0 = z_0 = a$, define y_n and z_n for each integer $n \geq 0$ by the rules

$$y_n = a \vee (b \wedge (c \vee (a \wedge (b \vee (c \wedge y_{n-1}))))),$$
$$z_n = a \wedge (b \vee (c \wedge (a \vee (b \wedge (c \vee z_{n-1}))))).$$

A. If $u, v \in F$, then $u \leq a \vee c$, $c \leq v$, and $a \vee (b \wedge v) \leq a \vee (b \wedge u)$ imply $b \wedge v \leq b \wedge u$. This statement and its dual further hold under cyclic permutations of a, b, and c.

Applying $(W4)$ to the inequality $b \wedge v \leq a \vee (b \wedge v) \leq a \vee (b \wedge u)$, we obtain that either $b \leq a \vee (b \wedge u)$, which yields $b \leq b \wedge u \leq a \vee c$; $v \leq a \vee (b \wedge u)$, which yields $c \leq a \vee b$; $b \wedge v \leq a$, which yields $b \wedge c \leq a$; or $b \wedge v \leq b \wedge u$. Since the first three alternatives are impossible, A holds.

B. For all $n \geq 1$ we have $b, c \not\leq y_n$; $y_n \not\leq a, b, c$; $z_n \not\leq b, c$; and $a, b, c \not\leq z_n$.

This follows from the fact that if $n > 0$, then $a \vee (b \wedge c) \leq y_n \leq a \vee (b \wedge (c \vee a))$, with the dual condition holding for z_n.

C. If $m > n \geq 0$, then $y_n < y_m$ and $z_m < z_n$.

It is certainly clear that $y_n \leq y_m$ and $y_0 < y_m$. Suppose that $y_{n-1} < y_{m-1}$ and further that $y_m \leq y_n$. Successive applications of A yield that $c \wedge y_{m-1} \leq c \wedge y_{n-1} \leq y_{n-1}$, and inasmuch as $c \not\leq y_{n-1}$ and $c \wedge y_{m-1} \not\leq a, b$, it follows that $y_{m-1} \leq y_{n-1}$, a contradiction. Thus $y_n < y_m$, and duality yields $z_m < z_n$.

Now define for each $n \geq 1$,

$$w_n = b \vee (y_n \wedge (z_n \vee c)).$$

We will complete the proof by showing that the set $\{w_1, w_2, \ldots\}$ satisfies $(W2')$ and $(W3')$.

D. $w_m \leq w_n$ implies that $m = n$.

[2] P. Whitman [89].

Suppose $y_m \wedge (z_m \vee c) \leq w_m \leq w_n$. Then $a, c \not\leq w_n$ and $a, c \not\leq b$ imply that $y_m \wedge (z_m \vee c) \leq y_n \wedge (z_n \vee c)$. Therefore $y_m \wedge (z_m \vee c) \leq y_n$ and $y_m \wedge (z_m \vee c) \leq z_n \vee c$. Now inasmuch as $c \not\leq y_n$ and $y_m \wedge (z_m \vee c) \not\leq a$, b, the first inequality in the preceding sentence yields that $y_m \leq y_n$, so that $m \leq n$. Moreover, since $y_m \wedge (z_m \vee c) \not\leq a, c$ and $a \not\leq z_n \vee c$, the second inequality yields $z_m \vee c \leq z_n \vee c$, and A gives $z_m \leq z_n$. Hence $m \geq n$, and we conclude that $m = n$.

To show that $(W2')$ and $(W3')$ are satisfied, let $m, n_1, \ldots, n_k$ be distinct positive integers. Suppose $y_m \wedge (z_m \vee c) \leq w_m \leq w_{n_1} \vee \cdots \vee w_{n_k}$. Then the only possibilities are $y_m \wedge (z_m \vee c) \leq w_{n_i}$ for some $1 \leq i \leq k, a \leq y_m \leq w_{n_1} \vee \cdots \vee w_{n_k}$, or $c \leq z_m \vee c \leq w_{n_1} \vee \cdots \vee w_{n_k}$. The first alternative yields that $w_m \leq w_{n_i}$, an impossibility. The second and third alternatives are also impossibile since $a, c \not\leq w_n$ for each n. Consequently $(W2')$ holds. Furthermore, since $w_{n_1} \wedge \cdots \wedge w_{n_k} \not\leq b$, the inequality $w_{n_1} \wedge \cdots \wedge w_{n_k} \leq w_m$ implies that $b \leq w_{n_1} \wedge \cdots \wedge w_{n_k} \leq y_m \wedge (z_m \vee c) \leq z_m \vee c$, an impossibility. Therefore $(W3')$ also holds, and the proof of 16.6 is complete.

We now have enough properties of free lattices to apply free lattice techniques to the solution of some general lattice-theoretic problems.

16.7: *If a lattice identity holds in each finite lattice, then this identity holds in every lattice.*[3]

PROOF: Obviously if an identity holds in every free lattice, then it holds in every lattice. Consequently to prove 16.7, we must show that if X is a finite set and $u, v \in W(X)$ are such that $u\Lambda \neq v\Lambda$, then there is a finite lattice L that does not satisfy the lattice identity

$$u = v.$$

Let M be the collection of all those lattice polynomials in $W(X)$ of rank at most rank u + rank v. Let L be that subset of $FL(X)$ consisting of all finite meets of the elements $p\Lambda(p \in M)$ together with the element

$$\bigvee\{x\Lambda \mid x \in X\}.$$

L is then a finite subset of $FL(X)$, L is closed under meets in $FL(X)$, and L contains the greatest element of $FL(X)$. Therefore under the partial order it inherits from $FL(X)$, L is a finite lattice. Moreover, L is generated by the elements $x\Lambda(x \in X)$, and it is clear that the identity $u = v$ does not hold in L.

Theorem 16.7 can be viewed in the context of certain special classes of lattices. For example, it is easy to see that a lattice identity holds in every distributive lattice if and only if it holds in the two-element chain. (Proof?)

[3] R. Dean [25].

But what about the class of modular lattices? Is it true that if a lattice identity holds in every finite modular lattice, then it holds in every modular lattice? The answer to this important question is unknown; with some temerity we conjecture that the answer is negative.

Our next application concerns α-universal systems. Given an infinite cardinal α, we define a partially ordered set P to be an α-*universal partially ordered set* if the cardinality of P is α and every partially ordered set of cardinality at most α can be weakly embedded in P. Similarly, a lattice L is an α-*universal lattice* if the cardinality of L is α and every lattice of cardinality at most α can be embedded in L. The two results to follow deal with the existence of such systems in the case $\alpha = \aleph_0$.

16.8: *A lattice freely generated by three elements is an $\aleph_0$-universal partially ordered set.*[4]

PROOF: With 16.6 in mind, we will show that if a lattice F is freely generated by an infinite subset $\{x_0, x_1, x_2, \ldots\}$, then any countable partially ordered set P can be weakly embedded in F. Enumerate the elements of P: $P = \{a_0, a_1, a_2, \ldots\}$. Set $s_0 = x_0$. Continuing by induction, if s_i has been defined for each $i = 0, \ldots, k-1$, set

$$U_k = \{s_i \mid i < k \text{ and } a_i \geq a_k\}, \qquad V_k = \{s_i \mid i < k \text{ and } a_i \leq a_k\},$$

and define

$$s_k = (x_k \wedge \textstyle\bigwedge U_k) \vee \bigvee V_k.$$

We will prove that P is weakly embedded in F by showing that, for all n and m, $a_n \leq a_m$ if and only if $s_n \leq s_m$.

A. $x_n \leq s_m$ *implies* $a_n \leq a_m$, *and* $s_n \leq x_m$ *implies* $a_n \leq a_m$.

The proof of A is by induction on $n + m$. When $n = m = 0$, both implications are trivial. If $x_n \leq s_m$, then either $x_n \leq x_m \wedge \bigwedge U_m \leq x_m$ or $x_n \leq s_i$ for some $s_i \in V_m$. In the first case $n = m$ so that $a_n = a_m$, and in the second case the induction hypothesis yields that $a_n \leq a_i \leq a_m$. On the other hand, if $s_n \leq x_m$, then $x_n \wedge \bigwedge U_n \leq x_m$, and we must have either that $x_n \leq x_m$ or $s_i \leq x_m$ for some $s_i \in U_n$. Therefore either $a_n = a_m$ or $a_n \leq a_i \leq a_m$.

B. $a_n \leq a_m$ *implies* $s_n \leq s_m$.

Assume that $a_j \leq a_k$ and that B is true whenever $n + m < j + k$. If $k > j$, then $s_j \in V_k$, and therefore $s_j \leq s_k$. If $k < j$, then $s_k \in U_j$, so that $x_j \wedge \bigwedge U_j \leq s_k$. Further, our assumption yields that $s_i \leq s_k$ for all $s_i \in V_j$, whence $s_j \leq s_k$.

[4] P. Crawley and R. A. Dean [22]. A general result yielding the existence of α-universal partially ordered sets and α-universal lattices for uncountable α has been obtained by B. Jónsson [56].

C. $s_n \leq s_m$ implies $a_n \leq a_m$.

Again we use induction, so assume that $s_j \leq s_k$ and that C holds whenever $n + m < j + k$. Then $x_j \wedge \bigwedge U_j \leq s_k$, and four possibilities arise:

(1) $x_j \leq s_k$.
(2) $s_i \leq s_k$ for some $s_i \in U_j$.
(3) $x_j \wedge \bigwedge U_j \leq x_k \wedge \bigwedge U_k \leq x_k$.
(4) $x_j \wedge \bigwedge U_j \leq s_{k_1}$ for some $s_{k_1} \in V_k$.

If (1) occurs, then $a_j \leq a_k$ by A. The induction assumption and (2) yield that $a_j \leq a_i \leq a_k$. If (3) holds, then either $x_j \leq x_k$ or $s_i \leq x_k$ for some $s_i \in U_j$, so that either $a_j = a_k$ or $a_j \leq a_i \leq a_k$. In the case that (4) holds, we repeat the argument above, obtaining a necessarily finite decreasing sequence of positive integers $k = k_0 > k_1 > \cdots > k_l$ such that $s_{k_h} \in V_{k_h}$ for each $h = 1$, ..., l. For the terminal element s_{k_l}, possibilities (1), (2), or (3) can hold, but not (4). Therefore $a_j \leq a_{k_l}$, and we conclude that $a_j \leq a_{k_l} \leq \cdots \leq a_{k_1} \leq a_k$.

16.9:   *An $\aleph_0$-universal lattice does not exist.*[5]

PROOF: Since any countable lattice contains only countably many finitely generated sublattices, 16.9 will follow if we show that *there are $2^{\aleph_0}$ noniso-morphic lattices generated by three elements*. The proof of this statement uses the idea of the *set $C(p)$ of components* of a polynomial $p \in W(X)$, defined inductively for each p as follows: If $p \in X$, then $C(p) = \{p\}$; if $p = (p_1 \wedge p_2)$ or $p = (p_1 \vee p_2)$, then $C(p) = \{p\} \cup C(p_1) \cup C(p_2)$.

Now let $X = \{a, b, c\}$ be a three-element set. To simplify notation, for the remainder of this proof *we will identify a polynomial p with its equivalence class $p\Lambda$ in $FL(X)$*. Let w_n ($n = 1, 2, \ldots$) be the infinite set of polynomials constructed in the proof of 16.6 that freely generates a sublattice of $FL(X)$, and set

$$A = \{a \wedge (b \vee c), a \vee (b \wedge c), b \wedge (a \vee c),$$
$$b \vee (a \wedge c), c \wedge (a \vee b), c \vee (a \wedge b)\} \cup \bigcup_{n < \infty} C(w_n).$$

Let $H = \{h_1, h_2, \ldots\}$ be a countably infinite set. Let 2^ω denote the set of all functions on the positive integers to $\{0, 1\}$, and for each $\sigma \in 2^\omega$ construct a partially ordered set H_σ by defining in H a partial order by the rules

$$h_1 < h_3 < h_5 < \cdots;$$
$$h_{2n} < h_{2n-1}, \quad \text{if } \sigma(n) = 0;$$
$$h_{2n-1} < h_{2n}, \quad \text{if } \sigma(n) = 1.$$

Clearly for any $\sigma, \tau \in 2^\omega$, the partially ordered sets H_σ and H_τ are isomorphic if and only if $\sigma = \tau$.

[5] P. Crawley and R. A. Dean [22].

Next, for each $\sigma \in 2^{\omega}$, construct a partially ordered set G_{σ} by defining a partial order in the set $A \cup H$ as follows. For $x, y \in A \cup H$, $x \leq y$ if one of the following hold:

(1) $x, y \in H$ and $x \leq y$ in H_{σ}.
(2) $x, y \in A$ and $x \leq y$ in $FL(X)$.
(3) $x \in A$ and $y \in H$, and for some $h_n \leq H$, $h_n \leq y$, and either $x \leq w_{2n-1}$ or $x \leq w_{2n}$ in $FL(X)$.

Two facts are readily verified. First, if $p, q \in A$ and $(p \vee q) \in A$, then $(p \vee q)$ is the least upper bound of p and q in G_{σ} [this depends on the fact that p, q and $(p \vee q)$ are components of the w_n's]. The dual statement also holds. Second, for each n, h_n is the least upper bound of w_{2n-1} and w_{2n}. Consequently, if K_{σ} is the normal completion of G_{σ} and if L_{σ} is the sublattice of K_{σ} generated by a, b, and c, then $G_{\sigma} \subseteq L_{\sigma}$, and bounds existing in G_{σ} are preserved in L_{σ}.

Notice that in G_{σ}, $x > a$ implies $x \geq a \vee (b \wedge c)$, and $x < a$ implies $x \leq a \wedge (b \vee c)$, with analogous implications holding for b and c. Therefore in the normal completion and hence in L_{σ} these implications also hold. This shows that a, b, and c are both meet- and join-irreducible. And as L_{σ} is generated by a, b, and c, they are the only such elements. It follows that if φ is an isomorphism of L_{σ} onto L_{τ}, then the restriction of φ to $\{a, b, c\}$ is a permutation in $\{a, b, c\}$. If φ induces the identity permutation in $\{a, b, c\}$, then the restriction of φ to the set A is the identity map, and therefore the restriction of φ to H_{σ} is an isomorphism of H_{σ} onto H_{τ}, so that we must have $\sigma = \tau$.

Finally, suppose that the collection L_{σ} ($\sigma \in 2^{\omega}$) includes seven distinct lattices that are isomorphic. Since there are only five nontrivial permutations of three elements, there must exist three of the seven isomorphic lattices, say L_{ρ}, L_{σ}, and L_{τ}, with isomorphisms φ_1 and φ_2 of L_{σ} and L_{τ} onto L_{ρ}, respectively such that the restrictions of φ_1 and φ_2 to $\{a, b, c\}$ are equal. Consequently, if, $\varphi = \varphi_2^{-1}\varphi_1$, then φ is an isomorphism of L_{σ} onto L_{τ} with the property that φ restricted to $\{a, b, c\}$ is the identity map. But this implies that $\sigma = \tau$, a contradiction. We conclude that each isomorphism class in the set of lattices L_{σ} ($\sigma \in 2^{\omega}$) contains at most six members, so that the collection L_{σ} ($\sigma \in 2^{\omega}$) includes a continuum number of nonisomorphic lattices, each, of course, generated by three elements.

Our final application of free lattice techniques provides the proof of a theorem promised in Chap. 4.

16.10: *Every lattice can be embedded in some uniquely complemented lattice.*[6]

[6] R. P. Dilworth [30]. Cf. C.C. Chen and G. Grätzer [14].

PROOF: The proof of 16.10 is based on the concept of a free extension. Specifically, given a lattice L, we say that a lattice F is *freely generated over L* by an element w if L is a sublattice of F, the elements of L together with w generate F, and whenever a function f maps $L \cup \{w\}$ to a lattice M in such a way that the restriction of f to L is an isomorphism, then f extends to a homomorphism of F to M.

Given the lattice L and some element w not in L, we can easily construct a lattice freely generated over L by w. Let X be the set consisting of w and all the elements of L, and let F be a free lattice freely generated by X. Then considering L as a subset of X, the identity map in L extends to a homomorphism φ of the sublattice of F generated by L to L. Let ζ be the least congruence relation in F such that

$$\varphi(u) = \varphi(v) \text{ implies } u \; \zeta \; v,$$

and form the factor lattice F/ζ. It is easy to check that the natural map $x \longrightarrow x\zeta$ of X to F/ζ is one-to-one (making use, for example, of the direct product of L and the two-element chain), and if we identify the elements of X with their images under this map, then the resulting lattice is readily seen to be freely generated over L by w.

The main step in the proof of 16.10 is the derivation of the following basic lemma: *Let L be any lattice with least element 0 and greatest element 1 such that each element in L has at most one complement, and let a be an element in L with no complement. Let F be freely generated over L by an element w not in L, and let γ denote the least congruence relation in F that collapses the quotients $1/a \vee w$ and $a \wedge w/0$. Then the natural map $x \longrightarrow x\gamma$ of L to F/γ is one-to-one, and the only elements in F/γ that have complements are $a\gamma$, $w\gamma$, and those elements $x\gamma$ such that $x \in L$ and x has a complement in L; moreover, each element in F/γ has at most one complement.*

Before proving this basic lemma, let us see how it gives the theorem we are seeking. If L is any lattice, by adjoining a new greatest element and a new least element, if necessary, we can assume that L has a greatest and a least element and that no other member of L has a complement. Under these circumstances we can apply the basic lemma repeatedly to the elements of L, embedding L in a lattice L_1 with the properties that L_1 has the same greatest and least elements as L, each element of L has a complement in L_1, and each element in L_1 has at most one complement. Repeating this with L_1 and continuing this procedure, we obtain an ascending sequence of lattices $L \subseteq L_1 \subseteq L_2 \subseteq \cdots \subseteq L_i \subseteq \cdots$ such that L_i has the same greatest and least elements as L_{i+1}, each element in L_i has a complement in L_{i+1}, and each element in L_{i+1} has at most one complement. And forming the set-union of the L_i's, we obtain a uniquely complemented lattice containing L as a sublattice.

Our proof of the basic lemma uses two auxiliary lattices M and M', each of which contains L as a sublattice and is generated by the elements of L together with one additional element v. Since the definition of M' is dual to the definition of M (although in general M' is not the dual lattice of M), we will describe only the lattice M. In essence M is the free system which is generated under the join operation by L and an additional generator v such that $a \lor v = 1$. Specifically, let M be the set of ordered pairs

$$M = \{\langle b, j \rangle \mid b \in L, j \in \{0, 1\}, \text{ and } b \geq a \text{ implies } j = 0\},$$

together with the partial order defined by

$$\langle b, j \rangle \leq \langle c, k \rangle \text{ if } c = 1 \text{ or if } b \leq c \text{ and } j \leq k.$$

It is routine to check that M is a lattice in which meets and joins are given by the following formulas:

$$\langle b, j \rangle \land \langle c, k \rangle = \langle b \land c, j \land k \rangle \qquad \text{if } b, c \neq 1,$$
$$\langle b, j \rangle \land \langle 1, 0 \rangle = \langle b, j \rangle,$$
$$\langle b, j \rangle \lor \langle c, k \rangle = \begin{cases} \langle b \lor c, j \lor k \rangle & \text{if } \langle b \lor c, j \lor k \rangle \in M, \\ \langle 1, 0 \rangle, & \text{if } \langle b \lor c, j \lor k \rangle \notin M. \end{cases}$$

The map $b \longrightarrow \langle b, 0 \rangle$ is certainly an isomorphism of L to M, and to simplify subsequent notation, we identify the elements of L with their images under this map. Observe that with this identification M is generated by the elements of L together with the element

$$v = \langle 0, 1 \rangle;$$

0 and 1 are the least element and greatest element of M, respectively, and

$$a \lor v = 1, \qquad a \land v = 0.$$

We need four elementary properties of M.

A. If $x, y \in M$ and $x \lor y \geq v$, then either $x \lor y = 1$, $x \geq v$, or $y \geq v$.

B. If $x \in M$ and $x \lor v \geq a$, then $x \geq a$.

C. If $x, y \in M$ and $x \lor y = 1$, then $x \geq c$ and $y \geq d$, where $c, d \in L$ and $c \lor d \geq a$.

D. If $x, y \in M$ and $1 > x \lor y \geq b$ with $b \in L$, then $x \geq c$ and $y \geq d$, where $c, d \in L$ and $c \lor d \geq b$.

The proofs of A-D are short and quite easy; will give the proofs of A and D and leave the other two as exercises. To prove A, write $x = \langle b, j \rangle$ and $y = \langle c, k \rangle$, and assume that $x \lor y \neq 1$. Then $x \lor y = \langle b \lor c, j \lor k \rangle$, and $x \lor y \geq v$ implies that $j \lor k = 1$ and hence that $j = 1$ or $k = 1$. But this means that either $x \geq v$ or $y \geq v$. Moving to the proof of D, if $x = \langle c, j \rangle$ and $y = \langle d, k \rangle$, then $x \lor y \geq b$ implies that $c \lor d \geq b$, and clearly $x \geq \langle c, 0 \rangle = c$ and $y \geq \langle d, 0 \rangle = d$.

Now as F is freely generated over L by $w \notin L$, there is a homomorphism h of F onto M such that $h(w) = v$ and the restriction of h to L is the identity map. Observe that

$$h(a \vee w) = a \vee v = 1 \qquad \text{and} \qquad h(a \wedge w) = a \wedge v = 0.$$

Therefore if θ_h is the congruence relation belonging to h, the quotients $1/a \vee w$ and $a \wedge w/0$ are collapsed by θ_h. But since γ is the least congruence relation in F collapsing these quotients, $\gamma \leq \theta_h$. Consequently, as the restriction of h to L is one-to-one, it follows that the natural map $x \longrightarrow x\gamma$ of L into F/γ is also one-to-one.

E. The following implications hold for each $x \in F$:

(1) For all $b \in L$, $h(x) \geq b$ implies $x\gamma \geq b\gamma$.
(2) $h(x) \geq v$ implies $x\gamma \geq w\gamma$.

Let K be the collection of all those elements $x \in F$ for which (1) and (2) hold. Clearly, all the elements of L as well as the element v belong to K. Therefore if we prove that K is a sublattice of F, then it follows that $K = F$ and hence that E is true.

First we show that K is closed under join. Assume $y, z \in K$ and $x = y \vee z$. Suppose $b \in L$ is such that $h(x) = h(y) \vee h(z) \geq b$. If $h(y) \in L$ and $h(z) \in L$, then the fact that y and z satisfy (1) shows that $y\gamma \geq h(y)\gamma$ and $z\gamma \geq h(z)\gamma$, so that $x\gamma = y\gamma \vee z\gamma \geq h(y)\gamma \vee h(z)\gamma = h(x)\gamma \geq b\gamma$. If $h(y) \notin L$ or $h(z) \notin L$, then either $h(y) \geq v$ or $h(z) \geq v$, and by (2) we infer that either $y\gamma \geq w\gamma$ or $z\gamma \geq w\gamma$. Under any circumstances $x\gamma = y\gamma \vee z\gamma \geq w\gamma$. Now if $h(y) \vee h(z) = 1$, then C guarantees that there are elements $c, d \in L$ such that $h(y) \geq c$, $h(z) \geq d$, and $c \vee d \geq a$, and using (1), we obtain that $y\gamma \geq c\gamma$ and $z\gamma \geq d\gamma$. Hence $x\gamma \geq c\gamma \vee d\gamma \geq a\gamma$, and therefore $x\gamma \geq a\gamma \vee w\gamma = 1\gamma \geq b\gamma$. On the other hand, if $h(y) \vee h(z) \neq 1$, then D and our assumption that $h(x) \geq b$ yield the existence of elements $c, d \in L$ such that $h(y) \geq c$, $h(z) \geq d$, and $c \vee d \geq b$. Again (1) applies, and we conclude that $y\gamma \geq c\gamma$ and $z\gamma \geq d\gamma$, and hence that $x\gamma \geq c\gamma \vee d\gamma \geq b\gamma$. Thus x satisfies (1).

To show that x also satisfies (2), suppose that $h(x) = h(y) \vee h(z) \geq v$. If either $h(y) \geq v$ or $h(z) \geq v$, then from (2) we get that $x\gamma = y\gamma \vee z\gamma \geq w\gamma$. If $h(y) \not\geq v$ and $h(z) \not\geq v$, then both $h(y)$ and $h(z)$ belong to L, and $h(y) \vee h(z) = 1$ by A. Invoking (1), we obtain that $y\gamma \geq h(y)\gamma$ and $z\gamma \geq h(z)\gamma$, giving $x\gamma = y\gamma \vee z\gamma \geq h(y)\gamma \vee h(z)\gamma = 1\gamma \geq w\gamma$. Thus x satisfies (2), and we conclude that K is closed under join.

The proof of closure under meet is easier. If $x = y \wedge z$, where $y, z \in K$, and $h(x) \geq b$ with $b \in L$, then $h(y) \geq b$ and $h(z) \geq b$; consequently $y\gamma \geq b\gamma$ and $z\gamma \geq b\gamma$, so that $x\gamma = y\gamma \wedge z\gamma \geq b\gamma$. Condition (2) follows similarly, and therefore K is closed under meet.

F. If $b \in L$ and $w\gamma \geq b\gamma$, then $b = 0$.

G. If $x \in F$ and $w\gamma \lor x\gamma \geq a\gamma$, then $x\gamma \geq a\gamma$.

For if the assumptions of F are satisfied, since $\theta_h \geq \gamma$, we have $v = h(w) \geq h(b) = b$, which implies $b = 0$. Under the assumptions of G, $v \lor h(x) = h(w) \lor h(x) = h(w \lor x) \geq h(a) = a$, and by B and E we infer that $x\gamma \geq a\gamma$. One further observation: The duals of statements F and G necessarily hold also, inasmuch as F and G do not involve the lattice M.

At this point note that by dualizing the foregoing procedure we obtain a lattice M' together with a homomorphism h' of F to M' such that the dual of E holds for this map h'.

Suppose now that $x, y \in F$ are such that $x\gamma$ and $y\gamma$ are complements in F/γ. Since $\gamma \leq \theta_h$, as observed above, we have $h(x) \lor h(y) = 1$, and therefore one of the following must hold:

(1) $h(x), h(y) \in L$ and $h(x) \lor h(x) = 1$.
(2) $h(x) \geq v$.
(3) $h(y) \geq v$.

Dually we also have at least one of the following:

(1') $h'(x), h'(y) \in L$ and $h'(x) \land h'(y) = 0$.
(2') $h'(x) \leq v$.
(3') $h'(y) \leq v$.

We will complete the proof of the basic lemma and hence of 16.10 by showing that under any circumstances either $\{x\gamma, y\gamma\} = \{w\gamma, a\gamma\}$ or there exists a pair of complements $c, d \in L$ such that $x\gamma = c\gamma$ and $y\gamma = d\gamma$. It suffices to deal with the cases when (1) and (1'), (1) and (2'), (2) and (2'), or (2) and (3') hold; the rest follow from these by symmetry or duality.

If (1) and (1') hold, then E and its dual yield that $h'(x)\gamma \geq x\gamma \geq h(x)\gamma$ and $h'(y)\gamma \geq y\gamma \geq h(y)\gamma$, and as the map $z \longrightarrow z\gamma$ $(z \in L)$ is one-to-one, we have

$$h'(x) \lor h'(y) \geq h(x) \lor h'(y) \geq h(x) \lor h(y) = 1,$$

$$h(x) \land h(y) \leq h(x) \land h'(y) \leq h'(x) \land h'(y) = 0.$$

Thus $h(x)$ and $h'(x)$ are complements of $h'(y)$ in L, and the assumptions of the basic lemma require that $h(x) = h'(x)$. Similarly, $h(y) = h'(y)$. Therefore $x\gamma = h(x)\gamma$ and $y\gamma = h(y)\gamma$, as desired.

In the case that (1) and (2') hold, apply the dual of E and then E to obtain that $x\gamma \leq w\gamma$ and $h(x)\gamma \leq x\gamma \leq w\gamma$. By F we get that $h(x) = 0$, and hence that $h(y) = 1$. Again E applies to give $y\gamma \geq 1\gamma$. Consequently $y\gamma = 1\gamma$ and $x\gamma = 0\gamma$.

If (2) and (2') hold, then the inequalities $h(x) \geq v \geq h'(x)$ together with

E and its dual yield that $x\gamma \geq w\gamma \geq x\gamma$. This and the assumption that $x\gamma \vee y\gamma = 1\gamma$ gives $w\gamma \vee y\gamma \geq a\gamma$, and from G we infer that $y\gamma \geq a\gamma$. By duality $y\gamma \leq a\gamma$. Thus $x\gamma = w\gamma$ and $y\gamma = a\gamma$.

Finally, if (2) and (3') hold, then with E and its dual we obtain that $x\gamma \geq w\gamma \geq y\gamma$. But this means that $x\gamma = x\gamma \vee y\gamma = 1\gamma$ and $y\gamma = 0\gamma$. This completes the proof.

A substantial part of the theory of free lattices has not been touched in this chapter; we have been more concerned with the application of free lattice techniques to more general problems and have dealt but little with the problems involving free lattices themselves. Some examples of the work in this area might be mentioned. The papers of B. Jónsson [59], F. Galvin and B. Jónsson [41], B. Jónsson and J. E. Kiefer [62], R. A. Dean [26], and R. McKenzie [67], for instance, are concerned with the problem of describing the sublattices of free lattices. And in a somewhat different direction, free lattices generated by partially ordered sets are considered by R. P. Dilworth [30], R. A. Dean [24, 27], H. Rolf [77], and P. Crawley and R. A. Dean [22].

17

VARIETIES
OF
LATTICES

In the preceding chapters we have studied four different classes of lattices defined by lattice identities, the classes of modular, Arguesian, and distributive lattices and the class of all lattices. In this final chapter we will take a general look at classes of lattices defined by identities and study a few of their properties as well as some additional specific examples.

If X is a countably infinite set, any lattice identity is determined by a pair of elements in the word algebra $W(X)$. Indeed, if $u, v \in W(X)$, a lattice L satisfies the identity

$$u = v$$

if and only if $f(u) = f(v)$ for every homomorphism f of $W(X)$ to L. Now for each set $\mathcal{E}$ of lattice identities, we define $\mathbf{V}(\mathcal{E})$ to be the class of all those lattices that satisfy every identity in $\mathcal{E}$. And when a class $\mathbf{K}$ of lattices has the property that $\mathbf{K} = \mathbf{V}(\mathcal{E})$ for some set of identities $\mathcal{E}$, we say that $\mathbf{K}$ is a *variety*.

When $\mathcal{E}$ is empty, $\mathbf{V}(\mathcal{E})$ is the class of all lattices and hence includes every other variety. On the other hand, if $\mathcal{E}$ consists of the single identity $x = y$, where x and y are distinct elements of X, then $\mathbf{V}(\mathcal{E})$ is the class of all one-element lattices, which is included in every other variety. Note further that if $\mathcal{E}_i (i \in I)$ is any family of sets of identities, then

$$\mathbf{V}(\bigcup_{i \in I} \mathcal{E}_i) = \bigcap_{i \in I} \mathbf{V}(\mathcal{E}_i).$$

Consequently the intersection of a family of varieties is again a variety, and it follows that the varieties form a complete lattice, which we will refer to as the *lattice of varieties*.[1] It is a nontrivial fact that *the lattice of varieties is distributive*.

---

[1] The reader might well object to speaking of a lattice whose elements are "classes." However, we speak of the lattice of varieties for convenience and to more clearly suggest the relationship between the various varieties. Moreover, in this instance, there is no difficulty in equivalently defining the lattice of varieties in such a way that the elements of the lattice are, for example, certain subsets of $W(X)^2$.

Given a class **K** of lattices, it is clear from the remarks of the preceding paragraph that there is a least variety $\mathbf{K}^v$ containing the class **K**. In fact, if $\mathcal{E}(\mathbf{K})$ denotes the set of those identities satisfied by every lattice in **K**, then $\mathbf{K}^v = \mathbf{V}(\mathcal{E}(\mathbf{K}))$. In practice this description of $\mathbf{K}^v$ is not very helpful, for the determination of the identities that hold in every lattice in a given class is almost invariably very difficult. G. Birkhoff has discovered an alternative description involving only the formation of direct products, sublattices, and homomorphic images that is much more useful. A derivation of Birkhoff's theorem is our first objective in this chapter, and this requires some preliminary remarks.

Let **K** be a class of lattices, and let $P\mathbf{K}$, $S\mathbf{K}$, and $H\mathbf{K}$ denote, respectively, the class of all those lattices that are isomorphic with direct products of lattices in **K**, the class of all lattices isomorphic with sublattices of lattices in **K**, and the class of all homomorphic images of lattices in **K**. Under any circumstances the class **K** is contained in each of the classes $P\mathbf{K}$, $S\mathbf{K}$, and $H\mathbf{K}$. On the other hand, the conditions $\mathbf{K} = P\mathbf{K}$, $\mathbf{K} = S\mathbf{K}$, and $\mathbf{K} = H\mathbf{K}$ are equivalent, respectively, to the statements that **K** is closed under the formation of isomorphic images of direct products, sublattices, and homomorphic images of members of **K**. In addition, it is not difficult to check (proof?) that

$$P S \mathbf{K} \subseteq S P \mathbf{K}, \qquad P H \mathbf{K} \subseteq H P \mathbf{K}, \qquad S H \mathbf{K} \subseteq H S \mathbf{K},$$

and from these relations we infer that the class $HSP\mathbf{K}$ is closed under the formation of direct products, sublattices, and homomorphic images.

We also need to extend the notion of free lattice. Given a class **K** of lattices, we say that a lattice F is **K**-*freely generated* by a subset X if F is generated by X and any map of X to a lattice L in **K** extends to a homomorphism of F to L. Notice that we do not require F to belong to **K**. In particular, under our definition, if the lattice F is **K**-freely generated by X and the class **K** contains a class **L**, then F is also **L**-freely generated by X. We are mainly interested in **K**-freely generated lattices, however, when they belong to **K**: *If a class* **K** *of lattices contains at least one lattice with more than one element and* $\mathbf{K} = P\mathbf{K} = S\mathbf{K}$, *then for each cardinal* $\alpha > 0$ *there exists* $F \in \mathbf{K}$ *such that* F *is* **K**-*freely generated by a subset of cardinality* α. To prove this, let L be a free lattice freely generated by a set X of cardinality α. Set

$$\Sigma = \{\theta \in \Theta(L) \,|\, L/\theta \in \mathbf{K}\}$$

and $\sigma = \bigwedge \Sigma$. Then L/σ is a subdirect product of the lattices L/θ $(\theta \in \Sigma)$; i.e., L/σ is isomorphic with a sublattice of a direct product of members of **K** and hence belongs to **K**. Observe next that inasmuch as **K** contains a lattice T having two distinct members, for any two distinct elements $x, y \in X$ there is a homomorphism of L to T under which x and y have distinct images. This shows that $x\sigma \neq y\sigma$, and therefore the map $x \longrightarrow x\sigma \,(x \in X)$ is one-to-one. Consequently the set $X/\sigma = \{x\sigma \,|\, x \in X\}$, which generates L/σ, has car-

dinality α. Finally, given any map of X to a lattice $K \in \mathbf{K}$, this map extends
to a homomorphism h of L to K. If θ_h is the congruence relation belonging
to h, then $\theta_h \geq \sigma$, and it follows that the map $a\sigma \longrightarrow h(a)$ $(a \in L)$ is a homomorphism of L/σ to K. This is enough to guarantee that L/σ is $\mathbf{K}$-freely generated by X/σ.

We can now derive Birkhoff's theorem.

17.1:   *For each class* $\mathbf{K}$ *of lattices,* $\mathbf{K}^v = HSP\mathbf{K}$.[2]

PROOF: Since the theorem is obvious when $\mathbf{K}$ contains only one-element
lattices, we can assume that $\mathbf{K}$ contains at least one lattice with more than one
element. Set $\mathbf{L} = HSP\mathbf{K}$. Clearly, each lattice in $\mathbf{L}$ satisfies every identity in
$\mathcal{E}(K)$, whence $\mathbf{K}^v = \mathbf{V}(\mathcal{E}(\mathbf{K})) \supseteq \mathbf{L}$. Suppose that $L \in \mathbf{K}^v$. Since $\mathbf{L} = P\mathbf{L} = H\mathbf{L}$,
we can invoke the result above, obtaining a lattice $F \in \mathbf{L}$ such that F is
$\mathbf{L}$-freely generated by a subset X of cardinality $|L|$. Form the word algebra
$W(X)$, and extend the identity map in X to a homomorphism φ of $W(X)$ to
F. In addition let ψ be a homomorphism of $W(X)$ onto L; here we use the fact
that $|X| = |L|$. At this point, assume that $u, v \in W(X)$ are such that $\varphi(u) = \varphi(v)$. Pick any lattice $K \in \mathbf{K}$ and any homomorphism f of $W(X)$ to K. Since
K also belongs to $\mathbf{L}$, the restriction of f to X extends to a homomorphism g
of F to K. And inasmuch as the restriction of φ to X is the identity map, the
restriction of $g\varphi$ to X equals the restriction of f to X. But this implies that
$g\varphi = f$, so that

$$f(u) = g(\varphi(u)) = g(\varphi(v)) = f(v).$$

Since this holds for any homomorphism f of $W(X)$ to a member of $\mathbf{K}$, it follows
that the identity $u = v$ belongs to $\mathcal{E}(\mathbf{K})$; therefore this identity is satisfied by L.
Consequently $\psi(u) = \psi(v)$, and we have proved that, for every $u, v \in W(X)$,
$\varphi(u) = \varphi(v)$ implies $\psi(u) = \psi(v)$. From this we infer that there is a homomorphism h of F onto L such that $\psi = h\varphi$, and as $F \in \mathbf{L}$ and $\mathbf{L} = H\mathbf{L}$, we
conclude that $L = h(F) \in \mathbf{L}$. Thus $\mathbf{K}^v \subseteq \mathbf{L}$, completing the proof.

As a corollary to Birkhoff's theorem we obtain that *a class* $\mathbf{K}$ *of lattices
is a variety if and only if* $\mathbf{K} = P\mathbf{K} = S\mathbf{K} = H\mathbf{K}$. Another useful fact is that
two varieties having the same subdirectly irreducible members are equal.
(Proof?)

The foregoing results also show that a variety $\mathbf{V}$ contains a lattice $\mathbf{V}$-
freely generated by a set of any given cardinality. Let us define a lattice F
to be a *free* $\mathbf{V}$-*lattice generated by* X if $F \in \mathbf{V}$ and F is $\mathbf{V}$-freely generated by
X. As in the case of free lattices, two free $\mathbf{V}$-lattices generated by sets of the
same cardinality are isomorphic. For the familiar varieties of distributive
and modular lattices, a little more can be said. For example, if n is a positive
integer, the free distributive lattice generated by n elements is finite; however,

---

[2] G. Birkhoff [9]. Actually this formulation is due to A. Tarski [83]. Birkhoff's
theorem and the prefatory remarks are valid for very general algebraic systems.

the number of elements in this lattice is not known if $n > 7$.[3] The proof of finiteness is left as an exercise with this hint: Show that the free distributive lattice generated by n elements is isomorphic with the lattice of all o-ideals of the Boolean algebra of all subsets of an n-element set. Things are not so nice for modular lattices. The free modular lattice generated by n elements is infinite when $n > 3$. (The proof of this is also an exercise. *Hint:* Find an infinite projective plane generated by four points.) The diagrams in Fig. 17-1 represent the free distributive lattice and the free modular lattice generated by three elements.[4] (The reader should verify this claim.)

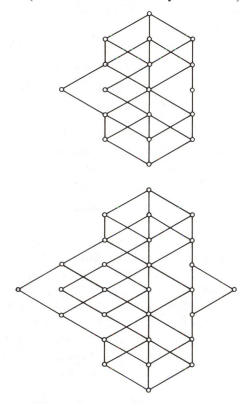

Fig. 17-1

The benefits of the fact that congruence lattices are distributive again become apparent as we study varieties, for this property allows a significant improvement of Birkhoff's theorem. To formulate this result, we need the concept of an ultraproduct, and this, in turn, rests on the idea of an ultrafilter.

[3] Cf. R. Church [15].

[4] The free modular lattice generated by three elements was first described by R. Dedekind [28].

Given a set I, any nonempty member of the lattice of filters of the Boolean algebra of all subsets of I will be referred to as a *filter in I;* i.e., a nonempty set U of subsets of I is a filter in I if (1) $A \cap B \in U$ whenever $A, B \in U$, and (2) $A \in U$ whenever $A \supseteq B$ and $B \in U$. A filter in I is *proper* if it does not contain the empty set $\varnothing$. A maximal proper filter in I is called an *ultrafilter in I;* in other words, an ultrafilter in I is simply an atom in the lattice of filters of the Boolean algebra of all subsets of I. Alternatively, *if U is a proper filter in I, then following statements are equivalent:* (1) *U is an ultrafilter;* (2) *for all* $A \subseteq I$, *either* $A \in U$ *or* $I - A \in U$; *and* (3) *for all* $A, B \subseteq I$, *if* $A \cup B \in U$, *then* $A \in U$ *or* $B \in U$. (The proof is an exercise.)

Now let L_i $(i \in I)$ be a family of lattices. Let U be an ultrafilter in I. Form the direct product $P = \mathsf{X}_{i \in I} L_i$, and define a relation θ_U in P by the rule

$$x \, \theta_U \, y \text{ if } \{i \in I \,|\, x(i) = y(i)\} \in U.$$

Then θ_U is a congruence relation in P (proof?), and the factor lattice P/θ_U is called an *ultraproduct* of the lattices $L_i (i \in I)$—more specifically, *the ultraproduct of the* L_i $(i \in I)$ *by* U.

For each class $\mathbf{K}$ of lattices, let $P_s\mathbf{K}$ and $P_u\mathbf{K}$ denote the classes consisting of all lattices that are isomorphic with subdirect products and with ultra-products, respectively, of members of $\mathbf{K}$. The following theorem, due to B. Jónsson, is the improvement of Birkhoff's theorem we are seeking.

17.2: *For each class* $\mathbf{K}$ *of lattices,* $\mathbf{K}^v = P_s HSP_u \mathbf{K}$.[5]

PROOF: It is clear that $P_s HSP_u \mathbf{K} \subseteq \mathbf{K}^v$, so we need to show that each member of $\mathbf{K}^v$ belongs to $P_s HSP_u \mathbf{K}$. Also, since each lattice in $\mathbf{K}^v$ is a subdirect product of subdirectly irreducible members of $\mathbf{K}^v$, it is enough to prove that each subdirectly irreducible lattice in $\mathbf{K}^v$ belongs to $HSP_u \mathbf{K}$. Assume, therefore, that $K \in \mathbf{K}^v$ and that K is subdirectly irreducible. By Birkhoff's theorem there is a family of lattices L_i $(i \in I)$, each of which is a member of $\mathbf{K}$, a sublattice L of the direct product $\mathsf{X}_{i \in I} L_i$, and a congruence relation $\theta \in \Theta(L)$ such that $K \cong L/\theta$. For each pair of elements $x, y \in L$, set

$$I(x, y) = \{i \in I \,|\, x(i) = y(i)\}.$$

And for each subset $A \subseteq I$, define the congruence relation $\varphi(A)$ in L by

$$x \, \varphi(A) \, y \text{ if } A \subseteq I(x, y).$$

[$\varphi(A)$ is just the congruence relation belonging to that homomorphism of L to $\mathsf{X}_{i \in A} L_i$ given by $x \longrightarrow x_A$, where x_A is the restriction of x to A.] Notice that inasmuch as $A \subseteq B \subseteq I$ implies $\varphi(A) \geq \varphi(B)$, and $A \cup B \subseteq I(x, y)$ if and only if $A \subseteq I(x, y)$ and $B \subseteq I(x, y)$, we have

$$\varphi(A \cup B) = \varphi(A) \wedge \varphi(B) \qquad \text{all } A, B \subseteq I.$$

[5] B. Jónsson [60].

Now let U be a maximal proper filter in I with the property that

$$A \in U \text{ implies } \varphi(A) \leq \theta.$$

We will show that U is an ultrafilter. If this is not the case, there is a subset $D \subseteq I$ such that neither D nor its complement $D' = I - D$ belongs to U. Therefore, because of the maximality of U, there must exist $A, B \in U$ such that $\varphi(D \cap A) \not\leq \theta$ and $\varphi(D' \cap B) \not\leq \theta$. But $\varphi(A \cap B) \leq \theta$ and $\Theta(L)$ is distributive, so

$$\theta = \theta \vee \varphi(A \cap B) = \theta \vee \varphi([D \cap A \cap B] \cup [D' \cap A \cap B])$$
$$= \theta \vee [\varphi(D \cap A \cap B) \wedge \varphi(D' \cap A \cap B)]$$
$$= [\theta \vee \varphi(D \cap A \cap B)] \wedge [\theta \vee \varphi(D' \cap A \cap B)].$$

L/θ, however, is subdirectly irreducible, and therefore θ is irreducible in $\Theta(L)$. consequently either $\theta = \theta \vee \varphi(D \cap A \cap B)$ or $\theta = \theta \vee \varphi(D' \cap A \cap B)$, and hence either $\varphi(D \cap A) \leq \varphi(D \cap A \cap B) \leq \theta$ or $\varphi(D' \cap B) \leq \varphi(D' \cap A \cap B) \leq \theta$, a contradiction. Thus U is an ultrafilter in I.

Define the congruence relation φ_U in L by

$$x \; \varphi_U \; y \text{ if } I(x, y) \in U,$$

and note that L/φ_U is isomorphic with a sublattice of the ultraproduct of the lattices $L_i (i \in I)$ by U. If $x, y \in L$ are such that $x \; \varphi_U \; y$, then $I(x, y) \in U$, so that $\varphi(I(x, y)) \leq \theta$. As the congruence relation $\varphi(I(x, y))$ identifies x and y, we infer that $x \; \theta \; y$. It follows that $\varphi_U \leq \theta$, and consequently L/θ is a homomorphic image of L/φ_U. Thus $K \in HSP_uK$, completing the argument.

The real utility of Jónsson's theorem is made apparent by the following lemma.

17.3:   *If K is a finite set of finite lattices, then $P_uK = K$.* [6]

PROOF: If $L \in P_uK$, then there is a family of lattices $L_i (i \in I)$, each belonging to K, and an ultrafilter U in I such that L is isomorphic with the ultraproduct of the $L_i (i \in I)$ by U; i.e., $L \cong P/\theta_U$, where $P = \chi_{i \in I} L_i$. For each $K \in K$, set $I_K = \{i \in I \mid L_i = K\}$, and note that inasmuch as $\bigcup_{K \in K} I_K = I \in U$ and K is finite, we must have $I_K \in U$ for some $K \in K$. Now it is easy to see that U_0, the set-intersection of U and the set of all subsets of I_K, is an ultrafilter in I_K, and in view of $I_K \in U$, that L is isomorphic with the ultraproduct of the lattices $L_i (i \in I_K)$ by U_0. Thus we may assume that all the lattices $L_i (i \in I)$ are equal to a single lattice K.

For each $a \in K$, let x_a be that element of P such that $x_a(i) = a$ for all $i \in I$. Then the map $a \longrightarrow x_a \theta_U \; (a \in K)$ is a homomorphism of K to P/θ_U, and this homomorphism is necessarily one-to-one since $\varnothing \notin U$. This

---

[6] Cf. T. Frayne, A. C. Morel, and D. Scott [38].

homomorphism is also onto, for if x is any member of P, and, as above, $I(x, x_a) = \{i \in I \mid x(i) = x_a(i)\}$, then the finiteness of K and the condition $\bigcup_{a \in K} I(x, x_a) = I \in U$ yield that $I(x, x_a) \in U$ for some $a \in K$, so that $x \, \theta_U \, x_a$. We conclude that $L \cong P/\theta_U \cong K$.

Combining 17.2 and 17.3, we get

17.4: *If* **K** *is a finite set of finite lattices, then* $\mathbf{K}^v = P_s H S \mathbf{K}$. *In particular, every subdirectly irreducible lattice in* $\mathbf{K}^v$ *belongs to* $HS\mathbf{K}$. [7]

17.5: *If K and L are nonisomorphic subdirectly irreducible lattices, K is finite, and L has at least as many elements as K, then there is an identity that holds in K but not in L.* [8]

PROOF: Since L can not be a homomorphic image of a sublattice of K, 17.4 shows that L does not belong to the variety $\{K\}^v$; i.e., L does not satisfy every identity that holds in K.

The statement of the preceding theorem is false without the assumption that the lattice K is finite. For example, if u is a rational vector space of countably infinite dimension, v is a rational vector space of uncountable dimension, and K and L are the lattices of all finite subspaces of u and v, respectively, then both K and L are subdirectly irreducible (in fact, simple), and they are certainly nonisomorphic. On the other hand, any finitely generated sublattice F of L is a sublattice of the lattice of subspaces of some finite dimensional subspace of v, and hence F is isomorphic with a sublattice of K, and K itself is isomorphic with a sublattice of L. Consequently a lattice identity holds in K if and only if it holds in L.

At this point it is possible to describe the structure of a small part of the lattice of varieties, at least near the bottom. We have already remarked that the least element of this lattice is the variety, **0** consisting of all one-element lattices. If a variety **V** contains a lattice with more than one element, then **V** contains a two-element chain and hence any sublattice of a direct product of two-element chains. In view of 11.3, this means that **V** contains all distributive lattices. It follows that the variety **D** of all distributive lattices is a unique atom in the lattice of varieties. Further, any variety containing a nondistributive lattice also contains either M_5, the five-element modular nondistributive lattice, or N_5, the five-element nonmodular lattice. Consequently, if $\mathbf{M}_5$ and $\mathbf{N}_5$ denote the least varieties containing M_5 and N_5, respectively, $\mathbf{M}_5 = \{M_5\}^v$, $\mathbf{N}_5 = \{N_5\}^v$, then $\mathbf{M}_5$ and $\mathbf{N}_5$ cover **D**, and any variety properly larger than **D** contains either $\mathbf{M}_5$ or $\mathbf{N}_5$. In addition the distributivity of the lattice of varieties implies that $\mathbf{M}_5 \vee \mathbf{N}_5$ covers both $\mathbf{M}_5$ and $\mathbf{N}_5$.

We call fill out the picture a bit more. Let M_6 and U_8 denote the lattices

---

[7] B. Jónsson [60].

[8] B. Jónsson [60], A. L. Foster and A. F. Pixley [37].

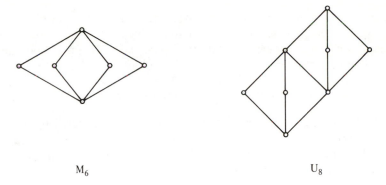

M_6 U_8

Fig. 17-2

shown in Fig. 17-2. Both M_6 and U_8 are subdirectly irreducible, and neither is a homomorphic image of a sublattice of the other. Also, it is easily checked that the only other subdirectly irreducible lattices that are homomorphic images of sublattices of either M_6 or U_8 are M_5 and the two-element chain. Therefore if $\mathbf{M_6} = \{M_6\}^v$ and $\mathbf{U_8} = \{U_8\}^v$, it follows from 17.4 that $\mathbf{M_6} \neq \mathbf{U_8}$ and that both $\mathbf{M_6}$ and $\mathbf{U_8}$ cover $\mathbf{M_5}$ in the lattice of varieties. Thus the picture of the lattice of varieties, so far, looks as shown in Fig. 17-3. Shortly we will see the $\mathbf{M_6}$, $\mathbf{U_8}$, and $\mathbf{M_5} \vee \mathbf{N_5}$ are the only varieties that cover $\mathbf{M_5}$.

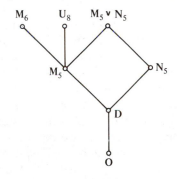

Fig. 17-3

Despite the seemingly small number of varieties near the bottom, K. Baker [4] and R. McKenzie [66] have shown that *the lattice of varieties has cardinality* $2^{\aleph_0}$. In fact, Baker shows that there are $2^{\aleph_0}$ varieties of modular lattices.

A set of identities characterizing the variety $\mathbf{N_5}$ has been discovered by McKenzie [67]: $\mathbf{N_5}$ is precisely that class of lattices satisfying the two identities

$$x \wedge (y \vee z) \wedge (y \vee w) \leq [x \wedge (y \vee (z \wedge w))] \vee (x \wedge z) \vee (x \wedge w),$$

$$x \wedge (y \vee (z \wedge (x \vee w))) = [x \wedge (y \vee (x \wedge z))]$$
$$\vee [x \wedge ((x \wedge y) \vee (z \wedge w))].$$

(The reader is urged to consult McKenzie's paper for the proof of this difficult result.) A second description of $\mathbf{N}_5$ can be given in terms of certain lattice configurations. Defining a lattice L to be of *width n* if n is the maximal number of pairwise noncomparable elements in L, we have

17.6: $\mathbf{N}_5 = \mathbf{T}^v$, *where* $\mathbf{T}$ *is the class of all lattices of width* 2.[9]

PROOF: We will actually prove the following equivalent statement: N_5 *is the only subdirectly irreducible lattice of width* 2. Let L be a subdirectly irreducible lattice of width 2. For the purposes of this proof, define a *pentagon* to be a quintuple $\langle a, b, c, u, v \rangle$ such that $a, b, c, u, v \in L$ and

$$u > a > b > v, \qquad c \wedge a = v, \qquad c \vee b = u.$$

Since L is necessarily nondistributive, it contains a sublattice isomorphic to N_5, and hence L has at least one pentagon.

A. If $\langle a, b, c, u, v \rangle$ is a pentagon and x/y is a proper quotient of L that is weakly projective into a/b, then x/y is a subquotient of a/b.

To prove A, it suffices to show that any transpose of a subquotient of a/b is a subquotient of a/b. Suppose therefore that x/y is a lower transpose of r/s and that r/s is a subquotient of a/b. The assumption that x/y is proper, i.e., that $x > y$, requires that $x \not\leq s$. If $x \not\geq s$, then x and s are noncomparable, and since s and c are certainly noncomparable, it follows that x and c are comparable. But $x \leq r \leq a$, and therefore the condition $x \geq c$ yields that $a \geq c$, a contradiction, and the condition $x \leq c$ yields that $x \leq a \wedge c = v \leq b \leq s$, also a contradiction. Thus it must be that $x \geq s$. This, of course, means that $x/y = r/s$ and consequently that x/y is a subquotient of a/b. A dual argument handles the case when x/y is an upper transpose of r/s.

At this point observe that inasmuch as L is subdirectly irreducible, there is a proper quotient p/q weakly projective into every proper quotient of L. In particular if $\langle a, b, c, u, v \rangle$ is any pentagon, then p/q is weakly projective into a/b and hence a subquotient of a/b by virtue of A. Moreover, if $a > x > b$, then both $\langle a, x, c, u, v \rangle$ and $\langle x, b, c, u, v \rangle$ are pentagons, and hence p/q must be a subquotient of both a/x and x/b, an impossibility. It follows that *if* $\langle a, b, c, u, v \rangle$ *and* $\langle a', b', c', u', v' \rangle$ *are pentagons, then* $a = a'$ *and* $b = b'$; *in addition* $a \succ b$, *and* a/b *is weakly projective into every proper quotient of* L.

B. Let $\langle a, b, c, u, v \rangle$ be a pentagon, and let x/y be weakly projective into r/s. Then $r \wedge u = s \wedge u$ implies $x \wedge u = y \wedge u$.

Again it is enough to prove B in the following three cases: x/y is a subquotient of r/s, x/y is a lower transpose of r/s, and x/y is an upper transpose

[9] O. T. Nelson, Jr. [70].

of r/s. In the first case $r \wedge u = s \wedge u$ implies that

$$x \wedge u = x \wedge r \wedge u = x \wedge s \wedge u = s \wedge u \leq y \wedge u \leq x \wedge u,$$

and hence that $x \wedge u = y \wedge u$. Similarly, in the second case, $r \wedge u = s \wedge u$ implies that $x \wedge u = x \wedge r \wedge u = x \wedge s \wedge u = y \wedge u$.

The third case requires a little more work. To handle it, suppose x/y is an upper transpose of r/s, $r \wedge u = s \wedge u$, and further that $x > y$ and hence that $r > s$. Observe that $r \nleq y$, for otherwise $x = r \vee y = y$. Thus if r and y are comparable, then $r \geq y$, and this yields that $x/y = r/s$ and hence that $x \wedge u = y \wedge u$. We can assume, therefore, that r and y are noncomparable. Next observe that if $y \geq x \wedge u$, then $y \wedge u \geq x \wedge u \geq y \wedge u$, so that $x \wedge u = y \wedge u$. Suppose, on the other hand, that $y < x \wedge u$. Under these circumstances $y < u$ and

$$r \vee y = x \geq r \vee (x \wedge u) \geq r \vee y,$$

whence $r \vee (x \wedge u) = x$. Also,

$$r \wedge (x \wedge u) = r \wedge u = s \wedge u = (r \wedge y) \wedge u = r \wedge y,$$

which shows that $\langle x \wedge u, y, r, x, r \wedge u \rangle$ is a pentagon and therefore that $a = x \wedge u$ and $y = b$. Now r and $y = b$ are noncomparable, and r and c are noncomparable, so it must be that r and c are comparable. This leads to a contradiction, however, for $r \geq c$ implies that $b = y \geq s \geq s \wedge u = r \wedge u \geq c$, and $r \leq c$ implies that both $r \leq u$ and $s \leq u$ and hence that $r = r \wedge u = s \wedge u = s$. Consequently the condition $y < x \wedge u$ is impossible, so we can further assume that y and $x \wedge u$ are noncomparable. This assumption, together with the noncomparability of r and y, requires that r and $x \wedge u$ are comparable. The condition $r \leq x \wedge u$ is impossible since it yields that $s \leq r \leq u$ and hence that $r = r \wedge u = s \wedge u = s$. Therefore $r \geq x \wedge u$, and we infer that

$$x \wedge u = x \wedge r \wedge u = r \wedge u = s \wedge u \leq y \wedge u \leq x \wedge u,$$

completing the proof of B.

Suppose now that $\langle a, b, c, u, v \rangle$ is any pentagon and $x \in L$. If $x \nleq u$, then $x \vee u > u$, and as a/b is weakly projective into $x \vee u/u$, lemma B asserts that $a = a \wedge u = b \wedge u = b$, a contradiction. Thus $x \leq u$, and duality yields that $x \geq v$. Summarizing, *if $\langle a, b, c, u, v \rangle$ is any pentagon, then u and v are, respectively, the greatest and least elements if L, $u = 1$ and $v = 0$.*

For the remainder of the proof let $\langle a, b, c, 1, 0 \rangle$ be a fixed pentagon. We will show that $L = \{a, b, c, 1, 0\}$. Assume that $x \in L$ exists with $x \notin \{a, b, c, 1, 0\}$. Suppose further that $x > c$. If $a \wedge x = b \wedge x$, then $\langle a, b, x, 1, a \wedge x \rangle$ is a pentagon, showing that $a \wedge x = 0$, and this means that $\langle x, c, a, 1, 0 \rangle$ is a pentagon, which implies that $x = a$ and $b = c$, an impossibility. Therefore we must have $a \wedge x > b \wedge x$. Set

$$y = c \vee (b \wedge x).$$

Certainly, $x \geq y$, and so $b \wedge x \geq b \wedge y \geq b \wedge x$, whence $b \wedge x = b \wedge y$. If in addition $a \wedge y = b \wedge x$, then $\langle a, b, y, 1, b \wedge x \rangle$ is a pentagon, forcing $b \wedge x = 0$, and this in turn implies that $\langle x, c, b, 1, 0 \rangle$ is a pentagon, contrary to the fact that $b \neq c$. Thus $a \wedge y > b \wedge x$. But under these conditions $c \vee (b \wedge y) = c \vee (b \wedge x) = y$, implying that $\langle a \wedge y, b \wedge y, c, y, 0 \rangle$ is a pentagon and hence that $x \geq y = 1$, a contradiction. Consequently $x > c$ is impossible, and duality yields that x and c are noncomparable.

Suppose next that $x > a$. Then $x \wedge c \neq 0$, for if $x \wedge c = 0$, then $\langle x, a, c, 1, 0 \rangle$ would be a pentagon, an impossibility. Set

$$z = a \vee (x \wedge c).$$

Clearly, $x \geq z$. In addition $z > a$, for otherwise we would have $a \geq x \wedge c$ and hence that $x \wedge c = 0$. Further $x \wedge c \geq z \wedge c \geq x \wedge c$, so $z \wedge c = x \wedge c$. Set

$$w = b \vee (x \wedge c),$$

and note that $z \geq w \geq x \wedge c$ and $z \wedge c = w \wedge c = x \wedge c$. If $z > w$, then $\langle z, w, c, 1, x \wedge c \rangle$ is a pentagon, contradicting the fact that $x \wedge c \neq 0$. Therefore $z = w$, and this implies that $\langle a, b, x \wedge c, z, 0 \rangle$ is a pentagon, again a contradiction since $z \leq x < 1$. We conclude that it is impossible for $x > a$, and as x and c are noncomparable and a and c are noncomparable, the only other possibility is that $x \leq a$. Duality yields that $x \geq b$, and inasmuch as $a \succ b$, we infer that either $x = a$ or $x = b$, a final contradiction. Thus $L = \{a, b, c, 1, 0\}$ and the proof of 17.6 is complete.

We can also write an identity that, together with the modular law, characterizes the variety $\mathbf{M}_5$. This we will derive as a consequence of the following basic structure theorem for modular lattices. Here U_{10} denotes the lattice shown in Fig. 17-4.

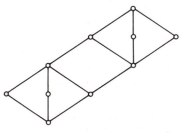

U_{10}

Fig. 17-4

17.7: *A subdirectly irreducible modular lattice having more than five elements contains a sublattice isomorphic with one of the lattices* M_6, U_8, *or* U_{10}.[10]

PROOF: The proof begins with five lemmas concerning projectivities in an arbitrary modular lattice L.

A. If a/b and c/d are two quotients of L having a common upper transpose, then they have a common upper transpose whose largest element is $a \vee c$.

B. If a/b and c/d are quotients of L having a common upper transpose, then either $a \wedge c = b \wedge d$ or a/b and c/d have proper subquotients a_1/b_1 and c_1/d_1, respectively, which have a common lower transpose.

To prove A, suppose x/y is a common upper transpose of a/b and c/d, and set $y_1 = y \wedge (a \vee c)$. Then

$$a \vee y_1 = a \vee (y \wedge (a \vee c)) = (a \vee y) \wedge (a \vee c) = x \wedge (a \vee c) = a \vee c,$$

and certainly $a \wedge y_1 = a \wedge y = b$. Similarly, $c \vee y_1 = a \vee c$, and $c \wedge y_1 = d$. Thus $a \vee c/y_1$ is the required common upper transpose of a/b and c/d.

To prove B, let x/y be a common upper transpose of a/b and c/d. Since $a \wedge y = b$ and $c \wedge y = d$, we have $b \wedge d = a \wedge y \wedge d = a \wedge d$ and, similarly, $b \wedge d = b \wedge c$. Now suppose $a \wedge c > b \wedge d$. Then $a_1 = b \vee (a \wedge c) > b$ and $c_1 = d \vee (a \wedge c) > d$, and the quotients a_1/b and c_1/d both have $a \wedge c/b \wedge d$ as a common lower transpose.

The next lemma involves quotients of sublattices isomorphic to M_5. Given any lattice K, a quotient a/b of K will be referred to as a *lower quotient* if $a \succ b$ and b is the least element of K, and dually a/b will be called an *upper quotient* if $a \succ b$ and a is the greatest element of K.

C. If a/b and c/d are proper quotients of L having a common upper transpose and if $a \wedge c = b \wedge d$, then there exists a sublattice $K \cong M_5$ such that two lower quotients of K are upper transposes of a/b and c/d, respectively.

Let x/y be a common upper transpose of a/b and c/d. As in the proof of B, we have $b \wedge d = a \wedge d = b \wedge c$, in addition to the assumption that $a \wedge c = b \wedge d$. Therefore

$$a \wedge (b \vee d) = b \vee (a \wedge d) = b \vee (b \wedge d) = b,$$

and clearly $a \vee (b \vee d) = a \vee d$. Thus $a \vee d/b \vee d$ is an upper transpose of a/b, and, similarly, $b \vee c/b \vee d$ is an upper transpose of c/d. Set $y_1 = y \wedge (a \vee c)$. The calculation used in the proof of A shows that $a \vee y_1 =$

[10] B. Jónsson [61]. Cf. also G. Grätzer [43].

$c \vee y_1 = a \vee c$, $a \wedge y_1 = b$, and $c \wedge y_1 = d$. Consequently

$$(a \vee d) \vee y_1 = (b \vee c) \vee y_1 = (a \vee d) \vee (b \vee c) = a \vee c.$$

In addition, $y_1 \geq b$ and $y_1 \geq d$, so

$$(a \vee d) \wedge y_1 = (a \wedge y_1) \vee d = b \vee d,$$

and, similarly, $(b \vee c) \wedge y_1 = b \vee d$. Further

$$(a \vee d) \wedge (b \vee c) = b \vee ((a \vee d) \wedge c) = b \vee d \vee (a \wedge c) = b \vee d.$$

Hence $\{a \vee c, a \vee d, b \vee c, y, b \vee d\}$ is a sublattice of L isomorphic with M_5, completing the argument.

D. *Let $\{v, a, b, c, w\}$ be a sublattice of L isomorphic with M_5, where $v > a$, $b, c > w$. If $x \in L$ and $v > x \geq a$, then*

$$S = \{v, x, b \vee (x \wedge c), c \vee (x \wedge b), (x \wedge b) \vee (x \wedge c)\}$$

is a sublattice of L isomorphic with M_5.

The proof of D consists simply of verifying that the necessary relations hold. Observe first that since $x \geq a$, $b \vee (x \wedge c) \geq b$, and $c \vee (x \wedge b) \geq c$, the join of any two of the elements x, $b \vee (x \wedge c)$, or $c \vee (x \wedge b)$ must be v. Now

$$x \wedge (b \vee (x \wedge c)) = (x \wedge c) \vee (x \wedge b) = x \wedge (c \vee (x \wedge b)),$$

and

$$\begin{aligned}(b \vee (x \wedge c)) \wedge (c \vee (x \wedge b)) &= ([b \vee (x \wedge c)] \wedge c) \vee (x \wedge b) \\ &= (b \wedge c) \vee (x \wedge c) \vee (x \wedge b) \\ &= (x \wedge b) \vee (x \wedge c),\end{aligned}$$

and as $v > x$, it follows that S is a sublattice of L isomorphic to M_5.

E. *Let a/b and c/d be proper quotients of L such that a/b is projective in four steps to c/d. Suppose further that no proper subquotient of a/b is projective in fewer than four steps to a subquotient of c/d. Then L contains a sublattice isomorphic to either U_8 or U_{10}.*

Let $a/b = a_0/b_0, a_1/b_1, \ldots, a_4/b_4 = c/d$ be a sequence of quotients such that a_i/b_i is a transpose of a_{i-1}/b_{i-1} for each $i = 1, 2, 3, 4$. Because of duality, without loss of generality we can suppose that a_1/b_1 is an upper transpose of a_0/b_0. And as a/b is not projective in fewer than four steps to c/d, it follows that a_2/b_2 is a lower transpose of a_1/b_1, a_3/b_3 is an upper transpose of a_2/b_2, and a_4/b_4 is a lower transpose of a_3/b_3. In view of A and its dual, we can also assume that

$$a_1 = a_0 \vee a_2, \qquad b_2 = b_1 \wedge b_3, \qquad a_3 = a_2 \vee a_4.$$

Furthermore, if $a_0 \wedge a_2 \neq b_0 \wedge b_2$, then B asserts that a_0/b_0 and a_2/b_2 contain proper subquotients e/f and g/h, respectively, having a common lower transpose x/y, and as a_2/b_2 is a lower transpose of a_3/b_3, it follows that x/y is a lower transpose of a subquotient of a_3/b_3 and hence that e/f is projective in three steps to a subquotient of $a_4/b_4 = c/d$, contrary to assumption. The same argument applies to a_2/b_2 and a_4/b_4, and the dual argument to a_1/b_1 and a_3/b_3, yielding that

$$a_0 \wedge a_2 = b_0 \wedge b_2, \qquad b_1 \vee b_3 = a_1 \vee a_3, \qquad a_2 \wedge a_4 = b_2 \wedge b_4.$$

Now C and its proof imply that a_0/b_0 and a_2/b_2 are lower transposes of two lower quotients of the sublattice

$$\{a_1, a_0 \vee b_2, b_0 \vee a_2, b_1, b_0 \vee b_2\},$$

which is isomorphic to M_5, and the dual of C implies that a_1/b_1 and a_3/b_3 are upper transposes of two upper quotients of the sublattice

$$\{a_1 \wedge a_3, b_1 \wedge a_3, a_1 \wedge b_3, a_2, b_2\},$$

which is also a copy of M_5. Indeed, a_1/b_1 is an upper transpose of $a_1 \wedge a_3/b_1 \wedge a_3$. Suppose $(a_1 \wedge a_3) \vee b_0 \neq a_1$. If we set

$$w = (a_1 \wedge a_3) \vee b_0,$$

then $a_1 > w \geq b_0 \vee a_2$ inasmuch as $a_1 \wedge a_3 \geq a_2$. Thus D applies to the element w and the first copy of M_5 above, yielding that w is an atom of a sublattice $S \cong M_5$ whose least element is $(w \wedge b_1) \vee (w \wedge (a_0 \vee b_2))$. Set

$$u = b_1 \vee (w \wedge (a_0 \vee b_2)), \qquad v = (b_1 \wedge a_3) \vee (u \wedge a_2).$$

The element u is then the image of w under the isomorphism of $a_1/b_0 \vee a_2$ onto a_1/b_1, and v is the image of u under the isomorphism of a_1/b_1 onto $a_1 \wedge a_3/a_3 \wedge b_1$. Consequently $a_1 \wedge a_3 > v \geq a_3 \wedge b_1$, and D shows that $a_1 \wedge a_3/v$ is an upper quotient of a sublattice $T \cong M_5$. Moreover,

$$(a_1 \wedge a_3) \vee (w \wedge b_1) = w \wedge ((a_1 \wedge a_3) \vee b_1) = w \wedge ((a_1 \wedge a_3) \vee a_2 \vee b_1)$$
$$= w \wedge ((a_1 \wedge a_3) \vee a_1) = w \wedge a_1 = w,$$

so that

$$(a_1 \wedge a_3) \vee [(w \wedge b_1) \vee (w \wedge (a_0 \vee b_2))] = w \vee (w \wedge (a_0 \vee b_2)) = w.$$

As $u \geq b_1 \geq b_1 \wedge a_3$ and $w \geq a_1 \wedge a_3$, we get

$$v = u \wedge ((b_1 \wedge a_3) \vee a_2) = u \wedge (b_1 \vee a_2) \wedge a_3 = u \wedge a_1 \wedge a_3$$
$$= u \wedge w \wedge a_1 \wedge a_3 = [b_1 \vee (w \wedge (a_0 \vee b_2))] \wedge w \wedge a_1 \wedge a_3$$
$$= [(w \wedge b_1) \vee (w \wedge (a_0 \vee b_2))] \wedge (a_1 \wedge a_3).$$

Hence $a_1 \wedge a_3/v$, which is an upper quotient of T, is a lower transpose of a lower quotient of S. Consequently S and T together generate a sublattice of L that is isomorphic with either U_8 or U_{10}. Summarizing, we have shown that if $(a_1 \wedge a_3) \vee b_0 \neq a_1$, then the conclusion of E holds.

We can assume, therefore, that $(a_1 \wedge a_3) \vee b_0 = a_1$, and by duality and symmetry that $(b_0 \vee b_2) \wedge a_3 = b_2$, $(a_1 \wedge a_3) \vee b_4 = a_3$, and $(b_2 \vee b_4) \wedge a_1 = b_2$. From these conditions we infer that

$$(a_1 \wedge a_3) \vee (b_0 \vee b_2) = a_1, \qquad (a_1 \wedge a_3) \wedge (b_0 \vee b_2) = b_2,$$
$$(a_1 \wedge a_3) \vee (b_2 \vee b_4) = a_3, \qquad (a_1 \wedge a_3) \wedge (b_2 \vee b_4) = b_2.$$

Computing further,

$$\begin{aligned}
a_0 \wedge (b_0 \vee a_2 \vee b_4) &= b_0 \vee (a_0 \wedge (a_2 \vee b_4)) \\
&= b_0 \vee (a_0 \wedge a_1 \wedge (a_2 \vee b_4)) \\
&= b_0 \vee (a_0 \wedge (a_2 \vee (a_1 \wedge b_4))).
\end{aligned}$$

And as

$$a_1 \wedge b_4 = a_1 \wedge a_3 \wedge b_4 \leq a_1 \wedge a_3 \wedge (b_2 \vee b_4) = b_2,$$

we obtain that

$$a_0 \wedge (b_0 \vee a_2 \vee b_4) = b_0 \vee (a_0 \wedge a_2) = b_0 \vee (b_0 \wedge b_2) = b_0.$$

In addition,

$$\begin{aligned}
a_0 \vee (b_0 \vee a_2 \vee b_4) &= a_0 \vee a_2 \vee b_4 = a_1 \vee b_4 = a_1 \vee b_2 \vee b_4 \\
&= a_1 \vee (a_1 \wedge a_3) \vee (b_2 \vee b_4) = a_1 \vee a_3.
\end{aligned}$$

Thus $a_1 \vee a_3/b_0 \vee a_2 \vee b_4$ is an upper transpose of a_0/b_0, and by symmetry it is also an upper transpose of a_4/b_4. But this means that a/b is projective in two steps to c/d, contrary to the hypotheses. Consequently our assumption at the beginning of this paragraph is untenable, and the proof of E is complete.

Proceeding now with the proof of 17.7, assume that L is a subdirectly irreducible modular lattice with more than five elements. If the dimension of L is exactly 2, then L has at least four atoms and hence contains a sublattice isomorphic to M_6. We may suppose, therefore, that L contains a four-element chain

$$a > b > c > d.$$

Since L is subdirectly irreducible, the meet of the two congruence relations $\theta_{a,b}$ and $\theta_{b,c}$ can not be the least congruence relation in L. Hence some proper subquotient of a/b is projective to some subquotient of b/c. Choose a sequence of proper quotients

$$a_0/b_0, \; a_1/b_1, \; \ldots, \; a_n/b_n$$

such that a_0/b_0 is a subquotient of a/b, a_n/b_n is a subquotient of b/c, each a_i/b_i is a transpose of a_{i-1}/b_{i-1}, and no proper subquotient of a/b is projective in fewer than n steps to a subquotient of b/c.

Since no proper subquotient of a/b can be a transpose of a subquotient of b/c, we certainly have $n \neq 1$. In addition, $n \neq 2$, for if a_2/b_2 were a subquotient of b/c, and, for example, a_1/b_1 were an upper transpose of both a_0/b_0 and a_2/b_2, then $b_1 \geq b_0 \geq b \geq a_2$ and hence $b_2 = a_2 \wedge b_1 = a_2$, contrary to the fact that a_2/b_2 is proper. Now when $n \geq 4$, E applies, yielding the conclusion of 17.7. So the only remaining case to consider is when $n = 3$.

Assume then that some proper quotient a_0/b_0 of a/b is projective in three steps to a subquotient a_3/b_3 of b/c. Repeating the argument of the preceding two paragraphs for the quotients a_3/b_3 and c/d, we can also assume that some proper subquotient u/v of a_3/b_3 is projective in three steps to a subquotient of c/d. Pick quotients $u/v = u_0/v_0$, u_1/v_1, u_2/v_2, u_3/v_3 such that u_3/v_3 is a subquotient of c/d and each u_i/v_i is a transpose of u_{i-1}/v_{i-1}. Notice that u_1/v_1 must be a lower transpose of u/v; otherwise u_1/v_1 would be projective in two steps to a quotient that lies entirely below v_1, an impossibility as shown in the preceding paragraph. Therefore an application of the duals of B and C shows that u/v is an upper transpose of an upper quotient of some copy of M_5. As a subquotient of a_3/b_3, u/v is projective in three steps to a subquotient of a_0/b_0, and by the dual of the argument just given, u/v is a lower transpose of a lower quotient of another copy of M_5. These two copies of M_5 must generate a sublattice isomorphic with either U_8 or U_{10}, and the proof of 17.7 is complete.

17.8: M_5 *is precisely that class of lattices that satisfy the modular law and the identity*

$$x \wedge (y \vee z) \wedge (y \vee w) \wedge (z \vee w) \leq (x \wedge y) \vee (x \wedge z) \vee (x \wedge w). \text{[11]}$$

PROOF: It is easy to check that this identity holds in M_5 but fails to hold in M_6, U_8, and U_{10}. Consequently, if L is a subdirectly irreducible modular lattice that satisfies the identity, then 17.7 shows that L has at most five elements and hence is isomorphic with either M_5 or the two-element chain, whence $L \in M_5$. As a variety is determined by its subdirectly irreducible members, the conclusion of 17.8 follows.

Theorem 17.7 also makes it clear that *the only varieties that cover* $\mathbf{M}_5$ *in the lattice of varieties are* $\mathbf{M}_6$, $\mathbf{U}_8$, *and* $\mathbf{M}_5 \vee \mathbf{N}_5$.[12] For if $\mathbf{V}$ is a variety of modular lattices that properly contains $\mathbf{M}_5$, then $\mathbf{V}$ contains either M_6 or U_8 (U_8 is a homomorphic image of U_{10}). Therefore either $\mathbf{V} \supseteq \mathbf{M}_6$ or $\mathbf{V} \supseteq \mathbf{U}_8$.

Little progress has been made in determining those varieties that cover $\mathbf{N}_5$; it is not even known if there are finitely many. In this connection the reader might verify that the four lattices in Fig. 17-5 each generates a variety that covers $\mathbf{N}_5$.

The foregoing results illustrate some of the basic techniques used in the investigation of lattice varieties. For a number of additional results concerning both individual varieties as well as the lattice of varieties itself, the

[11] B. Jónsson [61].
[12] B. Jónsson [61]. Cf. also G. Grätzer [43].

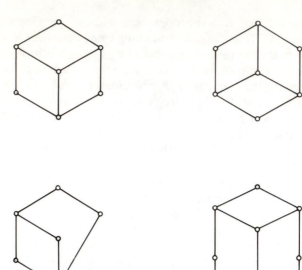

Fig. 17-5

reader is urged to consult the papers of B. Jónsson [60, 61], R. McKenzie [66, 67], K. Baker [4, 5], and Dang Xuan Hong [53].

REFERENCES

1. I. Amemiya and I. Halperin, Complemented modular lattices, *Can. J. Math.* **11** (1959), 481–520.

2. E. Artin, Coordinates in affine geometry, *Reports Math. Colloq. Notre Dame* (1940).

3. K. Baker, A generalization of Sperner's lemma, *J. Combinatorial Theory* **6** (1969), 244–245.

4. K. Baker, Equational classes of modular lattices, *Pacific J. Math.* **28** (1969), 9–15.

5. K. Baker, Equational axioms for classes of lattices, *Bull. Amer. Math. Soc.* **77** (1971), 97–102.

6. J. G. Basterfield and L. M. Kelly, A characterization of sets of n points which determine n hyperplanes, *Proc. Camb. Phil. Soc.* **64** (1968), 585–588.

7. G. Birkhoff, On the combination of subalgebras, *Proc. Camb. Phil. Soc.* **29** (1933), 441–464.

8. G. Birkhoff, Combinatorial relations in projective geometries, *Annals of Math.* **36** (1935), 743–748.

9. G. Birkhoff, On the structure of abstract algebras, *Proc. Camb. Phil. Soc.* **31** (1935), 433–454.

10. G. Birkhoff, Rings of sets, *Duke Math. J.* **3** (1937), 442–454.

11. G. Birkhoff, Subdirect unions in universal algebra, *Bull. Amer. Math. Soc.* **50** (1944), 764–768.

12. G. Birkhoff, *Lattice Theory*, rev. ed. New York: American Mathematical Society, 1948.

13. G. Birkhoff and M. Ward, A characterization of Boolean algebras, *Annals of Math.* **40** (1939), 609–610.

14. C. C. Chen and G. Grätzer, On the construction of complemented lattices, *J. Algebra* **11** (1969), 56–63.

15. R. Church, Enumeration by rank of elements of the free distributive lattice with seven generators, *Notices Amer. Math. Soc.* **12** (1965), 724.

16. H. H. Crapo and G.-C. Rota, *On the Foundations of Combinatorial Theory*: *Combinatorial Geometries*, prelim. ed. Cambridge: M.I.T. Press, 1970.

17. P. Crawley, The isomorphism theorem in compactly generated lattices. *Bull. Amer. Math. Soc.* **65** (1959), 377–379.

18. P. Crawley, Lattices whose congruences form a Boolean algebra, *Pacific J. Math.* **10** (1960), 787–795.

19. P. Crawley, Decomposition theory for nonsemimodular lattices, *Trans. Amer. Math. Soc.* **99** (1961), 246–254.

20. P. Crawley, Direct decompositions with finite dimensional factors, *Pacific J. Math.* **12** (1962), 457–468.

21. P. Crawley, Regular embeddings which preserve lattice structure, *Proc. Amer. Math. Soc.* **13** (1962), 748–752.

22. P. Crawley and R. A. Dean, Free lattices with infinite operations, *Trans. Amer. Math. Soc.* **92** (1959), 35–47.

23. A. C. Davis, A characterization of complete lattices, *Pacific J. Math.* **5** (1955), 311–319.

24. R. A. Dean, Completely free lattices generated by partially ordered sets, *Trans. Amer. Math. Soc.* **83** (1956), 238–249.

25. R. A. Dean, Component subsets of the free lattice on n generators, *Proc. Amer. Math. Soc.* **7** (1956), 220–226.

26. R. A. Dean, Sublattices of free lattices, *Lattice Theory*, Proc. of Symp. in Pure Math., II. Providence: American Mathematical Society, 1961, pp. 31–42.

27. R. A. Dean, Free lattices generated by partially ordered sets and preserving bounds, *Can. J. Math.* **16** (1964), 136–148.

28. R. Dedekind, Über die drei Moduln erzengte Dualgruppe, *Math. Annalen* **53** (1900), 371–403.

29. R. P. Dilworth, The arithmetical theory of Birkhoff lattices, *Duke Math. J.* **8** (1941), 286–299.

30. R. P. Dilworth, Lattices with unique complements, *Trans. Amer. Math. Soc.* **57** (1945), 123–154.

31. R. P. Dilworth, Note on the Kurosch-Ore theorem, *Bull. Amer. Math. Soc.* **52** (1946), 659–663.

32. R. P. Dilworth, A decomposition theorem for partially ordered sets, *Annals of Math.* **51** (1950), 161–166.

33. R. P. Dilworth, The structure of relatively complemented lattices, *Annals of Math.* **51** (1950), 348–359.

34. R. P. Dilworth, Proof of a conjecture on finite modular lattices, *Annals of Math.* **60** (1954), 359–364.

35. R. P. DILWORTH and P. CRAWLEY, Decomposition theory for lattices without chain conditions, *Trans, Amer. Math. Soc.* **96** (1960), 1–22.

36. R. P. DILWORTH and C. GREENE, A counterexample to the generalization of Sperner's theorem, *J. Combinatorial Theory* **10** (1971), 18–21.

37. A. L. FOSTER and A. F. Pixley, Algebraic and equational semimaximality; equation spectra II, *Math. Z.* **93** (1966), 122–133.

38. T. FRAYNE, A. C. MOREL, and D. SCOTT, Reduced direct products, *Fund. Math.* **51** (1962), 195–228.

39. O. FRINK, Complemented modular lattices and projective spaces of infinite dimension, *Trans. Amer. Math. Soc.* **60** (1946), 452–467.

40. N. FUNAYAMA and T. NAKAYAMA, On the distributivity of a lattice of lattice-congruences, *Proc. Imp. Acad. Tokyo* **18** (1942), 553–554.

41. F. GALVIN and B. JÓNSSON, Distributive sublattices of a free lattice, *Can. J. Math.* **13** (1961), 265–272.

42. V. GLIVENKO, Sur quelques points de la logique de Brouwer, *Bull. Acad. Sci. Belgique* **15** (1929), 183–188.

43. G. GRÄTZER, Equational classes of lattices, *Duke Math. J.* **33** (1966), 613–622.

44. G. GRÄTZER and E. T. SCHMIDT, Ideals and congruence relations in lattices, *Acta Math. Acad. Sci. Hung.* **9** (1958), 137–175.

45. G. GRÄTZER and E. T. SCHMIDT, On congruence lattices of lattices, *Acta Math. Acad. Sci. Hung.* **13** (1962), 179–185.

46. C. GREENE, A rank inequality for finite geometric lattices, *J. Combinatorial Theory* **9** (1970), 357–364.

47. M. HALL and R. P. DILWORTH, The imbedding problem for modular lattices, *Annals of Math.* **45** (1944), 450–456.

48. I. HALPERIN, Complemented modular lattices, *Lattice Theory*, Proc. of Symp. in Pure Math., II. Providence: American Mathematical Society, 1961, pp. 51–64.

49. L. H. HARPER, The morphology of geometric lattices.

50. J. HASHIMOTO, On direct product decomposition of partially ordered sets, *Annals of Math.* **54** (1951), 315–318.

51. J. HASHIMOTO, Ideal theory for lattices, *Math. Japonicae* **2** (1952), 149–186.

52. J. HASHIMOTO, Direct, subdirect decompositions and congruence relations, *Osaka Math. J.* **9** (1957), 87–112.

53. DANG XUAN HONG, Covering relations among lattice varieties, *Pacific J. Math.* **40** (1972), 557–603.

54. B. JÓNSSON, On the representation of lattices, *Math Scand.* **1** (1953), 193–206.

55. B. JÓNSSON, Modular lattices and Desargues' theorem, *Math. Scand.* **2** (1954), 295–314.

56. B. Jónsson, Universal relational systems, *Math. Scand.* **4** (1956), 193–208.

57. B. Jónsson, Representation of modular lattices and relation algebras, *Trans. Amer. Math. Soc.* **92** (1959), 449–464.

58. B. Jónsson, Representations of complemented modular lattices, *Trans. Amer. Math. Soc.* **97** (1960), 64–94.

59. B. Jónsson, Sublattices of a free lattice, *Can. J. Math.* **13** (1961), 256–264.

60. B. Jónsson, Algebras whose congruence lattices are distributive, *Math. Scand.* **21** (1967), 110–121.

61. B. Jónsson, Equational classes of lattices, *Math. Scand.* **22** (1968), 187–196.

62. B. Jónsson and J. E. Kiefer, Finite sublattices of a free lattice, *Can. J. Math.* **14** (1962), 487–497.

63. B. Jónsson and G. S. Monk, Representations of primary Arguesian lattices, *Pacific J. Math.* **29** (1969), 95–140.

64. A. Kurosh, Durchschnittsdarstellungen mit irrededuziblen Komponenten in Ringen und sogenannten Dualgruppen, *Mat. Sbornik* **42** (1935), 613–616.

65. F. Maeda, *Kontinuierliche Geometrien.* Berlin: Springer-Verlag, 1958.

66. R. McKenzie, Equational bases for lattice theories, *Math. Scand.* **27** (1970), 24–38.

67. R. McKenzie, Equational bases and non-modular lattice varieties, *Trans. Amer. Math. Soc.* **174** (1972), 1–43.

68. J. E. McLaughlin, Atomic lattices with unique comparable complements, *Proc. Amer. Math. Soc.* **7** (1956), 864–866.

69. M. L. Mousinho, Modular and projective lattice, *Summa Brasil. Math.* **2** (1950), 95–112.

70. O. T. Nelson, Jr., Subdirect decompositions of lattices of width two, *Pacific J. Math.* **24** (1968), 519–523.

71. J. von Neumann, Continuous geometries, *Proc. Nat. Acad. Sci. U.S.A.* **22** (1936), 92–100.

72. J. von Neumann, Examples of continuous geometries, *Proc. Nat Acad. Sci. U.S.A.* **22** (1936), 101–107.

73. J. von Neumann, *Continuous geometry* (I. Halperin, ed.). Princeton: Princeton University Press, 1960.

74. T. Ogasawara and U. Sasaki, On a theorem in lattice theory, *J. Sci. Hiroshima Univ., Ser. A* **14** (1949), 13.

75. O. Ore, On the foundations of abstract algebra, II, *Annals of Math.* **37** (1936), 265–292.

76. O. Ore, Theory of equivalence relations, *Duke Math. J.* **9** (1942), 573–627.

77. H. Rolf, The free lattice generated by a set of chains, *Pacific J. Math.* **8** (1958), 585–595.

78. G.-C. ROTA, On the foundations of combinatorial theory, I. Theory of Möbius functions, *Z. Wahrscheinlichkeitstheorie und Verw. Gebiete* **2** (1964), 340–368.

79. M. H. STONE, The theory of representations for Boolean algebras, *Trans. Amer. Math. Soc.* **40** (1936), 37–111.

80. E. SZPILRAJN, Sur l'extension de l'ordre partiel, *Fund. Math.* **16** (1930), 386–389.

81. T. TANAKA, Canonical subdirect factorizations of lattices, *J. Sci. Hiroshima Univ.*, *Ser. A* **16** (1952), 239–246.

82. A. TARSKI, Sur les classes closes par rapport à certaines opérations élémentaires, *Fund. Math.* **16** (1929), 181–305.

83. A. TARSKI, A remark on functionally free algebras, *Annals of Math.* **47** (1946), 163–165.

84. A. TARSKI, A lattice-theoretical fixpoint theorem and its applications, *Pacific J. Math.* **5** (1955), 285–309.

85. H. TVERBERG, On Dilworth's decomposition theorem for partially ordered sets, *J. Combinatorial Theory* **3** (1967), 305–306.

86. M. WARD, A characterization of Dedekind structures, *Bull. Amer. Math. Soc.* **45** (1939), 448–451.

87. T. WHALEY, Large sublattices of a lattice, *Pacific J. Math.* **28** (1969), 477–484.

88. P. WHITMAN, Free lattices, *Annals of Math.* **42** (1941), 325–330.

89. P. WHITMAN, Free lattices. II, *Annals of Math.* **43** (1942), 104–115.

90. P. WHITMAN, Lattices, equivalence relations, and subgroups, *Bull. Amer. Math. Soc.* **52** (1946), 507–522.

INDEX

ultrafilter, 180
ultraproduct, 180
unique comparable complements, 32
unique irredundant decompositions, 50
uniquely complemented lattice, 32
upper bound, 4
upper continuous lattice, 15
upper-directed set, 148
upper quotient, 187
upper transpose, 76

variety, 176

weak embedding, 70
weak representation, 98
weakly atomic lattice, 13
weakly projective quotients, 76
well-ordering, 64
width, 184
word algebra, 12